Screen, Culture, Psyche

Screen, Culture, Psyche illuminates recent developments in Jungian modes of media analysis, and illustrates how psychoanalytic theories have been adapted to allow for the interpretation of films and television programmes, employing post-Jungian methods in the deep reading of a whole range of films. Readings of this kind can demonstrate the way that some films bear the psychological projections not only of their makers but of their audience, and assess the manner in which films engage the writer's own psyche. Seeking to go beyond existing theories, John Izod explores the question of whether Jungian screen analysis can work for ordinary filmgoers – can what functions for the scholar be said to be true for people without a background in Jung's ideas?

Through detailed readings of a number of films and programmes, John Izod builds on the work previously done by Jungian film analysts, and moves on to contemplate the level of audience engagement. Offering deep readings of films directed by Kubrick and Bernardo Bertolucci, as well as satirical comedy, documentaries and twenty-first century Westerns, the book explores the extent to which they manage to make the psychological impact on spectators that films of a similar kind have done on Jungian writers. The author concludes that the screen texts with the best likelihood of impacting the culture of the audience through their collective psychological force fall at opposite ends of the size and budget range: highly personal documentaries, and the most affecting of mainstream genre movies.

This innovative text will be essential reading for psychoanalysts and therapists, as well as students and scholars of film with an interest in understanding how screen products work psychologically to engage the viewer.

John Izod is Professor of Screen Analysis and Head of the Department of Film & Media Studies at the University of Stirling where he has taught since 1978. He has published numerous articles, and is the author of two previous Jungian studies of films and television programmes.

Screen, Culture, Psyche

A post-Jungian approach to working with the audience

John Izod

Routledge
Taylor & Francis Group
LONDON AND NEW YORK

First published 2006 by Routledge
27 Church Road, Hove, East Sussex BN3 2FA

Simultaneously published in the USA and Canada
by Routledge
270 Madison Avenue, New York, NY 10016

Routledge is an imprint of the Taylor & Francis Group, an informa business

Typeset in Times by Garfield Morgan, Mumbles, Swansea
Printed and bound in Great Britain by TJ International Ltd, Padstow, Cornwall
Paperback cover design by Terry Foley, Anú Design

This publication has been produced with paper manufactured to strict environmental standards and with pulp derived from sustainable forests.

British Library Cataloguing in Publication Data
A catalogue record for this book is available from the British Library

Library of Congress Cataloging-in-Publication Data
Izod, John, 1940–
Screen, culture, psyche : a post-Jungian approach to working with the audience / John Izod.
p. cm.
Filmography:
Includes bibliographical references and index.
ISBN 0-415-38016-2 – ISBN 0-415-38017-0
1. Motion pictures–Psychological aspects. I. Title.
PN1995.I97 2006
791.4301'9–dc22

2005033832

ISBN10: 0-415-38016-2 (hbk)
ISBN10: 0-415-38017-0 (pbk)

ISBN13: 978-0-415-38016-4 (hbk)
ISBN13: 978-0-415-38017-0 (pbk)

For Grahame and Angela Smith
Pamela Rayner
and in fond memory of
William Rayner and Trevor Whittock

My teachers and friends who enrich their teaching with iridescent visions of the narrative arts' tapestries, changing the lives of all who know them

Contents

Acknowledgements

Chapters 1 and 2 were written with Jana Branch who left me the beneficiary of an intellectual debt that I cannot sufficiently acknowledge except in warmly reciprocating her friendship. Those chapters are used here with her generous permission. I owe thanks for advice and affection to Joanna Dovalis, Don Fredericksen, Luke Hockley, Richard Kilborn, Jane Ryan and Philip Schlesinger.

A short version of Chapter 1 was published as '*Barry Lyndon* and the limits of understanding' in *Kinema* 20 (Fall 2003), 5–18. 'Bernardo Bertolucci's *The Dreamers* (2003): the politics of youth remembered', *Kinema* 22 (Fall 2004), 43–62 comprised a truncated working of the present Chapter 5. Chapter 6 is a development of 'Anima and the political dynamics of cultural change: the case of *S1møne*' in *Literature/Film Quarterly* 34(1) (2006). And a shorter version of my analysis of trends in the Western genre in Chapter 8 was published as 'Westerns and global imperialism' in *Spring* 73 (2005), 1–20. The author is grateful to the editors of these journals for permission to use them here.

Introduction

Post-Jungian screen studies

The purpose of this book is to extend post-Jungian approaches to the analysis of films and television programmes. My intention is twofold: firstly to develop an emphasis that connects Jungian work on films to the cultures in which they are screened; secondly, and linked to the first objective, to explore what can be revealed by Jungian readings about the impact of selected texts on their audiences. I shall attempt to assess whether these films could have functioned for audiences in ways which Jungian analysis suggests that they might.

The first substantive applications of C. G. Jung's theories to cinema were published by Don Fredericksen in 1979–80. He examined the nature and significance of the psychoanalyst's concept of symbolism and then tested that framework in an analysis of Basil Wright's documentary *Song of Ceylon* (1935) (Fredericksen 1979, 1980, 2001). A decade later a number of scholars continued the process of adapting Jungian theories to the study of cinema and to a lesser extent television. The best of this work included Beebe (1990, 1996, 2001); Izod (1992); and Rushing and Frentz (1991, 1993). Since the turn of the century, the profile of Jungian screen studies has been further raised by three books: a collection of papers gathering together some of the best work in the field (Hauke and Alister 2001); a study of Jungian theory in the context of detection and detective movies (Hockley 2001); and my own volume in which some of the main features of Jungian theory are explored as they relate both to the process of reading the screen and to explication of archetypal figurations embodied in a number of media texts (Izod 2001).

The primary focus of the bulk of this work, my own included, has been on analysing screen texts and icons to show how Jungian ideas offer new ways of understanding characters, images and narratives where they manifest archetypal images and invoke myths. By way of secondary emphasis, previous writing also demonstrated how screen characters who bear the strong marks of archetypal characteristics can compensate for the psychological needs of spectators. Movies are patently capable of relaying archetypal figures and myths through present-day stories. Myths of the West, of the hero and of the perfect, beloved seductress, are just three recurrent types that will be touched on in the following chapters. Such myths, while fresh-minted for present-day audiences, also embody a vitalising history, for they link back in structure, form and (most important of all) the impulses governing their making and reception to the oldest recorded stories.

For Jungians, the fascination of myths starts with the way they connect the present imaginings of today's filmmakers back through the generations, but it reaches far beyond the simple observation of such links.

Myths and ideology

Myths are not innocent of values. The boldest evidence for that is found in Roland Barthes's Marxist thesis 'Myth Today' (1973). He argued that contemporary myths evacuate history of its factual basis so as to give priority to the connotation that things have always been, and will continue to be, governed by unchanging values. In a famous analysis of an image on the cover of *Paris Match* showing a young black Algerian in uniform saluting the Tricolour, he made the point that the picture was not presented as a still of a named individual on parade at a specific occasion. Rather it was framed to be understood as celebrating the enduring rightness of French imperialism. For Barthes, myth invariably masked the consequences of imperialist politics and capitalist economics from a well-deceived public. No accident, then, that this image was published at the time when French government of Algeria was being bloodily contested in a war which eventually led to the independence of that African nation.

Barthes's sombre analysis does not lack penetration when dealing with advertising, commerce and political propaganda. Indeed, we shall see when discussing the Western genre in Chapter 8 that mythology can have just the function he described. However, Barthes abandoned observation in favour of wish-fulfilling fantasy when he insisted that a Marxist society would be free of myths. Paradoxically his argument that mythology must always have an ideological dimension was if anything reinforced by his bizarre assertion (which history had already demonstrated to be wildly erroneous) that Marxism would lead to the death of myth. Steeped in ideology, this fantasy became his own and fellow neo-Marxists' myth from which they had evacuated the all too often brutal history of Marxist regimes.

Myths and the healing imagination

An altogether different perspective has been adopted by Jungians. They see myths as contributing to the regulation and balancing of the psychic system. For them, myths are eloquent expressions of psychological patterns which have healing potential because they can make available to consciousness buried urges, fears and delights and thus enhance the psychological well-being of the individual. However, myths are by definition stories that gain the willing assent of many people and are held in common. Thus they permit a degree of insight into the hidden currents of more than the individual psyche alone. They arise from and in turn stimulate impulses activated in the unconscious of large numbers of people. Since they express the concerns (whether verbalised or not) of many people, myths are also a means by which both individuals and communities strengthen their sense of identity.

Mainstream pleasures

Films can arouse intense pleasure in audiences. Indeed mainstream movies, in the attempt to assure their backers of good financial returns, invariably try to please their customers. And the pleasures an audience can take are many. They include delight in the aesthetic qualities of artistically modulated images and sound. They may be the ingenuity of the storytelling: for example, there can be enjoyment in trying to work out the twists and turns of a thriller's plot. For other spectators, thinking about thematic content offers deep rewards. But the dependable bedrock, the *sine qua non* of mainstream movies, is emotional gratification. Clearly the virtual pleasures that movies offer encompass a wide spectrum of emotions: fear and horror, disgust and revulsion, lust and hatred; as well as courage and delight, attraction and engagement, desire and love. However, in mainstream production the spectrum of emotions invoked is incomplete for commercial (hence ideological) reasons: although the filmmaker who can make audiences laugh has a promising career, the director who attempts to afflict them with a sense of the tedium of existence (as Michelangelo Antonioni and Jean-Luc Godard sometimes purposely did) is not going to find a ready home in Hollywood. Similarly, the director who, rather than deploying dependable feel-good chemistry, leaves audiences feeling bad about themselves is taking a serious commercial risk, albeit possibly a noble one.

Jungian work has the capability to analyse and point up the significance of the kinds of pleasure that movies offer.

Feeling and emotion

Jung's differentiation of *feeling* from the over-mastering force that *emotion* exerts helps us distinguish the different degrees to which the audience can engage with a film. He described feeling as a process that imparts a definite value to a given content in the mind: one likes or dislikes it. It is a subjective process which, in expressing a sort of valuation, functions as a form of judgement. As such, it is 'neither more nor less than an ordinary thinking process' (Jung 1921: 434). Cinema-goers who respond to a film by saying, for example, that they like the hero for her or his clean-cut looks, clarity of thought or swift action are describing their feelings. So too if they explained that they disliked the film because, for instance, its storyline seemed to them implausible or its soundtrack left much to be desired. Theirs would be the general type of feeling-toned response to the cinema-going experience.

Emotion is experienced when feeling intensifies to the point where it causes nervous agitation or physical innervations (Jung 1921). It is a primary force exercised by the unconscious, and the individual has little control over it (Samuels *et al.* 1986: 11). Jung saw this as a force so strong that he sometimes reversed the usual formulation, saying that emotion possesses the individual rather than the other way about. It would indeed be hard to overemphasise its significance in the shaping of human affairs since igniting the emotions makes possible the forging anew of an individual's consciousness: 'Emotion is the moment when steel meets flint and a spark is struck forth, for emotion is the chief source of consciousness. There is no change from darkness to light or from inertia to movement without emotion' (Jung 1954c: 96).

Without the emotions there is no progress; they are essential to the reshaping of a person's life not only by initiating the new but also (whether welcome or not) by acting like fire and burning the old order in the psyche so as to clear the way for rebirth (Jung 1954c). In sum, Jung asserted that the inner progress toward a fuller encounter with the self (a journey of discovery he called individuation) was by no means driven by the intellect. Rather, emotion and intuitions point the way, so that self-discovery comes through the subject's response to affect.

Although we shall be working primarily with the emotional excitation caused by movies, because it is there that the intervention of archetypally informed images (often in the guise of mythological material) is most plainly seen, it is worth remembering that films can and do work with feelings as well as emotions.

Positive and negative effects of myth

Jungian work on screen texts is exciting to undertake because it can illuminate the analyst through the mental processes undergone in casting light on the text. In this respect the formal work done by the Jungian critic differs from other spectators' enjoyment mainly in that the former has to hold the focus for longer. Although most of the films and television programmes discussed here are presenting a simulated reality, the emotions they engender in the spectator are real enough even where they have no object in the analyst's actual world. The instance in Chapter 6 of *S1møne*, a film which features a fantasy star who arouses high passions among her fans, backs up that observation.

Emotions supply the trunk road that carries two-way traffic between the unconscious and consciousness. So the Jungian interpreter of a text may well find that contemplation of what originated on screen helps illuminate some dark corners in his or her own mind. Again, the same can happen to every spectator, the difference being that the Jungian screen analyst contemplates the text for long periods and reads it in accordance with a pre-existing methodology (Izod 2001: 15–32). Such an illumination can contribute to the process of homeostasis or regulation of that individual's psyche – a potentially positive aspect of the work the analyst does on myth. Indeed, I have argued elsewhere that it is a benefit which any member of the audience may enjoy through emotional engagement with a film (Izod 2001).

It is necessary, however, to speak of the converse, the risk that myths may lead to an inflation. When emotion-charged ideas and images surface from the unconscious and seize an overexcited admiration, they may seduce the conscious mind into forgoing its balancing and controlling function. The ego then ceases to perform in its usual manner, keeping the promptings of the unconscious in harmony with consciousness. This is a risk to which not only Jungian, but all work that engages with deep emotions is exposed; and indeed, as I shall argue later, it is a risk to which the passions aroused by an intense and popular film may expose the audience in general. It seems to me that a measure of inflation has occurred to the extent that we post-Jungian film readers have ignored Barthes's arguments about the ideological function of myth. We have not sufficiently accounted for ideology in our work, and the two modes of understanding myth have been implicitly taken as diametric opposites. However, they should be deployed to complement each other. Jung himself, always conscious of the cultural dimension of symbols and their location in social discourse, would not have found this strange.

Myths, religion and the screen

Myths are closely bonded to religion. This is the case not only because they are accepted as self-evident truths by large numbers of people: the connection is robust because myths express for every epoch both celebration of what large numbers of people believe and the communal search to advance understanding of the incomprehensible aspects of life and the universe. In some myths relayed via the screen, the rituals of quasi-religious celebration and enquiry plainly occur. For example, the life paths of leading characters in certain films that have no concern whatever with organised religion nevertheless follow a trajectory comparable to those of the messiahs (not to mention the prophets and devils) of the established faiths. Those stories often have the characteristics of hero myths. Such characters (all the more vividly if they are played by recognised stars) convey to the enthralled congregation in the cinema's darkened arena something of the numinous intensity previously invested in the human gods of organised religion. Jungian readings can enhance understanding of these figures by focusing on their quasi-divine aspect and many such studies, including my own *Myth, Mind and the Screen* (2001), have investigated the spiritual potential of cinema. That, however, is not my main purpose in what follows.

Film has one significant positive advantage over organised religions which potentially makes it more effective as a prompt to, and reflection of, changes in communal psychology; but the same factor also makes it less potent than the established faiths as a force in forming beliefs adopted by large sectors of society. The churches are shackled to a symbolism which is almost impossible for them to change. They are locked to it by the dogma that they have to adopt to give the institutional canon of their faith its authority. By contrast, each film has the freedom, should its creators wish to take advantage of it, to remake ancient symbols in ways that have deep meaning for the audiences to whom it is released. That occurs because those symbols arise from, and in return engage with, impulses emerging from the unconscious of not only the film's makers but also its future spectators. Turning this observation around, however, we have also to recognise that, in their own individual right, almost all films suffer the concomitant disadvantage (compared with formal religions) that their symbols have currency only for a relatively short time. They have the mixed blessing that they do not play out their dramas against an authoritative and dogmatic framework of ethical rules that attempts to govern – as many faiths do – not only the moral conduct but also the acceptable thoughts of their followers.[1] Lacking that framework, however, they also lack the cultural mechanism that sustains the continuity of authority. Mythology on the screen is adaptable and flexible, but (notwithstanding the access granted by videotape and DVD) can be argued to be evanescent because its reception by audiences is tied to the surface style of the films that carry it. And style on the screen – in a style-conscious age – is subject to changes in fashion no less than any other consumer good. The popular audience for an old film falls away faster than the materials on which it is recorded. I shall discuss this issue further in Chapter 6.

Yet having said that, in every decade the life-challenging conundrums which characters on screen have to resolve can require spectators to face the

1 It is worth noting that the cinema cannot entirely ignore morality. In most nations films have to pass through gatekeeping procedures in the pre-censorship of scripts and censorship of finished product. Although this is a cumbersome business (because it of necessity requires censors to work in lowest common denominator terms for an audience which conceptually is insufficiently differentiated), nonetheless censors' powers position them as authorised guardians of society's politically dominant moral values.

basic issue upon which all morality is founded: the necessity, if they are to mature as individuals, of knowing themselves. Although there is no single master film text that triggers a higher degree of self-awareness, some of the endless succession of movies that pass across our screens do, from a Jungian perspective, have that power. Once again, however, it is necessary to speak not only of the positive potential of what might be described as auto-therapeutic work but also of the risk of inflation in the reading of the film. Where quasi-religious themes are in play, there exists a real danger that enthusiasm fired by emotion may overwhelm the consciousness of not only the individual but also the collective, as we shall see.

Post-Jungian readings, culture and ideology

Looking at the ways in which post-Jungian readings imply that screen myths might work on audiences entails considering how those myths relate to the cultural and ideological values to which the films' audiences were exposed at the time of the product's release. We shall find that questioning the psychological effect of films frequently brings the political context and the intervention of the medium itself into consideration. As Andrew Samuels (2001: 28) argues, the connection between the psychological and the political cannot be ignored in either the domestic domain or society at large: 'Individuals live not only their own individual lives but also the life of the times. (Jung is always quoted as telling his students that "when you treat the individual you treat the culture".) People cannot be seen in isolation from the society and culture that has played a part in forming them'. And, 'Politics of both a destructive and a creative kind show up in family patterns, gender relations, connections between wealth and (mental) health, control of information and accompanying imagery, and in religious and artistic assumptions' (p. 5).

In the microcosm, since people have a political self, the political events of a lifetime will have contributed to their individual political myth. In the macrocosm, politics is inevitably psychological – both emotional and irrational. Whether in religious fundamentalism, nationalism or ethnic cleansing, politics embodies the psyche of a people (Samuels 2001: 5, 28). Samuels's observations are pertinent in a study of the psychological impact of film and television because the majority of people know most of the great political upheavals of their lifetimes – be they war, change of government or loss of charismatic leaders – as mediated occurrences. It seems to follow that both the individual self and the collective consciousness may be shaped in part both by the psychological impact of high political drama and by the political impact of high psychological drama on the screen. It also seems likely that this may be the case whether that drama is occurring in a social or a fictional sphere.

Political and psychological inflation

In the very public arena of cinema and television with which we are concerned, the psychological and the political are constantly juxtaposed, while the media amplify their conjunction. The English-language tabloid media, which so espouse influence through sensationalised allegations about the current state of our culture, frequently claim that the psychological power of certain movies (not to speak of videotapes and video games) brings about a direct response in at least some members of the audience. They insist that screen fictions are the instrumental cause of socially undesirable behaviour. This topic is dug up whenever events, stories or characters on screen can be alleged to have aroused high emotions that are publicly shared. There are indeed times when the experience of watching a film will cause concern to numbers of people. On other occasions, however, it is the press coverage itself which starts things by stimulating anxiety in a cross-section of the public, many of whom will not have seen the film or programme in question. Either way, the tabloids latch onto anxiety and amplify it in a feedback loop of manufactured hysteria. What we see, to revert to Jungian terms, is a collective inflation orchestrated for venal reasons.

It works like this: where an incident has been reported which resembles the immoral actions of characters in a controversial film (it may be a crime or other form of anti-social behaviour), it will be alleged to have been committed as a result of copycat action. If the offenders can be shown to have seen the film in question, that is taken as proof of the connection. But even if there is no evidence of any crime having occurred as a consequence of audience exposure to that or a similar controversial film, the press may drum up the fear that crimes are *likely* to be committed in the future by members of the audience because such films incite them to maniacal conduct.

This is not the place to rehearse the vast, inconclusive literature on the effects of film and television programmes. But I do want to touch on whether there is any justification for the idea that films should be regarded as in some way dangerous. It is often argued that movies such as *The Silence of the Lambs* (Jonathan Demme, USA, 1990)[2] or *Natural Born Killers* (Oliver Stone, USA, 1994) incite imitation. A lawyer actually attempted to sue Oliver Stone on behalf of a client who had been shot by two runaway teenagers on a murderous rampage. When caught, they said that they had been inspired by repeated viewing of *Natural Born Killers.* The lawyer argued that the director as artist and Warner Brothers as distributor should share responsibility for murders that were tied by their

2 Analysed in Izod (2001: 105–23).

perpetrators and the press to the film (Moss 1998: 4). Stone's rebuff was characteristically terse: 'Has your father been brutalised? Sue Oedipus and call Hamlet as a witness. Do you hate your mother? Blame Medea and Joan Crawford' (cited in Moss 1998).

The allegation that films are in some sense the sole, direct cause of crimes carried out after their release (and sometimes in their name) is undoubtedly too crude to be persuasive. As Stephen Moss argues, it may be that among the causes of crime a film is one fragment in a grotesque jigsaw with many pieces, but zoom in on that one factor alone, and the larger social picture is lost (Moss 1998).

When films are reckoned as part of the larger picture, however, some do seem to contribute to the disturbance of certain vulnerable people. Trauma may be suffered either by an individual alone or as member of a group. David Hewison has written concerning insecure individuals watching film that not everyone has a sufficient degree of mastery over their symbolic experiences to enable them to play with symbols (2000: 291). That process of play, known as active imagining, I have described as a productive way of integrating film with personal experience so as to enhance individuation. The challenge in so attempting is to surrender a measure of control to a film's images and accommodate the psychological disruption they may produce (Izod 2001: 15–32). Hewison observed, however, that, contrary to what might be thought, it requires a strong and flexible ego to be able to tolerate the lessening of conscious control which is essential if the exercise of active imagining is to be productive. But many patients come to him with partial or fragmented ego development. Symbols are more likely to play with them than they to be able to play with symbols. He cites as a familiar phenomenon in the consulting room patients who read a film erroneously. They use the film to meet needs which press on them so heavily as not to let them see they are misreading the text. For such patients, a film may provide an illustration of how they see themselves, or may touch on memories of complexes so painful they have to 'rewrite' their experience of the movie (Hewison 2000: 291–3). Can a film be read erroneously as an encouragement to act cruelly by those whose drives already push them toward brutality? Has a psychological inflation occurred in such cases? Possibly this is what happened with the murderers who cited *Natural Born Killers* as their inspiration. Certainly their allegations about its effect were a troubling misinterpretation of a film more plausibly read as an attack on the tabloid American media that glorify violence.

Emotions, audiences and the cultural frame of reference

Each movie-goer is present in the cinema both as an individual and as one of a crowd. Where a film evokes strong emotions, a collective response may form – plainly evidenced by laughter, flinching, groans and occasionally applause. If the collective experience develops with great intensity, the individual may be overwhelmed by it, not least because the emotions that films generate usually touch us before we can guard against them. Once again, on-screen actions are virtual, but the emotions they arouse are real.

In general we expect mainstream feature films to try and excite emotion principally for the gratification of their audiences. But whilst this is characteristic of the dominant form in English-language cinema, it has never been a universal model for filmmaking. Propaganda films, for example, attempt to do the contrary. They seek to use viewers' emotion to focus their interpretation on a limited range of meanings designed to reinforce in their minds the values which the films' sponsors wish to propagate. This can be seen in the case of *Triumph of the Will* (Leni Riefenstahl, Germany, 1934). In its day, a favoured element in the monstrous Nazi propaganda machine – a key piece in that dreadful jigsaw puzzle – it sought to move people in support of their social and political programme. The film attempted to generate an overawed response inspired by the size and efficiency of Hitler's military power. It appears to have succeeded in its aim – but it is important to note that it did so within the cultural and political framework of its particular historical moment. In its day its propaganda message complemented a collective paranoia that already existed, intensifying the ugly mood. With the passage of time, however, *Triumph of the Will* became an unthreatening historical document.

In the chapters that follow, we shall not be analysing propaganda *per se*, but independent and authored films as well as television documentaries in addition to some mainstream movies. Nevertheless, propaganda, ideology, documentary *and* fiction are close bedfellows. The emotional impact of a feature film is no less bound to the time, circumstance and culture of its day than a current affairs programme on, say, an aspect of public health such as the dangers of obesity. Having said this, the impact of film on people's social behaviour – whether for good or evil – is negligible compared with the influence of the more fanatical expressions of religious belief. There are, sadly, innumerable examples past and present of religiously inspired political movements that through the ages have urged their followers to unspeakable acts of hatred against their fellow beings – often neighbours onto whom they project their own demons. *Triumph of the Will* was exceptionally influential for a film precisely because it was released into a symbolic arena already shaped by a political movement of quasi-religious intensity.

Other factors make it hard to deny, however, that feature films can exert some influence on social behaviour and psychology. Fiction, no less than factual, screen narratives and images can inculcate fashions, sell toys, goods and services, promote film stars and help set the agenda for widespread discussion of a whole variety of issues. Common speech often relies on quotes and anecdotes from popular films and television shows to convey ideas and meanings. Sachleben and Yenerall recognise that when the audience takes phrases or gestures which please them from the screen, those utterances may pass into common usage detached from the memory of their origins. They cite the example of Homer Simpson's characteristic grunt 'd'oh!' which for North Americans now refers to a bone-headed mistake and a lack of common sense or intelligence. In such instances, people's enjoyment of the source film can be seen to have registered in the collective consciousness (Sachleben and Yenerall 2004: 1). In short, cinema and television provide millions with common frames of reference in relation to many aspects of life, both social and private. The question remains whether the predicaments of characters on screen so touch the audience as to impact on their own psychological state.

Individualism, formal realism and 'identification'

Mainstream cinema in the West is predominantly devoted to exaltation of the individual as the focus and centre of all that is worthwhile. The ideology of individualism was massively strengthened in the second half of the twentieth century through the endeavours of the advertising and marketing industries in order to enhance the circulation of capital in the post-industrial age. This thrust impacted not only on commerce and design but also on themes, forms and style in the arts. Simon Frith, for example, points out that musical hybridity and syncretism are making for increasingly complex relationships between national and cultural identities and music. Whereas previously the experience of music had often contributed to the formation of politics (for example in both African-American and radical social movements in the USA), it seemed at the end of the twentieth century to be becoming much less powerful in constructing a collective identity. Now music tended to support individualism (Frith 1999: 224–6).

Mainstream cinema is deeply implicated in that ideology through the machinery of formal realism, a prime characteristic of much popular storytelling ever since the novel evolved. Among the elements required to endow a story with the characteristics of formal realism are that its main protagonists must have a developing personal history and be psychologically plausible. They should have not only an outer life of words and deeds, but also an inner one to which audience members give their assent. That assent is commonly won by an interplay between outer and inner life governed by narrative cause and effect. Typically, something which happens in the story world affects a protagonist. The character's inner response to that occurrence changes his or her mental state and causes a reaction which motivates the way he or she reacts. That reaction will probably be the next event in the story world, a word or deed which in due course will bring about its own effect on both the inner and outer life of one or more of the other protagonists. In mainstream movies the resultant chain of action and reaction which bridges inner and outer lives seeks to persuade viewers that they are witnessing main characters undergoing plausibly motivated and recognisable emotions. The requirement that audiences should be able to recognise the affect that protagonists are experiencing (supposedly essential if the box office is to prosper) sometimes leads filmmakers to telegraph emotions blatantly. This occurs because access to the inner life of protagonists motivated by the ongoing drama is reckoned to be an essential component if an audience is to 'identify' with them.

Most scripts depend on what is loosely termed 'identification' as a means of arousing the audience's interest in, and binding them to, the characters. Reliance on this mechanism has become so much the norm that British and American journalists writing about English-language movies have habituated to it, as if identification were an infallible aesthetic drug. In their reviews they refer to the degree to which a film encourages audiences to 'identify' with lead characters as the yardstick that makes it possible to gauge in advance its likely box office success. The charismatic nature of a film star's persona when augmented by the machinery of 'identification' is believed further to enrich the spectator's experience by giving them an intense feeling of what it is like to be the star character in question. All in all, 'identification' has become such a key index of quality in both movie production and consumption that its impact on audiences cannot be ignored.

Structure of sympathy, and empathy

Murray Smith has examined the phenomenon in detail. He points out that when the term is bandied about, it gestures vaguely toward a present-day 'folk theory'. This claims that we find ourselves becoming attached to characters who demonstrate qualities and values that somewhat resemble those which we like to think we ourselves should possess. Furthermore, it conveys the idea that we experience vicariously with those characters the emotions which they undergo (Smith 1995: 2). 'Identification' therefore is a topic worth our investigating as a mechanism through which the psychological predicaments of characters on screen may infiltrate spectators' minds.

Smith shows that the machinery of identification is both more intricate and draws viewers into a greater variety of imagined relationships with characters than is understood by most of those who rely laxly upon the concept. He prefers to describe the usual level of engagement as deriving from a 'structure of sympathy', and this he differentiates from empathy. The structure of sympathy is emphatically *not* an inert narrative system embedded in the text with which willy nilly the spectator 'identifies'. On the contrary, the spectator actively responds to stimuli from the text which he or she may find sufficiently engaging to organise his or her reactions in a structure of sympathy (Smith 1995: 82). It follows that one person may become involved in a structure of sympathy while someone else watching the same movie may be untouched by it.

The spectator engages in three kinds of text-led activity to produce this structure. The first is recognition, often taken for granted because it is a staple function of formal realism. Recognition refers to the spectator's construction of character. Usually in film it coheres 'around the image of a body, as an individuated and continuous human agent' (Smith 1995: 82). Although this process is not usually considered in terms relating to the folk concept of identification, its importance is readily grasped from the care with which film producers select actors for their look, movement and vocal qualities as signifiers of meaning. To put it crudely, villains and heroes seldom look alike.

The second process Smith names is alignment. He describes it as akin to the literary notion of focalisation. It is brought about in part by the degree to which the narration restricts itself to the actions of a single character. In addition, it is governed by the extent of access to the internal state of a character, a function which may vary from one character to another within a narrative. Alignment thus refers to the systematic apportioning of knowledge among characters and between them and the spectator (1995: 83).

The third process is allegiance. It depends upon the spectator having what he or she believes to be reliable access to the character's state of mind and on understanding the context of the character's actions. The spectator then makes a moral evaluation of the character on the basis of this knowledge. He or she categorises the character's actions as, for example, harmful, and then experiences affective or emotional arousal deriving from the categorisation of those actions (probably, in the instance mentioned, anger). Many factors, Smith adds, contribute to the process of moral evaluation and hence to allegiance: among them character action, iconography and music are particularly significant (Smith 1995: 84–5).

If we enter the structure of sympathy by engaging with a character on the basis of recognition, alignment and allegiance (and, remember, we don't have to), 'our responses are at a tangent to those of the character: they are acentral, sympathetic rather than empathic' (Smith 1995: 85). Empathy, in contrast, is central imagining. Smith finds it to be distinct from sympathy or acentral imagining by virtue of the subject's emptying out his or her own qualities 'in order to simulate the states of the target subject: it is not a question of sharing but of imaginative substitution' (p. 96). However, the division between the two modes of imagining is far from absolute, not least because Smith sees that central imagining or empathy is not confined (as folklore implies) to involuntary responses which the individual subject cannot avoid, but may also be voluntary. This recognition provides an important key in adapting Smith's work to a post-Jungian theoretical milieu.

Smith distinguishes two types of involuntary empathic responses. An autonomous reaction occurs when, for example, we experience a shock identical to that which the character feels – where, for example, we, like the character, are startled by a loud, unexpected gunshot. Unlike the other forms of empathy, this response does not arise from an engagement with the character (p. 102). But the second type of involuntary response, affective mimicry, does deepen engagement with the character concerned. Affective mimicry is the phenomenon which filmmakers think of as the power of the close up and the reaction shot. It occurs when the facial and bodily cues given forth by another person cause us reflexively to simulate the basic, broad affect that person is experiencing. On screen, the large and focused dimensions of a character's visible (and, we should add, audible) cues augment their impact on the spectator. Meanwhile, information provided by the total narrative context enables us to refine our grasp of the emotions being experienced by the character (Smith 1995: 98–9, 101–2).

Some empathic responses are voluntary and Smith refers to them as emotional simulation. This is part of the process of discovering more about the behaviour of a person in a situation concerning which we have limited knowledge: 'We imaginatively project ourselves into their situation, and hypothesize as to the emotion(s) they are experiencing' (1995: 97). This is obviously pertinent to many characters in fiction as through trial and error we build ourselves a picture of their affective states by simulating them. However, as Smith points out:

> If this is correct, then one of the very mechanisms through which we form beliefs about the traits and occurrent states of characters – the kind of information on which the structure of sympathy depends – is, in fact, a form of empathy. For in simulating an emotion or any other intentional state, we are not merely recognizing or understanding it, but centrally imagining it.
>
> (Smith 1995: 98)

According to Smith there are, nevertheless, two key differences between the structure of sympathy (acentral imagining) on the one hand and empathy (central imagining) on the other. Sympathetic phenomena require comprehension of narrative and characters. Empathic phenomena do not. In the case of sympathetic responses, the spectator cognitively recognises an emotion and responds with a different but appropriate emotion based on his or her evaluation of the character. With empathic responses, the spectator simulates or experiences the very affect or emotion that the character is feeling (1995: 102).

For Smith, empathic responses usually function within the structure of sympathy to help the spectator gain an understanding of the fictional world and its characters. Empathic responses are 'constantly filled out, modified, sometimes overturned by our cognitive construction of the narrative (that is, by what we come to know through our ordinary perceptual, conceptual, and inferential processing)' (1995: 103).

However, Smith concedes that in some circumstances the contrary may be true. As a form of involuntary empathy, affective mimicry has an extraordinary power to disrupt and force a reorganisation in the reading of a film's moral structure. It may produce responses which overwhelm the structure of sympathy: Hitchcock, for instance, sometimes used mimicry deliberately to run counter to sympathy (1995: 103–4).

Emotional investment

Smith's demonstration that the machinery of 'identification' is intricate and that it draws viewers into a wide variety of imagined relationships with characters is compatible with a Jungian perspective. But Jungians see empathy as having greater significance than Smith allows. Although giving due weight to the force of affective mimicry, he does not recognise that the phenomenon he describes as emotional simulation can also overwhelm sympathy. As we shall see, Jungians would argue that when we imaginatively project ourselves into a character's situation, and hypothesise as to the emotions he or she is experiencing, it is possible, even if this be a voluntary mental investment, to feel so moved by those emotions that empathic responses dominate our processing of narrative data. Should the spectator so engage with the text, something resembling a spontaneous process of projection and projective identification can occur. Then the film becomes much more than a text that encourages simulation but an imaginary space deeply invested with personal libido which consequently partakes of both fantasy and the real world.

An important paper by Ira Konigsberg on the transitional phenomena of cinema illuminates this idea. Although Konigsberg is developing post-Freudian and Lacanian theoretical perspectives, the psychological dynamic he describes as being invoked in the watching of films accords with post-Jungian thought. In using the phrase 'transitional phenomena' Konigsberg picks up a term originating with D. W. Winnicott to refer to those intermediate objects such as teddy bears which children select to substitute for the mother when they begin to separate out from her. As the child grows into adulthood such transitional phenomena become diffused into an intermediate space. Part private fantasy and part based in observation, this transitional space assists the individual in dealing with the tensions between inner and outer reality by bringing the two worlds into relation. For Konigsberg, the images on the cinema screen provide us with just such a transitional, subjective-objective world (1996: 873–4). They are both tied to the real world yet not of it, being, as two-dimensional images subject to both spatial and temporal composition and editing, more like the images that populate our imaginations. The viewer then imposes on those images something that does not exist in actuality but is a product of his or her own interactions with them (1996: 881):

> In the silent, darkened theater, removed from a direct confrontation with reality, and perceiving images that seem half-real and transitional we slip into a state of half-wakefulness, into a reverie that weakens our defenses and sets loose our own fantasies and wishes to interact and fuse with the characters and even the landscape that we see on the screen. I do not have to describe for you the way in which we loosen hold of ourselves at times and become fastened to what we see on the screen, but not completely fastened – a merging takes place, a sense of the characters as me and not-me, as part of my subjective world and part of objective reality. What actually transpires is a process of introjection followed by projection, a process by which we . . . take in the images and then project ourselves into them as they appear before us – a process of introjection and projective identification.
>
> (1996: 885–6)

> In the dynamics I am describing, the introjection of the film images triggers an internal process by which we invest these images with our own psychic and emotional overlays and then project them back out, along with our own involvement, onto their imprints on the screen – a process that continues, back and forth, as we watch the film. I need only remind you of the sudden jolt we feel, of our sense of loneliness and incompleteness as we are forced to pull back into ourselves, as our ties with the images on the screen are suddenly severed when the film ends.
>
> (1996: 886)

We may note, by the way, that one of the merits of Konigsberg's piece is that it shows (which Smith's exclusive concern with characters does not permit) how spectators may respond in an engaged manner to not only characters but the film *as a whole* – a broader dimension that also harmonises with a Jungian approach.

Konigsberg specifies, as an integral part of the process that he delineates, an oscillation between introjection and projection. The experience of Jungian analysts indicates that where introjection is followed by projective identification, the flow of libido back and forward between subject (the person experiencing the feeling) and object may be either conscious or unconscious. Introjection principally, but projection to a lesser degree, both facilitate an empathic response (see Jung 1921: 290, 452; Samuels *et al.* 1986: 85–6, 105–6, 113–14). Such a system of images circulating between the spectator's inner and outer worlds gives empathy greater significance in the film-watching process than Smith accepts. Rather than being limited to either affective mimicry or the testing of hypotheses concerning the emotional state of a character, the Jungian idea of empathy recognises that the subject makes an emotional investment in the image. Indeed, where the spectating subject invests libido massively, the image may end up so heavily freighted that it holds unconscious contents that warp the text to an empathic reading rendered unique to that spectator by the pressure of his or her needs.

At their most intense, films excite the emotions of their viewers to the point where some spectators redraft the map of their known universe. Knowledge of all things numinous carries a high-voltage energy charge and the cinema is no exception. When movies cause the emotions to run high, they bear with them all the concomitant risks associated with the uncertainty whether the individual spectator will use the stimulus for good (enhancing, say, knowledge of self and the world) or bad (the damaged personality suffering further harm, or the reinforcement of bigotry). From a Jungian point of view, for the person with a relatively healthy personality, this is a challenge not to be evaded. If such a person is to mature as an individual, he or she must sooner or later face up to and develop an understanding of an inescapable part of the human condition, namely the latent potential for evil no less than good. Thus while a few films do expose a minority of viewers to the danger of negative inflation to which I referred earlier, the case for emotionally dangerous or subversive films is at bottom the same as for every other art form. They have the capability to switch on the surprising kick light that throws an estranging flare into the darkness, peels the inner eyes to look afresh and starts the process of enquiry. That, as I said before, can lead to the enhancing of the psychological well-being by making available to consciousness concealed urges, fears and delights.

Culture and psyche

As indicated earlier, screen texts that feature myths and archetypal imagery can only be fully understood by reaching beyond the lone spectator's interest in them to a shared engagement on the part of significant sectors of the audience. Jungian theories are always concerned with collective experience of the symbolic and are therefore prime in the psychological exploration of culture. It is tautological to aver that a measure of collective consciousness will accompany the intense reaction to any given film for as long as popular reliving of that movie experience endures. However, the concept of collective consciousness, although it sits comfortably with the familiar idea of culture as a social construct, is not alone a sufficient account of the shared cinematic experience in which the excitation of symbolic material occurs. Erich Neumann's summary of Jung's words about the bilateral existence of symbols indicates why:

> Like the individual symbol, the social symbol valid for the group is 'never of exclusively conscious or exclusively unconscious origin,' but is produced by the 'equal collaboration of both.' The symbol therefore has a rational side 'which accords with reason,' and another side which is 'inaccessible to reason, since it is composed not only of data of a rational nature, but of the irrational data of pure inward and outward perception.'
>
> (Neumann 1954: 366–7 citing Jung 1921: 477–8, revised)

In common with all cultural forms, films are vehicles for symbolic energy charged not only with collective consciousness but also with shared, irrational material that has its source in the unconscious. Jung used the term 'the collective unconscious' to refer to phenomena that appeared to animate the psychological landscape of the human species; but some post-Jungians have developed the concept of 'the cultural unconscious' which for three reasons functions better as an indicator of the provenance of this partially formed energy. Firstly, however vast the audience for even a Hollywood blockbuster, that audience remains no more than a minor sector of the human species as a whole, though its international composition may be impressive. Secondly, no film with its characters and the stars who play them is ever received with unanimous acclaim by all those who see it. Thirdly, symbols found in screen texts (like other cultural forms) must indeed, to conform to Jung's meaning of the word, have a dimension that receives energy from the unconscious. However, those energies appear to lie nearer to the surface than the deep, collective unconscious from which are sourced the major archetypes of all human experience. Jung himself likened the unconscious to concentric spheres of variable depths; but, other than by distinguishing the personal from the collective, he did not differentiate them. The cultural unconscious, a term first used by Joseph Henderson (1984) is helpful because it points to an intermediate zone from which unconscious or semi-conscious arousals disturb and sway consciousness but without the potentially cataclysmic consequences which can occur when contents irrupt from the collective unconscious. It may be partly for this reason that the collective consequences of shocking movies are seldom socially uncontained. I shall develop and apply the idea of the cultural unconscious in Chapter 6.

The broad significance in psychosocial terms of the contest over culture is highlighted by Anthony Stevens. He sees culture as having the same function as instinct in mammalian societies as 'the means by which adaptive wisdom is passed from one generation to the next' (1991: 123). Although the accumulated wisdom of the generations does not become obsolete, cultural traditions would nonetheless stultify were they not challenged and renewed. Ideally a homeostatic, or self-correcting balance is struck between the conservation of traditional values and new, probably youthful, drives for change. For Stevens that contest mirrors the young hero's urgent efforts to break away from the ambit of his or her parents and forge both his or her own life and psychological independence (1991: 124–5). In Stevens's judgement, the balance between old and new has been thrown out of kilter by on the one hand a reduction in interest in the spiritual quality of western culture and on the other an increased obsession with material development and personal gratification. In short, he sees our values as a culture are predominantly adolescent, unsuited to the carrying of the wisdom of the ages (1991: 186).

Leaving aside, as Stevens does, the inconvenient fact that a large proportion of the audience for the screen (and all commercially-funded culture) actually comprises adolescents and young adults, there is hardly a target more easy or satisfying to hit with the charge of sponsoring adolescent values than the ceaseless flow of English-language film and television. The stuff pours out from the great production machines on an industrial scale. Indeed, there is fascinating Jungian work to be done analysing the supposedly adolescent nature of, say, the blockbuster action movie. So much of this and related genres has afflicted the cultural forms they have taken over with an elderly, constipated feel. Far from being insurrectionary, it is seldom anarchic, joyful, enraged or even exuberant material. Much of it passes for adolescent because it requires the spectator to experience an endless succession of aural and visual sensations and shocks. Here we find time and again the culture of the *senex* inculcating the *puer* – the elderly in heart and mind inflicting their ossifying culture on the young. Although both the *senex* and *puer aeternus* will be found as character types in what follows (both archetypes govern *Besieged*'s Jason Kinsky in Chapter 4), study of the blockbuster as pseudo-adolescent culture must wait for another occasion. This volume is concerned with analysing a selection of mature films as a means of reflecting on the criteria set out above.

Chapter 1, co-written with Jana Branch, shows how a film which frustrates audiences' appetite for identification and emotional gratification allows us to see the strength of the machinery of desire in mainstream cinema. In his 1975 film *Barry Lyndon*, Stanley Kubrick offered audiences exquisite aesthetic pleasures both for the eye and ear. Images of some of the finest eighteenth-century European great houses and gardens were complemented by pastiches of the paintings and music of the age. But this was not sufficient to beguile the mass audience. Whereas in *Tom Jones* (Tony Richardson, UK, 1963), another film that originated in a picaresque novel, spectators were given points of view from within the scene and offered the illusion of being caught up in the action, in *Barry Lyndon* the dramatic style was flattened. This and other aesthetic devices removed any chance that spectators might become emotionally engaged in the story. Audiences observed the characters' lives as if from a distance rather than lived them vicariously. Kubrick simultaneously encouraged the twentieth-century expectation that the protagonists can be known intimately, while frustrating it.

Kubrick's work is featured again in the second chapter which, like the first, was written with Jana Branch. *Eyes Wide Shut*, unlike *Barry Lyndon*, hovers poised between a recognisable world of daily New York actuality and a fantasy world which looks almost the same. That illusory dimension of things springs from the characters' psychological dispositions. Those dispositions interlock so tightly, individual to group, group to individual, that the leading protagonists, Bill and Alice Harford, are pressured to live out a destructive collective fantasy which has its roots in decorously masked avidity for power. The chapter articulates the interaction of numerous robust archetypal figures but concludes by querying whether *Eyes Wide Shut* could have exercised its audiences in quite the way it troubled its protagonists.

There follow three chapters exploring psychological currents in Bernardo Bertolucci's latest films. A deep reading of *Stealing Beauty* reveals that, nearly 30 years after he declared that it would be impossible to connect his interest in politics and psychology with his aesthetics, he found the mechanism for doing so in a film which examines the relationship between art, artists and the lives of those around them. His dramatisation provided spectators with an opportunity to feel the energy of anima politics in family relationships. *Besieged* centres on an unlikely connection between unequals – a young medical student parachuted into Rome from her East African home and the owner of the house where she cleans and finds lodgings. Bertolucci and his co-writer Clare Peploe treat with great subtlety the edgy relationship which eventually develops despite the master-servant configuration of their first contact. As the plot progresses, a delightful feeling tone is established, generated by the potential for mutual discovery between these two. And they achieve this while implicating the social and cultural milieus of the characters in forming their dispositions, a device which cunningly adds to the uncertainty of the outcome. *The Dreamers* extends the social range and weaves sex, psychoanalysis, memory, dreaming, history, revolution and filmic style into a rich tapestry. It reveals spectacularly the strengths and weaknesses of a mature authorial style: wonderfully sophisticated and delightful in dealing with serious issues it seems nevertheless not sufficiently to have taken into account the circumstances and culture of the largest sector of the audience (the under 25s) to have achieved the political impact Bertolucci said he wanted the film to make.

Chapter 6 rounds out a circuit by bringing us to Hollywood, the most powerful source of myths in the western world. *S1møne* satirises the extravagant vacuity of Hollywood production at its most bone-headed. It reprises the Pygmalion story (previously recalled in *My Fair Lady*) and returns to a myth that resurfaces probably because it undermines the tendency of male heroes to succumb to sexism. *S1møne* enthusiastically evokes and punctures the male vanity which some media men flatter themselves is their creativity. These delusions are the materials through which writer and director Andrew Niccol mocks both the industry and (even more interestingly for the argument of this book) the audiences who so passionately desire to be gulled. In his film we find passions urged by images electrified by the cultural unconscious goading the on-screen audience to wildly irrational acts of fandom. *S1mone*'s actual audiences, though amused, were smaller and more restrained.

Documentary, with its roots in observable fact, is a sub-genre which might not be expected to reveal mythological foundations. However, documentaries often take story form, and even when they do not, they have no choice but to adopt a point of view, whether it be the filmmakers' or the commissioning broadcasters'. Despite their supposed objectivity, they are not hermetically closed off from myth. And some documentaries present images, people or narratives that have archetypal resonances. Chapter 7 discusses three kinds of documentary innovated in the past 20 years. It first considers some archetypal figures which appeared in mass-market docu-soaps of the 1990s. Then it looks at the poetic documentary and the input of an authorial imagination which declares itself in order to add to the viewer's pleasurable engagement with the film. The chapter closes with an examination of first-person documentary and demonstrates how a remarkable example of self-therapy exerts the force of emotions to the degree that it stirs some viewers into a deep experience of the filmmaker's distress, and encourages some among them to seek help in the long process of recovering from domestic torment suffered in their own past lives.

Chapter 8 argues that a key to the Western genre's formidable strengths and weaknesses is that it has constituted a primary locus where battle has been joined for the collective white soul of the United States of America. The dominant ideology of the genre is examined in so far as it impinges on the psychological characteristics of both the characters and the myth of the West itself. The genre has the capability to function as allegory (energised by the play with archetypal images) that provides an armature upon which may be woven readings bearing on moral, political, economic and spiritual issues. Two detailed readings of films released in 2003 demonstrate how closely the genre can mirror concerns that occupy the minds of its American audiences, though the reflection of those concerns is not necessarily perceived as such by the spectators.

A recurring problem faces the Jungian who writes about film and television. It arises because the underlying theory is not as well known in this field of study as Freud's ideas, which, together with Lacan's development thereof, dominated the field since the 1970s. The issue is whether to recapitulate Jung's thought and justify adapting it to screen analysis every time one uses it. Having deployed quite extensively those parts of post-Jungian theory that were needful in my previous two books, I have decided against repeating the task on this occasion. Those who need basic grounding in Jung's ideas are referred to the guide to further reading on page 225.

On post-Jungian schools

Nevertheless the reader may find it helpful to know how this book relates to the broad currents of post-Jungian thought in the early twenty-first century. Analysts who adopted Jung's writings and practice as their professional inheritance developed his ideas in differing ways as the years passed. Certain distinct emphases emerged in the course of this process; and it has been widely accepted since Andrew Samuels published *Jung and the Post-Jungians* in 1985 that three substantial groups can be identified. They are the classical, archetypal and developmental schools.

The developmental school

To begin with the last, the developmental school has sought to remedy two lacks in Jung's theorising. As Hester McFarland Solomon noted concerning the first of these omissions, 'Jung and his immediate followers did not focus on the depth psychological aspects of early infant and childhood development' (1997: 119). The second gap was a consequence of Jung and his immediate associates not having sufficiently studied the varieties of relationship that occur in the consulting room. Detailed study of what became known as transference and countertransference made it possible to anticipate and account for changes that occur in the association between analyst and client as analysis continues.

Freudians had always looked with intense interest at both questions, being particularly aware of their interrelationship in infantile transference (the process by which the child becomes psychologically invested in the parent, usually the mother). It is not that Jung ignored the development of the human personality but, as Samuels notes, his writings were scattered across his work because of the urgency with which his focus moved from the personal to the transpersonal or collective (1985: 133). Post-Jungians of the developmental school believed that Jung's want of extended theorising of this field left analytical psychology seriously handicapped in the consulting room (Solomon 1997: 119–20). The attention they devoted to rectifying these defects amounted to an attempt at repairing a damaging consequence of the rift between Freud and Jung. As Solomon remarks, the split had left the map of the human psyche seemingly divided between the two camps. Freud and his followers concentrated on the reductive method that sought to provide a comprehensive explanation of the development of personality from the earliest sources in the individual's psyche. Meanwhile Jung and his first followers focused teleologically on the functioning of mature states of the adult mind whereby all psychological events were thought to have a meaningful goal (Solomon 1997: 120–1).

Among its other capacities, developmental analysis throws light on the construction of the individual's personality and the sources of problems within it. Adapted to the 'reading' of characters in feature films, it can sometimes help the observer understand the behaviour of fictional people. We shall, for example, encounter characters in *Stealing Beauty* and *S1møne* (Chapters 3 and 6 respectively) the analysis of whom is enriched by a comprehension of their putative developmental case history. Having said this, however, the main thrust of my book, rather than engaging with reductive analysis, is directed toward interpreting archetypal images and speculating in an informed way about what they might mean for audiences.

The archetypal school

According to Michael Vannoy Adams, the archetypal school emerged in the late 1960s and early 1970s. It grew up in reaction to what James Hillman and his followers regarded as 'unnecessarily metaphysical assumptions in Jung and the complacent, rote application of Jungian tenets' (Adams 1997: 103). As Adams points out, a key element of this school's thinking is that they value the archetypal but discount the archetype. Hillman holds that an individual may identify any image (even the most banal) as being archetypal. Doing so indicates that from that person's perspective such an image has value and a certain typicality. The business of the archetypal psychoanalyst is to work with the image so identified by a client and to treat it as a material phenomenon. It is emphatically not to follow classical Jungians and look beyond the image to infer the prior existence of an archetype, for Hillman argued that the archetypal analyst must stick as close to the image as possible, helping clients to feel, experience, play with and respond to what their dreams and associations present them with. Archetypalists encourage their clients to appreciate that the fantasies produced by the imagination are the phenomena of reality, and as a consequence they decline to interpret images (Samuels 1985: 242; Adams 1997: 103–5).

Jung often advised that the interpretation of images should be delayed in order to let them ferment in the imagination and guide both client and analyst. Nevertheless, their eventual interpretation, often against a background of myth, is a key part of a classical analysis. Hillman faulted this process, finding that it intellectualised the experience and reduced the image to a general, pre-existing concept. Adams gives as an instance of such reduction the automatic linking of a concrete, dream image of a woman to the concept of the anima. Images of a variety of women with distinctive characteristics may be presented in an individual's dreams and associations. They are falsified if reduced to one single concept (1997: 108–9). Archetypal psychology 'values the particularity of all images over the generality of any concept' because for Hillman 'the imagination is truly autonomous, independent of the individual, transcendent to the subject' (in Adams: 109, 106). It has a 'transubjective' dimension.

This concept has points of contact with Jung's idea of the transpersonal or collective unconscious. It is explained by Samuels as the archetypalists' argument that the authority of fantasy imagery, even poetic imagery, comes from its being as old as humanity. In-depth imagining is both a condition and an expression of humans' existence as a species. In other words, images *are* phylogeny, themselves the very evolutionary history of the species (1985: 244). It follows that for Hillman, conventional notions of fantasy and reality are not opposed, but could swap places. Fantasy is always being embodied; whilst behind what is actual there is always a fantasy image (Samuels 1985: 245). It is an idea which in modern times has been eloquently demonstrated by Arthur C. Clarke in *The Promise of Space*. He advances the idea that there is a powerful interaction between science and literature. From the second half of the nineteenth century the fiction of space travel expressed a deepening hunger for interplanetary travel. These imaginings eventually enticed people into undertaking the great labour needed to convert dreams and aspirations into the intricate material technologies of actual space travel (1968: 21–32). In due time the actualities of space fight fed back not only into documentaries but also fictions.

The archetypal school set their face against reductionism partly because they believe it can falsify the particular phenomena of an individual's dreams and thereby misdirect analysis. But in addition they hold that it contributes to the moulding of a distinctive western epistemology in which myths usually draw upon and in turn augment the idea of a single god rather than a multiplicity of gods such as those of Ancient Greece. Archetypalists prefer polytheism to monotheism not as a matter of religious belief but because:

> the Gods and Goddesses are the names of powers or forces which have autonomy and are not conditioned by or affected by social and historical events, by human will or reasoning, or by personal and individual factors . . . they are felt to be informing powers that give shape to social, intellectual, and personal behaviour.
>
> (Miller 1981 cited in Samuels 1985: 242)

In his gloss on this, Samuels adds that Miller and Hillman interpret the rise of monotheism as a metaphor for the limitations placed on imagination and variety in contemporary western culture (1985: 243). For archetypal psychologists, a multiplicity and diversity of gods better reflects what they see as the fragmented, shifting and diverse nature of the individual's psyche (Adams 1997: 109–10). Jung too regarded the Olympian gods as having the potential metaphorically to represent personifications of psychic forces, albeit it by the twentieth century they had been dethroned from their former glory as autonomous psychic contents and were hidden in the garb of phobias, obsessions and other neurotic symptoms (Jung 1957: 37; Adams

1997: 110–11). In analysing films, recognising the values associated with a variety of gods can help identify diverse character types in the societies represented on screen and assist with the understanding of their psychological disposition (see Bolen 1985, 1990).

In so far as the ideas of the archetypalists relate to screen studies, I prefer to think of them as embellishing and reframing Jung's work rather than negating it. When the archetypal images experienced in common by a movie-going audience are held to be as old as humanity and themselves the very evolutionary history of the species, then the difference from classical Jungian hypotheses concerning the nature of archetypes is not great.

The classical school

The classical Jungian takes the archetype as the source of and shaping energy behind the generation of archetypal images. They do so even while recognising that an archetype is a theoretical concept not capable of proof precisely because it is a component of the unconscious. The term refers not to content, but to inherited modes of psychic functioning: until activated, the archetypes are forms without content; when activated they govern patterns of behaviour. They are the centres of energy around which ideas, images and affects cohere. As a fundamental dimension of the human psyche, archetypes are collective by nature. Because of this transpersonal status, the images and affects to the generation of which they contribute can take a particular intensity. Their significance is that people participate in the shared experience of stories and myths that are perceived as having numinous or religious significance through their creation and reception of symbolic and archetypal images that give form to the underlying archetypes.

While both the classical and the archetypal post-Jungian must respect the image, the classical analyst will tend to see it as the phenomenon through which the unconscious manifests itself. As David L. Hart remarks, the classical approach 'relies on a spirit of dialogue between conscious and unconscious', 'making conscious the unconscious life' (1997: 89). Some films are like dreams in having the capacity to furnish to the conscious mind a picture of the collective unconscious psychological state that has been overlooked or disregarded (see Hart 1997: 90). It is for this reason that the interpretation of films seems to me to be justified, after their emotional and numinous impact have been afforded due time and attention so that they resonate in the psyche. Interpretation of some films will be justified because, whether deliberately or unconsciously, the filmmakers have concealed deeper levels of meaning from their audiences. More trenchantly, interpretation can give conscious direction to a numinous text and bring what may be its magical or religious qualities to shared conscious experience.

Chapter 1

Barry Lyndon and the limits of understanding[1]

Introduction

I have chosen to begin with an analysis of a film which repudiates my thesis. *Barry Lyndon* (Stanley Kubrick, UK, 1975) refuses the kind of cohesion that I shall argue can occur between the psychology of characters and the metaphoric meaning for audiences of the story world. That cohesion will in some instances implicate audiences deeply, not merely engaging their emotions in the fiction but mirroring and playing back to them formative elements of their culture. *Barry Lyndon* refuses audiences this intimate engagement, most obviously by denying their appetite for 'identification' with the hero. However, the manner in which Kubrick blocks the spectator's appetite for psychological engagement demonstrates his complete understanding of the regimes that channel desire in mainstream fiction. Indeed, the disappointing box office returns of this gorgeous film can be seen to be a consequence of his having challenged audiences' reluctance to forego a sense of emotional fulfilment when the fiction reaches its culmination.

Barry Lyndon and eighteenth-century realism

In the instance of this film in particular, set as it is in a historical period, one might have expected that Kubrick's famously obsessive attention to authenticity would be directed toward taking the viewer into a more complete experience of the eighteenth century. It matches this expectation that the entire film was shot on location, much of it in great houses. The director of photography, John Alcott, has described the lengths to which he went to light from sources appropriate to the time ('Photographing' 1976). And the costume designer has spoken about selecting fabrics to ensure they looked

1 This chapter was written with Jana Branch.

exactly like the paintings of the period (Harlan 2001). Overall, however, the attention to historically accurate detail can be shown to have another objective because the very intensity of attention to authentic lighting, costumes, sets, language, music and manners ultimately exhausts the idea that it is possible to recreate the past.

Critics and audiences alike were fascinated with Kubrick's sumptuously framed vision of the life of Redmond Barry. Similarities between the director's compositions and eighteenth-century portrait and landscape paintings were immediately noted (Combs 1976: 4; Houston 1976: 79). In fact, the carefully composed attention to the frame has the effect of flattening what is being captured. This is not surprising since both painting and film reduce three dimensions to two; but Kubrick went further, using a range of cinematic devices to distract us from looking too deep. Among these, Martin Scorsese remarked on the director's unexpected use of the zoom lens and recognised that it has the precise effect of flattening the image like an eighteenth-century painting (in Harlan 2001). Then too, a Zeiss lens originally designed for NASA to use in satellite photography was, at Kubrick's instigation, adapted for the shoot. The 0.7*f* lens being exceptionally fast, Kubrick and Alcott were able to employ it on the interior night scenes, which they lit exclusively with candles. The low light levels obliged them to film with the lens wide open and as a consequence they had almost no depth of field. In addition, the characters in the court scenes followed high fashion of the time by wearing white make-up. The combination of light, lens and cosmetics all augmented the flattening effect.

Further flattening is achieved by the narration: it pre-empts suspense by telling us ahead of time what will happen. Finally, the dramatic style is flattened such that audiences observe characters' lives as if from a distance rather than live them vicariously as spectators did in *Tom Jones* (Tony Richardson, UK, 1963). *Barry Lyndon* was compared with this film since both originated in picaresque novels. However, contrary to *Barry Lyndon*, in the earlier film (in common with most mainstream cinema) spectators were given points of view from within the scene and offered the illusion of being caught up in the action. *Tom Jones* exploits the complex apparatuses of formal realism, *Barry Lyndon* refuses them.

All in all, Kubrick takes us as close as we can get to the lost actuality, yet what results is still a flat, choreographed approximation of what might have been, based on a collection of artefacts. The impression of studied superficiality led some critics to conclude that this was the whole of Kubrick's point. But when so much effort is made to draw our attention into the gorgeously composed frame, another suspicion immediately arises: what is just beyond the frame? What is this carefully arranged version of events trying so hard to keep out? What is Kubrick, from a twentieth-century perspective, trying to tell us through the agency of a life lived and told from an eighteenth-century perspective?

On the surface *Barry Lyndon* is a simple 'rise and fall' story taking its form and manner (as Thackeray had done for his nineteenth-century serialised plot) from eighteenth-century picaresque novels. Closer scrutiny shows, however, that numerous voices and perspectives contribute to the film's account of one man whose story, as a consequence, is not at all a simple linear tale. Even the function of Kubrick's painterly style in supposedly recreating the past comes into question because it is not only concerned with achieving a retrospective realism through portraits and landscapes that resemble Reynolds and Gainsboroughs. As Penelope Houston noted, such images as Leonard Rossiter's absurdly vainglorious Captain Quin prancing a jig, and the cuckolded Sir Charles Lyndon (Frank Middlemass) gobbling in fury over the card table, bring to mind the grosser caricatures of Gillray, Rowlandson and Hogarth (1976: 78–9).

Barry's fall and rise – and fall

The story of Redmond Barry (Ryan O'Neal) does not actually follow the simple bell curve of rise and fall which its two-part structure suggests. It is more like a switchback ride. At the start of the tale his father is killed in a duel. Thereafter, his mother (Marie Kean) is only sustained by the generosity of her brother-in-law, himself close to bankruptcy. Barry (as the narrator calls him throughout) thinks of himself as a gentleman, but mother and son are only by grace and favour able to maintain the status of gentlefolk. A succession of personal disasters soon robs the young man of even this standing. He loses his cousin and first love Nora (Gay Hamilton) to John Quin, a captain in the English army; fights a duel with his rival, and appears to win but has to flee to escape the law; is robbed by highwaymen of everything but the clothes he stands in; volunteers for service in an Irish regiment of the English army; and has his first experience of war in a battle where his mentor Captain Grogan (Godfrey Quigley) is killed.

Only when he steals an officer's horse, uniform and identity to desert from the army do things begin to improve: 'Barry felt once more that he was in his proper sphere, and determined never again to fall from the rank of a gentleman', the narrator comments (but the hero's newly-acquired name Fakenham hints at the doubtful validity of this claim). While deserting, he meets a German girl, Lischen (Diana Koerner) with whom he stays, and they become lovers (perhaps the happiest point in his young life); but the risk of discovery soon obliges him to move on. Sure enough, in his next encounter he is uncovered as an impostor by Captain Potzdorf (Hardy Kruger), one of the recruiting officers of the Prussian army, and is cashiered into the brutalising ranks of that Great Power.

When the Seven Years' War ends, his fortunes begin to rise again, albeit from an insecure base. Potzdorf transfers him into the service of the Minister of Police as a counterspy. His target is the Chevalier de Balibari

(Patrick Magee), an Irish libertine suspected of espionage on behalf of the Austrian empress. But Barry is so affected by meeting this elegant fellow-exile from his own country that he teams up with him. And when the Prussians decide to expel the Chevalier from their country, it is Barry wearing the old man's apparel whom they unwittingly convey across the border to freedom, missing his master who had slipped away the night before. Thereafter Barry joins the Chevalier at the gaming tables of Europe's courts. The older man's ingenuity as a cheat and Barry's willingness to use his sword to enforce bad debts enable them to fleece many a silk-clad gambler.

His taste for the lifestyle of the rich confirmed and, we are told, with youthful notions of romantic love dispelled, Barry sets about conquering the heart of a 'woman of fortune and condition'. He courts the Countess of Lyndon (Marisa Berenson) without waiting for the death of Sir Charles, her antiquated husband. But disease, long years of indulgence and apoplexy brought on by Barry's carnal insolence swiftly carry off the old man. A year later Barry marries Lady Lyndon, fathers a son, Bryan, on her and thereafter confines her to nursery and domestic duties. Now he occupies himself with pleasures of the flesh, stooping to infidelity even with his wife's maids.

It is not, however, his raffish behaviour that undoes him: that too closely resembles the conduct of other gentlemen to command notice outside the family. Three factors bring him down. One is the cold anger of his stepson, Lord Bullingdon, whose gorge rises with Hamlet-like disgust at his mother's hasty marriage to an opportunist who does not love her. His feelings are compounded in that Barry, although a tender father to his own son, acts like a harsh parent toward Bullingdon. As the boy (Dominic Savage) grows into manhood (Leon Vitali), his hatred of Barry grows in intensity and cunning, but is held in check by his cowardice. This stalemate breaks only when what the young man perceives as outrages done to his family reach a level he can no longer tolerate and he engages Barry in a duel.

The second factor leading to Barry's destruction is his inability to refuse his son Bryan anything he wants. As Mark Miller (1976) says, his tolerance and indulgence are unbounded because he tries to take on the role of the father he has always missed. Pitiably, this passion indirectly causes the child's death through Barry's inability to deny him a horse which is far too powerful, and from which Bryan falls. Loss of his shining boy destroys Barry's hopes (which mirror his own mother's) for a glowing future lived through the reflected glory of his offspring.

The third factor is Barry's attempt to gain a peerage. Had he not striven by fair means and foul to reach this goal, Bullingdon might not have found the courage to destroy him. The narrator says of Barry's endeavour:

> He made great sacrifices to bring it about. He lavished money here and diamonds there. He bought lands at ten times their value and

> purchased pictures and articles of virtue at ruinous prices. He gave repeated entertainments to those friends to his claim who, being about the royal person, were likely to advance it. And I can tell you, bribes were administered, and in high places too, so near the royal person of His Majesty that you would be astonished to know what noblemen condescended to receive his loans.

The narrator is mistaken in his first assertion. In the accompanying images we do see much evidence of lavish expenditure which maroons Barry far from his true social milieu. Whilst viewing a painting, for example, he admires gauchely 'the artist's use of the colour blue'. Nakedly, his only interests are the price of the picture and the cachet that owning it might bring. However, it is Lady Lyndon and Lord Bullingdon who make the sacrifices because the money squandered is theirs, as Bullingdon is well aware.

Limits of the narrator's understanding

Our picture of Barry's life is substantially shaped by the film's narration. Kubrick said that he used this device to get information across in an economical way – which it does. Also as intended, it gives hints in advance of the main plot developments, lessening the risk of their seeming contrived. In addition it ensures, by running ahead of events, that nothing comes as a surprise – everything seems inevitable (Ciment 1983: 170). At first hearing, therefore, the narrator appears omniscient, not only outlining Barry's history but doing so in a tone of voice (for example, deploying at Barry's expense mild irony arising from an overarching wisdom) which implies that his pronouncements should hold true for all eternity. Nonetheless there are distinct limits to his comprehension of his subject, limits characteristic of eighteenth- not twentieth-century values.

Kubrick emphasises the gap between our times and the eighteenth century by having all his characters (not only the narrator) deliver lines distinguished, even in times of exigency, by their literary formality. When highwaymen surprise Barry, perpetrators and victim converse in exquisitely balanced prose while the villains rob him at gunpoint. Though Barry begs to be allowed to keep his cash, being himself (after the duel with Quin) a fugitive from the law, the highwayman responds, 'Mr Barry, in my profession we hear many such stories. Yours is one of the most intriguing and touching I've heard in many weeks. Nevertheless, I'm afraid I cannot grant your request . . .'. Exchanges such as this delight our ears because of their incongruous and ironic delicacy; but we have to register the fact that no other fitting language is available to the characters themselves. It emphasises that we are watching a re-creation of history and observing characters who, in part because their language does not allow it, do not think in the ways we do.

What kind of person could the invisible narrator (Michael Hordern) be? He shares generic characteristics with other eighteenth-century narrators. Whilst the differences between Barry's solemn demeanour and that of the rambunctious Tom Jones are easily noticed, the narrators of Kubrick's film and Fielding's novel have qualities in common. Kubrick's is his own invention, since Thackeray had Barry relate his own story with an absurdly pompous flourish. A member of the educated elite, Kubrick's narrator attempts to tell Barry's story with sometimes amused paternal insight, and to report on the action (which for him is already in the past) like a fair judge of men. However, the presumption upon which the cycle of English-language picaresque novels (such as *Joseph Andrews*, *Tom Jones*, *Roderick Random* and, a century later, *Barry Lyndon*) relied, was that the rise and fall of the hero followed mainly from the moral worth of his deeds.[2] Here Kubrick's film breaks with its antecedents: though the narrator's measured intonation occasionally sounds like a moralist's, the actual words he uses seldom express moral judgement.

Like all the characters, the narrator is confined within the straitjacket of what eighteenth-century gentrified English was able to convey. So placed, he has a function comparable to that of Joseph Conrad's Marlowe in *Heart of Darkness* (1902) or the figure who literally occupies a corner of the frame, the journalist Thompson in Orson Welles's *Citizen Kane* (1941). Each is a shadowy character in his own right, and none is completely reliable in his observations since all are limited in their comprehension of what they witness by the ideologies which circumscribe them. The effect in *Barry Lyndon* is occasionally to open a divide between what we see and hear concerning the hero. The narrator reports, for example, that Barry has led his fellow Prussian conscripts in dissolute behaviour; but we see no evidence of ill conduct other than a coarsening of his complexion. Equally, the narrator builds the idea that the events to which he refers are linked causes and effects that have made Barry's life turn out in the way that he, the narrator, judges it to have done – but this pattern may not actually explain Barry's rise and fall. For instance, the narrator asserts that, on marrying, Barry 'by his own energy had raised himself to a higher sphere of society'. The evidence on screen, in contrast, suggests that at this point in his life Barry has for the most part either fallen by accident into misery or seized chance openings onto good fortune. His efforts to win Lady Lyndon amount to no more than a vigorous pursuit of the rituals of adulterous seduction in the courts of the nobility.

2 Kubrick named his hero 'Roderick' in one version of the screenplay.

The telling of Barry's life abounds with irony. Sometimes the narrator shows off his superior wisdom: 'Barry's father had been bred, like many other young sons of a genteel family, to the profession of the law; and there is no doubt he would have made an eminent figure in his profession had he not been killed in a duel – which arose over the purchase of some horses'. These words are spoken at the start of the film over voices uttering the ritual phrases that bring the confrontation to the moment when shots ring out and the distant figure of Barry's father falls dead. There is wry humour in the claim that we can be sure a man who has never practised law must have succeeded in it had his death not intervened. That the duel arose over a contract of sale – a matter which a lawyer should readily be able to settle – only compounds the irony.

Sometimes irony arises from the narrator's inevitable ignorance of the gap between his eighteenth-century perception of the way the world runs and that of the twentieth century. For example, in the second scene, Barry's mother strolls with a man who has given her a bouquet of wild flowers. The narrator informs us that Mrs Barry, 'after her husband's death, lived in such a way as to defy slander. Many a man who had been smitten by the charms of the spinster now renewed his offers to the widow; but she refused all proposals of marriage, declaring that she lived now for her son only, and the memory of her departed saint'. The ironic tone is present (for both eighteenth- and twentieth-century listeners) in Mrs Barry's description of the losing duelist as a saint. However, the narrator's words raise for the post-Freudian audience alone the concern that the mother's investment of her own future in Barry may put the son at risk. Indeed we shall see her in later years exercise undue influence over her son in urging his pursuit of a peerage.

Overall, the narrator adopts perspectives on Barry's story that alter with the circumstances of his subject's life. Consider our guide's shifting attitudes toward war and those who wage it. Early in the film, when an Irish regiment of the English army comes recruiting in Brady town, he seems to respond to the exhilaration of the local populace, reporting as the camera cuts close in on Nora's hungry gaze at Captain Quin, 'the whole country was alive with war's alarms, the three kingdoms ringing with military music'. A few weeks later, when Barry has joined the English army to escape his pursuers, the narrator refers to the regiment preparing to join 'their gallant armies fighting in Germany'. The tone alters with Barry's first taste of war.

With several hundred men facing slaughter, the narrator tells us that while it was 'only a skirmish . . . not recorded in any history books, it was memorable enough for those who took part'. In line abreast, the British regiment advances across open country, maintaining perfect formation as it marches on the French detachment. When the scarlet-clad soldiers come within range of the waiting French ranks, the latter fire volley after volley, scything down the British. Only occasionally cutting to static shots of the French as they wait for and then fire upon their attackers, Kubrick covers most of the action from travelling shots that either track just behind the first ranks of British soldiers, or march with the men alongside their leading rank, observing them through a long lens. When the first two volleys cut down numbers of men, we are only momentarily aware of the fact because we too march on and leave the fallen behind. For this brief moment there continues uninterrupted the sense of triumphal military action which the brilliant colours and meticulous geometry of the field of battle convey. Only when Captain Grogan takes a ball full in the chest do we halt as Barry carries his mentor off the field. Now we cannot help but see the agonies of the dying and the many corpses whose number Grogan is about to join. Only now, as Barry grieves over his friend and gives him a parting kiss, does the horror of the elegant but absurd military manoeuvre sink in.

We never learn the outcome of this battle. It is as though the fatuous, heroic rituals of war matter more to the kings and generals who command the combatants than the military outcome – but neither could possibly matter as much as the extravagant waste of life. Barry's and the narrator's perspectives here are closely linked in their repugnance as the latter anticipates Barry's desertion.

> After the death of his friend, Barry's thoughts turned from those of military glory to those of finding a way to escape the service . . . Gentlemen may talk of the age of chivalry, but remember the ploughmen, poachers and pickpockets whom they lead. It is with these sad instruments that your great warriors and kings have been doing their murderous work in the world.

With this we see, against the backdrop of a barn put to the torch, a ragged line of soldiers leading away the beasts they have pillaged for food, Barry among them, carrying a lamb in his arms. Like this animal which is about to be slaughtered, his innocence has been killed. Later, when Barry is cashiered into the Prussian army, we are told of, and see, a worse brutalisation of the conscripts, and Barry is said to have been caught up in this.

In contrast to these diatribes on the vain military ambitions of the nobility, the narrator notes the end of the Seven Years' War in a throwaway line, as if the disasters it visited on much of Europe were matters of no consequence: 'The War was soon ended and Barry's regiment was garrisoned in the capital'. As with the skirmish, so with the war: the narrator says nothing about its political or military outcomes. Furthermore, from that moment on, he has nothing more to say about the ethics of warmongering, now adopting the eighteenth-century notion of war as an occupation, simultaneously the sport of kings and a deadly job for the everyman, but not a moral issue.[3] The absence of a moral dimension to the concept of war helps us understand the way in which, until his expulsion from England, the parvenu Barry attaches himself to the very class of people who conducted those wars. Indeed, in due course he, of all people, raises a company of troops to ingratiate himself with George III, sending them to America to fight the rebels against the Crown.

As Barry moves up society's ladder, the narrator closes his eyes to the impact of the nobility on the people they govern. Instead he focuses exclusively on the inner court circles, and the cruelty and hypocrisy with which they use each other. Even in that limited sphere, the narrator's vision is tied close to Barry's point of view. He describes one scam which the young man performs for the Chevalier de Balibari at the card table, drawing attention to the effectiveness of the play without reference to the morality of cheating.

Barry and his fellow characters

To a lesser extent, the other characters also assess Barry, whether verbally or in their dealings with him. As with the narrator, what they say does not always match what Kubrick enables us to observe; and their interaction with Barry often reveals their personalities as much as his. For example, in the opening scenes, Nora, her brother, Quin and Grogan call him a boy. They are not exactly wrong, but are relying on a half truth because they all want to curb the man emerging in Barry.

It is not long after Captain Grogan has embraced Barry as a son that his generous mentor is killed. Barry's raw grief shows how much the loss of this second father hurts him and banishes his boyhood. Soon after, while deserting from the English army, he meets Lischen, a young woman whose husband has been swept away from home by the war. They fill each other's need for comfort, he stays and they become lovers. Lischen addresses him frankly and without the mildly sadistic cock-teasing that supplied Nora's prurient diversion. Although she is married and has an infant, this will be Barry's only experience of mutual, passionate love. The young woman cuts through his pretence of being Lieutenant Fakenham and learns his true name, a hint that she may have seen through his persona and engaged with the man naked in mind as well as body. If that is so, she is probably the only person ever to do so, Lady Lyndon being the only possible exception.

Others have a darker picture of Barry. Captain Potzdorf calls him a liar, impostor and deserter: these charges are true, but demonstrably not the whole truth. Later, the regiment's colonel describes Barry as a gallant

3 Apropos this view, 'cannon fodder' was not in that century an ironic term.

soldier but one who is so idle, undisciplined and unprincipled that he has done the men a great deal of harm. Whether Barry leads in misconduct (the colonel's verdict) or (as the narrator implies) has been drawn into bad ways by the men is a point left unresolved.

The Chevalier de Balibari is Barry's final mentor, the last man to lavish affection and care on him. Unhappily the lessons the younger man learns from this extravagant role model are of dubious value. The splendour of the Chevalier's appearance and his familiarity with the nobility boost Barry's desire to establish himself as a gentleman. However, although he proves adept at picking up the cardsharper's cheats from the older man, he lacks the aptitude to learn from the latter's accomplishment as a strategist. In this, the contrast between the two men is telling. The Chevalier plans his movements around the gaming tables of Europe to best advantage to preserve both his reputation and life. Barry (both before and after his marriage no less a wanderer than the Chevalier) is moved by circumstance and mischance. He will end his days as an unsuccessful gambler – a fate that the Chevalier can be expected to escape.

Despite his increasing dependence on his mentor's *savoir faire*, Barry parts company with him after his marriage to Lady Lyndon, travelling with his wife to her English estate. Thus his wedding coincides with the loss of his last adopted father. Barry's own failings as a parent, which become apparent over the following years, suggest that he has not absorbed a reliable model for that role from the few transient relationships he has had with father figures. Instead, he introduces his mother into his new household and so restores her influence over him.

Of all Barry's enemies, the deadliest is nearest him – his stepson, Lord Bullingdon. This young man, having nurtured for many years his unassailable (and largely justified) Oedipal sense of injury, launches a savage attack on his stepfather, choosing his timing carefully. He opts for the occasion when the Lyndons give a concert for 'the best people' as part of Barry's campaign for a peerage. Backed by a chamber orchestra, Lady Lyndon (harpsichord) and her chaplain the Reverend Runt (flute) are playing the sweet adagio from a concerto by J. S. Bach. The pretty illusion of hallowed domestic safety they are spinning is wrecked when Bullingdon leads Bryan clumping into the drawing room wearing his big brother's shoes. The older boy breaks the shocked silence to deliver a carefully rehearsed denunciation of his stepfather, seeking to ruin his reputation before the gathering which includes the very people who have the power to make or destroy him: 'It is not only the lowliness of his birth and the general brutality of his manners which disgusts me, but the shameful nature of his conduct toward Your Ladyship, his brutal and ungentlemanlike behaviour, his open infidelity, his shameless robberies and swindling of my property and yours'. Although this critique accurately hits some of Barry's vices, the motivation for Bullingdon's diatribe is the flaying of a parvenu by a born gentleman. However, for the distinguished company, his pinched snobbery is not exceptionable: it is Barry's reaction that they cannot forgive. Rather than challenge Bullingdon to a duel, the ritual means of redress acceptable to gentlemen, he fells the younger man with a terrible punch to the kidneys and, mad for blood, starts a murderous brawl. By shattering the rules of behaviour proper to a gentleman, Barry brings irreversible dishonour on himself, destroys his social standing and vindicates Bullingdon's condemnation.

It is easy to forget, because so much of the film features formal and public occasions, that Barry is loved by all his family, Bullingdon apart. Bryan's love is obvious and unconditional, encouraged by his success in manipulating his father. Mrs Barry's love is also unconditional, but she trades love for influence. Although more discreet than the little boy, she exercises her power over her son no less manipulatively.

Perhaps the most interesting, and certainly the most forlorn of the secondary characters is Lady Lyndon. Far from manipulating anyone, she seems more like a prisoner of her circumstances. At court, the rules of decorum govern her behaviour. In her own household her life and fortune are controlled in succession by her husbands, Mrs Barry and Lord Bullingdon. Meanwhile, from the Reverend Runt (Murray Melvin), her personal chaplain and constant companion, comes the chilly moralism which Bullingdon learns from him all too well.

Lady Lyndon seldom speaks, but the white mask of her face and her perennial lassitude signify the apathy of a woman who, when first seen, is caught between a valetudinarian spouse and the emptiness of a barren social life, and who has no function requiring greater commitment than decorum. So when Barry first meets her, his forcible entry into court circles surely endows him with the glamour of a wild rover. The contrast between the stifling manners of those who surround her and his purposeful vitality turns him into an irresistible figure.

Although she falls in love with him, the many abuses to which Barry subjects her soon confirm the hard lesson of her first marriage: that love and suffering are inseparably entwined in her life. Though she still attempts to freeze her face in the fashionably lifeless demeanour, it often gives away her feelings. Benjamin Ross (1995) says that the images which linger in the mind are of faces slowly and forlornly turning toward the objects of their desire. In no character is this yearning for love more constant than Lady Lyndon. Indeed, despite the endless shocks that life with Barry delivers her, we can see that some six years after their separation her feelings for him have not been extinguished. Our last sight of her is at the end of 1789. Cooped up by Bullingdon to do his bidding in her own home, she authorises payment of Barry's annuity. Grey haired now, pale and sad, her gaze wanders for a moment beyond the reach of her sexless son as her mind goes back to the times when the rigid decorum of her existence was disturbed by

Barry's unruly behaviour: she still harbours feelings for him, whether of love or enmity. Wordlessly her son recalls her to the dessicated propriety which he and the Reverend Runt have imposed on the household and hands her for signature yet another bill – apart from her feelings, Barry's only legacy.

Barry's elusive personality

What emerges from all this is a fragmented and diverse picture of Barry based on the differing experiences and points of view of the various characters who know him. The sum of these perspectives is insufficient to construct a rounded character in terms that a twentieth-century audience understands. Furthermore, we only get one hint of Barry's self-image when, as a bedtime tale for young Bryan, he invents a wildly exaggerated piece of derring-do. Rather than the recollections of his time as a soldier it pretends to be, it's a self-aggrandising fairy tale. In effect, he never speaks of his memories or reflections.

Barry is not predominantly loyal, brave, loving, romantic, brutal, malicious, mean, scheming, a liar, cheat or thief. Yet each of these traits emerges at one time or another within a particular situation, but neither consistently nor even passionately. He seems largely a man without individual will or moral vision – a man constructed by his surroundings (in contrast to a modern man, who believes he constructs himself). Who, then, is the real Barry Lyndon? Does the question itself – which undoubtedly interests us – depend on some form of post-psychoanalytic engagement with people? Kubrick's dual *modus operandi* is to blank off our enquiries about his psychological make-up while putting him in narrative circumstances which certainly arouse that interest. We are encouraged to try and empathise but blocked from doing so. There may not be just one Barry: rather, he may be a chameleon presence constantly redefined by the frame he finds himself in.

Though he tries hard to adapt to every changed circumstance, Barry does not actually fit in anywhere – less his personal failure than that of all the forces around him which have provided him with goals but not the means to realise them. His failure to find his place could be read as a comment on the failure at many levels (personal and domestic relationships, social stratification, military action and even political practice) of trying to mould the individual to rigid structures rather than asking how structures can be built to suit the needs of the individual (a modern psychological goal). As an amoral pawn of a sociopolitical system that is near the end of its usefulness, he does not spark much sympathy because he seems so unaware of any injustice either done to him or that he has himself perpetrated. The impersonal nature of all this is striking.

The backdrop of history

The vast upheavals of the turbulent epoch through which Barry lives make history the inescapable backdrop. The principal action begins in 1758, the second year of the Seven Years' War. Assuming Barry to be about 15 then, he must be about 40 in 1783, the *annus horribilis* of Bryan's death, the duel with Bullingdon and enforced return to Ireland. Lady Lyndon authorises his annuity in the year the Bastille was stormed, by which time he will have reached his mid-forties.

Much of what has been written thus far implies that the institutions of the old order determine every aspect of both Barry's and the other characters' existence, a view consistent with the era:

> Those who reconstructed European society and culture after the Thirty Years' War [1618–48] took as guiding principles *stability* in and among the sovereign nation-states, and *hierarchy* within the social structures of each individual state. For those who carried this task forward, it was important to believe that the principles of stability and hierarchy were found in all of the Divine plan, down from the astronomical cosmos to the individual family. Behind the inertness of matter, they saw in Nature, as in Society, that the actions of 'lower' things depended on, and were subordinate to, oversight and command by 'higher' creatures, and ultimately by the Creator. The more confident one was about 'subordination and authority' in Nature, the less anxious one need accordingly be about social inequalities. Likewise with the 'irrationality' of Emotion: if subjects ordered their lives indiscreetly, this gave rise to social disturbances of kinds that might be diverting to read about in the novels of Daniel Defoe, but were highly disagreeable to deal with in real life.
>
> (Toulmin 1990: 128)

Kubrick's narrator understands, as we have seen, that the Seven Years' War was a struggle in which the old, ossified order of kings and emperors of Europe squandered the lives of vast numbers of common people in order to secure the power of the nation-state and its attendant class structure. However, the events of Barry's later life overlap with the loosely linked upheavals of the American and French Revolutions which would lead eventually to extraordinary changes in both the sociopolitical sphere and the personal psyche.

We have seen how Barry is both a creature, and finally a supporter, of the old order. Neither he, King George III, Europe's aristocracy nor any other protagonist has the slightest inkling of the revolutionary nature of the changes that are underway or the newly restless moral consciousness that is emerging. Barry himself is not a rebel in the front lines, but his failure to find adequate solutions to his restlessness can be read as dissatisfaction that, even with a doubtful purpose, plants the seeds of revolution to be carried out by others.

Kubrick's films point up that attempts to impose order on the chaos of human impulses never wholly succeed. In *Barry Lyndon* the impact of both passions and culture register on the characters' lives the breakdown of the old order that is occurring unseen and off screen.

Breaching social codes

Contrary to most mainstream movies, these characters express roles rather than personalities, as Claude Michel Cluny noticed (1976: 100). Their pomaded, elegant appearance and their mannerisms are intended only as signifiers of social status, not as indicators of their inner thoughts. In any age where strict codes of conduct and fashion occur, those codes are meant to regulate the chaos of internal and external forces, nowhere more so than in Barry's world:

> . . . from the late-17th to the mid-20th century, [the hard-line contrast between reason and the emotions] shaped life in Europe on both the social and personal level. Like other elements in the scaffolding of Modernity, this contrast frequently 'went unsaid,' being embedded in the everyday social life of the nation-state. Calculation was enthroned as the distinctive virtue of human reason; and the life of the emotions was repudiated, as distracting one from the demands of clear-headed deliberation. In this social sense, 'emotion' became a code word for sex: to those who valued a stable class system, sexual attraction was a main source of social disruption . . . What began as a theoretical distinction in Descartes, between the intellectual power of human 'reason' and the physiological 'causes' of the emotions, turned into a practical contrast between (good) rationality and (bad) sentiment or impulsiveness.
>
> (Toulmin 1990: 134)

Even when hostilities break out, rigid social codes may retain their authority, as Kubrick had already shown in *Paths of Glory*. In *Barry Lyndon*, the ranks of French and British soldiers advancing on each other as bullets fly portray starkly the absurd lengths humans go to once committed to the idea of rationality at every level. Whereas in other species ritualised fighting among males allows them to establish dominance and hierarchy without inflicting mortal wounds, in eighteenth-century Europe this proposition is fatally lost to humankind.

Yet strict codes of conduct do not manage perfectly to suppress natural impulses. The disruption of order in *Barry Lyndon* springs from human passions. Barry's love for Nora threatens his uncle's family and is the root cause of Barry's having to leave home. Lady Lyndon's adulterous desire for Barry jeopardises her standing among 'the best people'. Equally, the lust for blood to which men are prone jeopardises the rules of the game. Although Barry loathes the regulated mass carnage of military service (despite adapting to it efficiently enough when coerced by the Prussians), he is always eager to fight his own battles with fists, sword or pistol. His name means 'a man keen as a spear', and his temper is infectious. When he punches Lord Bullingdon in front of his noble guests, the set-to arouses the other males. Bryan, the most protected of children, cannot conceal his delight at the mayhem; and that scion of the nobility Lord Hallam also enjoys the fight, struggling to erase the grin that briefly occupies his face. Since Barry's rage almost induces his fine guests to riot, it is no surprise that the gentry close ranks against him immediately after the fracas: they reaffirm the code of acceptable behaviour by repressing the recollection that they had wanted to become embroiled.

Breaching cultural codes

So much for the protagonists, but what is to be understood from the film text itself? Miller (1976) notes that its painterly compositions call attention to our presence, positioning us like visitors to an art gallery. But although 'they seem at first to require nothing more than cool detached perusal', they are actually an ambiguous device. Among their subtle effects, Kubrick's reverse zoom repeatedly dwarfs the actors inside larger landscapes so that we are left with a more intimate knowledge of the settings than we have of the characters themselves. We do well to recall that landscape gardens as seen in *Barry Lyndon* imposed order not only on nature but also on people, sometimes requiring entire villages be moved lest they interfere with a vista. Countless scenes zoom back from close shots and end by showing people as distant figures in huge scenery, identifiable only by their dress. They seem to have been positioned in accordance with a requirement that these scenes express the ordained purpose of the well-regulated social order. Furthermore, in the great houses the people seem to mimic the poses in the large portraits rather than the other way around. Elsewhere, Kubrick's compositions invoke memories of the lampoonists' satirical tableaux. Part of the dissonance of our viewing may be the distance between our modern viewpoint, which emphasises the power of the individual in relation to the world, and the world of the film, in which the settings (indoors and out) are so much larger than the people in them. All in all, the eighteenth-century environment portrayed seems full of forces that are much more determinant of individual destiny than the individual will.

Nevertheless, Michael Dempsey is right to comment that Kubrick's compositions should not be compared with paintings on a museum wall because they are not static: 'Moving images exist in time; they die. The central irony of *Barry Lyndon* is that all its awesome detailing of eighteenth-century life creates not the realism of a historian but the mirage of a dreamer; the film conjures up the past only to waft it away, as though it had never existed except in fantasy' (1976: 53). The ephemerality of the *mise-en-scène* (nowhere more subtle in its implication of fleet lives than in the candlelit scenes) is one of the factors that helps ready the mind of the spectator to approve the final title card. It simply notes that death has rendered all the characters equal. All their strivings are thereby stripped of significance.

To the impact of the painterly style must be added the cumulative effect of the music. Michel Sineux refers to the way that *Barry Lyndon* (in common with *2001* and *A Clockwork Orange*) is not a talking film in the conventional sense where dialogue acts as the principal vehicle for message and emotion. Rather, music dominates, with the consequence that these films are rooted in the emotional and the sensorial. They address the intellect via feeling and reach the conscious mind only after having energised the unconscious (1976: 36).

Almost all *Barry Lyndon's* music is as rigidly coded as the characters' behaviour. This is to say more than that it fits the time and places of the action, though it does that too. For example, 'The British Grenadiers' and 'Lillibullero' are heard during Barry's sojourn in the English army, and Frederick the Great's 'Hohenfriedberger March' plays when the Prussians have cashiered him. Beyond setting a rhythm for the troops' marches, however, this martial music projects a resolute cheeriness one function of which is to erase any negative emotions the conscript soldiers might be feeling. In addition, the marches have an authoritarian ring, unmistakable in Frederick's tune given that he was supreme commander of the Prussian army. Yet both that march and 'The British Grenadiers' are burlesqued as coarse drinking songs by soldiers of the respective armies – a further hint that the regulation of conduct is imperfect.

Handel's 'Sarabande', as adapted by Leonard Rosenman, has a function midway between the marches and the chamber music. It recurs throughout as a running commentary on the action. When first heard, it reflects the pomp and glory both of Barry's ambitions and of the old order at its proudest. As the film continues, variations play on the listening audience's mood: for example, during Barry's *annus horribilis* the mix foregrounds drums and pizzicato double bass to produce a funereal undertow to the theme. Overall the 'Sarabande' functions as a processional that relentlessly leads Barry, the narrator and the audience through his life's events. It becomes yet another ticking clock, a *memento mori* that prevents us from forgetting the inevitable end of Barry's story.

The scenes in which Barry aspires to the life of a gentleman are accompanied by chamber music. As Stephenson says, it suggests the power of emotions that are never allowed to surface (1981: 255). This music (another instance of the film's flattened surface) complements ironically the manners of the aristocracy through its structure, the symmetry and rigorous formal control of which dress its themes with an exquisite shell. Its elegance draws the listener's ear, yet may actually obstruct complete enjoyment because the pleasures of melody, harmony, repetition and development are so deliciously intricate and fulfilling that they can satisfy the listening mind and inhibit it from penetrating to the music's emotional core. Indeed there is no sign that the music touches the emotions of the characters at Lady Lyndon's concert. They seem to hear rather than listen.

There is one striking anachronism among the chamber pieces – Rosenman's adaptation of the second movement from Franz Schubert's Piano Trio in E-flat, op. 100. Here piano, violin and cello spin flowing and gorgeous lines which complement, enrich and entwine with each other. The passage, from the slow second movement, is heard twice and has the stronger impact in that it first underscores Barry's and Lady Lyndon's early meetings. The lambent melody suggests both the potential and the disappointments of love. Miller (1976) observes that the adaptation does not progress into Schubert's passionate middle section but repeats the major theme over and over again. It's a structural device that discreetly underlines Lady Lyndon's frustration, since she is alone in feeling love. Equally discreetly, it underscores Barry's failure to develop, by committing himself to an enduring and loving relationship, into a fully rounded human being.

On the second occasion the Trio is played, the adaptation has a darker timbre. This time it underscores the frustration of Barry's hopes in the social sphere. It also strengthens the framing of the action in the wider context of history. On crutches and with his leg amputated, Barry boards a coach to leave England forever. The personal cost of living by the rules of the old order is now inscribed on his body. As Miller notes, banished from the domain of old estates and family fortunes, the broken Barry resembles a metaphor for modern man coming into being at the time of the French Revolution. On the cusp of a new era, which might well have offered him a fuller life, the futility of his sacrifice is marked by Schubert's Trio as it heralds the arrival of the new Romantic and post-revolutionary era of individualised sensibility and mutual responsibility. Barry (who eventually returns unsuccessfully to the gaming table) never enters that new world. So there is frustration in this too – a frustration which, even though Barry is not conscious of it, the twentieth-century audience feels, longing for fulfilment on his behalf.

The modern perspective on an eighteenth-century tale

It is time to consider the position of the twentieth-century audience in more detail. They probably found it easier to recognise the emotional register of the chamber music than the English nobility of the eighteenth century. By the time of the film's release, the music industry had not only endowed most of these pieces with the status of classics, but had also made their melodies so popular that they added to the film's sense of nostalgia. Nevertheless, we 'get' the music at a cost.

I said earlier that part of the dissonance of our viewing may be the distance between our modern viewpoint, which emphasises the power of the individual in relation to the world, and the world of the film, where the settings and society are much larger and more robust than the people. Kubrick offers us the facsimile of a simpler time in the past but, by obliging us to discover it to be a *trompe l'oeil*, requires us to recognise that we ourselves have flattened history. Our nostalgic longings have stripped the past of its complexity and revised history to suit our own needs. Kubrick appears to use the techniques of film in his presentation of Barry (a protagonist characterised by his want of understanding) not to create history so much as to make us keenly aware of how the telling limits understanding.

The distancing effect reflects another historical accuracy: while people have always had interior lives, as an eighteenth-century man Barry would not have seen himself as he might have in our psychoanalytic age. The advent of psychoanalysis and psychology happened a century later alongside the rise of the middle class and its attendant reliance on consumerism (read: individual desire) – a social change resulting from radical transitions in economic as well as class structures. Given that Barry would not see himself as a bundle of motivations and desires, the usefulness of asking such questions about him comes into question. The film's reverse zooms stand out as a deliberate visual cue about the distance we have to acknowledge exists between the characters and scenery (however beautiful) and our understanding. Although it is seductive to want to say 'I understand', the distance, emphasised again and again, tells us that we can only observe and have to relinquish the desire to live vicariously.

Kubrick himself, however, like the film's audiences, did live in a frame that constructs the human being as focused on a conscious will which has a large measure of freedom, transformative ability and emotional agency. Inevitably we bring that perspective to our viewing of Barry's life which seems flat by comparison, focused on externals but lacking an internal engine that can truly effect change.

The language of longing

At the time of the film's release, Ryan O'Neal and Marisa Berenson were both criticised for poor acting and looking vapid and empty. In fact, their disguise of the emotion that we typically expect in a character-centred story is consistent with Kubrick's other techniques for downplaying interiority in favour of surface, whilst simultaneously tantalising us with desire to know more about those characters' inner lives.

The two emotions that do emerge most consistently from these characters are Barry's longing and Lady Lyndon's melancholy – both emotions that for the audience are easily associated with nostalgia. By hiding their interior lives, Kubrick prevents us from empathising too directly with the characters. We don't know exactly why Lady Lyndon is so sad or what propels Barry from one event to the next. We can guess or even project our own motivations into the scene, but the material Kubrick gives us is sparse. Rather, Barry's longing evokes the same feeling in ourselves, but our own longing is for something else and fastens upon the calmly composed image, the lost time, the beautiful frame that makes even war seem orderly.

Evidence for our longing is found in our response to the final sight of Barry, a jarring and unexpected freeze frame of his back as he steps, one-legged and off balance, into the carriage that will take him with his mother back to Ireland. The brutal view of his shattered frame makes us conscious of Barry stripped of the social masks that have hidden his inner nature from us and from himself. As the most uncomposed image in the film, it produces a discordant impact at the very moment when the on-screen record of him ends. It not only metaphorically consigns Barry in advance of time to his death, it also jolts us out of the frame within which Kubrick's careful control of the film's aesthetic conventions has held us throughout the preceding three hours. In this way it violates our longing.

The frustration of psychoanalysis

The confluence from within and in front of the screen of so much desire and longing in a film experience dominated by the emotional and sensorial (Sineux 1976: 36) suggests that it should respond with fruitful insights to a reading based on psychoanalytic principles. It is not hard to identify in it motifs that have both a symbolic and a mythological currency. Their presence would seem to suit a Jungian approach because Jungians' understanding of the nature and activity of the psyche focuses on bringing such images to consciousness.

Jung believed that the evolution of humanity through centuries of acculturation was marked by the long labour of successive generations to develop and sharpen consciousness. As it happens, he described those earlier generations in whom consciousness was emergent in a manner which resembles the psychological disposition of the characters in *Barry Lyndon*:

> His consciousness is still uncertain, wobbling on its feet. It is still childish, having just emerged from the primal waters. A wave of the unconscious may easily roll over it, and then he forgets who he was and does things that are strange to him. Hence primitives [read: *Barry*

> *Lyndon's* characters] are afraid of uncontrolled emotions, because consciousness breaks down under them and gives way to possession. All man's strivings have therefore been directed toward the consolidation of consciousness. This was the purpose of rite and dogma; they were dams and walls to keep back the dangers of the unconscious, the 'perils of the soul'.
>
> (Jung 1954a: 22)

Barry's largely unreflective existence as a wanderer marries with the idea that manifestations of consciousness in his time were much less robust than those to which our generation is accustomed. Furthermore, the relentless effort which all the sociopolitical forces in Barry's world devoted to the repression of emotion fits with the idea that, in an age that did not welcome expressions of individual consciousness, ritual had high value in inhibiting the obliterating onrush of the unconscious.

So what results when we examine Barry's personality using a Jungian matrix? It does not illuminate the recesses of his psyche in the way we might expect of a twentieth-century man. On the other hand, it does show signs of his identification with the collective symbols that serve to unify the (male dominated) social structures in the film. From the moment we first see Barry, he is, like all the characters, dressed to represent his assumed position in the social hierarchy. As he achieves upward mobility, however, rather than finding himself able at last to show his true face to the world, he has it obliterated by the aristocracy's mask of white make-up (Rourke 2001). In Jungian theory, the mask or persona is the face an individual turns to the world. As a consequence, it is substantially an archetype of social adaptation. Within a twentieth-century milieu, the domination of Barry's psyche by the persona would make his character unusually imbalanced. That, we shall find in Chapter 2, to be a distorting feature of Bill Harford's personality in *Eyes Wide Shut*. However, within his eighteenth-century social circle, Barry is no different from anyone else.

Today, a personality dominated by the persona results in the abnegation of the private, inner life. Of those individuals, Jung wrote: 'The construction of a collectively suitable persona means a formidable concession to the external world, a genuine self-sacrifice which drives the ego straight into identification with the persona, so that people really do exist who believe they are what they pretend to be' (1935: 193). Jung traced to this state of mind the source of various kinds of psychological distress for the twentieth-century individual, including behaviour which reverses in private the dominant disposition of the individual's public existence (pp. 193–4). However, our eighteenth-century hero shows no sign of suffering this kind of psychological reversal because, as we have seen, he adopts the appropriate persona for whatever social situation he finds himself in. His persona makes him, for good or evil, part of the collective. He fails to gain perfect acceptance only because it slips from time to time (which the masks of his peers never do), not because his peers find other aspects of his personality lacking.

The persona, in Jung's formulation, should be counterbalanced by an equally vigorous anima. In a man the anima typically presents itself as an arousing mental image of a woman (or a number of women). This recurring image, with its power to stir a man's emotions, represents those aspects of the inner world to which he is not giving due attention (Jung 1935: 192–5). Barry shows few signs that the women in his life (on whom he might be expected to project his anima manifestations) carry the energy charge of hope, fear, desire, love or loathing that would typify the anima of a modern man – a factor which reinforces the argument that his inner life is unknown to him, and certainly unknowable by us. With one exception, women exert a diminishing influence over him as the years pass. He suffers youthful anguish over Nora, but soon forgets her. Lischen might have been the perfect anima for a healthy young man – but his affair with her is transient. Lady Lyndon has no power over him. His mother, however, does exert ongoing influence. Even when he is almost 40 and should be his own master, she sets his strategic goals. These goals, however, have nothing to do with his inner or emotional life and everything to do with his social standing. In short, even she takes her son's persona to be the man. Her interference is catastrophic, as might be expected from psychoanalytic literature on men who remain belatedly attached to the maternal anima. Yet while there is no doubting Mrs Barry's influence, anima literature seems all but irrelevant because we have scant evidence for her stirring her son's emotions.

Where emotion plainly does overwhelm Barry is in his love for, and grief over Bryan. As an over-indulgent father who gave his joyous but ungovernable child a dangerous horse (i.e., too much power), Barry cannot escape responsibility for Bryan's death. In symbolic terms, his loss resonates with the destruction of the innocent aspects of his own headstrong nature. Children commonly represent the future to their parents, and when Bryan perishes, Barry's hopes die with him.

If we continue reading in this symbolic register, we must recognise that Barry has a second son, the melancholy Lord Bullingdon. The latter brings matters to a head by challenging his stepfather to a duel. Thanks to Barry's decision to turn his pistol aside at the very moment he has a socially acceptable opportunity to despatch his vengeful stepson, the young man survives. But, as a gentleman embodying the old order's values, Bullingdon has no hesitation in claiming his right to revenge and fires on Barry. Then he swiftly forces the injured man out of his world through the terms of the separation annuity which the latter must accept to survive. Bullingdon's pinched meanness (not untypical of his kind in the film) emphasises calculation (the value prized by the upper class) over emotion. So the fates of both Barry's sons – Bryan personifying emotion over calculation – underline the father's want of a future.

Barry's merciful action places emotion above calculation in a silent admission that he cannot follow the upper-class code to the death. As for the motivation driving Barry to his merciful gesture, perhaps experience of war and Bryan's death have left him realising the preciousness of life; perhaps he finds some belated familial affection for the youth; or maybe there is a limit to the pain he can inflict on his wife. The point is that we can only guess. No clues as to his mental state are vouchsafed.

To ensure our inability to operate on the film in this register, other symbolic evidence repulses consistent reading. For example, Barry is ambidextrous; but attempting a symbolic reading of this fact conjures up contra-indications and once again shows the limits for *Barry Lyndon* of this particular form of understanding. As a duellist both with pistol and sword, Barry employs the left hand which, by verbal association and tradition, is endowed with sinister, even death-dealing qualities. Yet he never actually kills anyone in a duel. Conversely, he fires his musket right-handed, and the Prussian infantry turns him into a proficient killer with that weapon. However, the right is symbolically the hand of openness and fair dealing.

Symbolic readings often lead to productive psychoanalytical readings in the Jungian scheme of things. But not here. Kubrick has placed several obstacles in the way of effective psychoanalytic interpretation of Barry. No current from Barry's unconscious ever becomes known to him in the way that a modern man might discover some inkling of his own motivation through dreams, interaction with family and associates or private illumination. There is, then, no sign of the kind of coming to consciousness which (whether they describe it that way or not) audiences for mainstream western cinema expect to share with their screen heroes. So something else is going on here. It can be located in Barry's happiness and unhappiness alike, both of which spring from his longing for freedom and acceptance – competing desires pursued in various projects within and outside the authorised social structure. Indeed, the pairing of individual freedom and social acceptance is an oxymoron in his world, poignantly expressed in his desire to be a gentleman. His expectation that such a position will free him to be whatever he wants whenever he wants is revealed to be a delusion. His attempts to be a 'gentleman' instead become a brutal lesson in the violent repression of individual desire in the powerful cause of social stability.

Seeing Barry wrecked – but by the film's account left unreflective – by his life's course is frustrating to today's viewer who is usually invited to see beneath the surface of heroes' lives. In the final outturn, Kubrick invites us to consider that physical, social and cultural structures reflect the capacity and limitations of their inhabitants' understanding – both within our own time and as we strive to know the eighteenth-century world of Barry. We are encouraged in our twentieth-century belief that we can know the main protagonists intimately, while we are simultaneously frustrated in our ambition by all the devices described. With *Barry Lyndon*, Kubrick reminds us that desire does not overcome distance; we can see but not know.

Chapter 2

The hero as failure: Stanley Kubrick's *Eyes Wide Shut*[1]

Introduction

Eyes Wide Shut (1999) differs from *Barry Lyndon* in that the principal protagonists can be analysed in ways which do reveal their psychological attributes. It is also possible to show how the minor characters have qualities that are archetypal in nature. As such, they illustrate aspects of the personalities of the principal figures.

The film faces its audiences with several quandaries which, as its deliberate aesthetic control indicates, are meant to perplex. Principal among them is the difficulty of anchoring the diegesis to a situated story world. It seems to swim between dream and displaced actuality. The action is slow and Tom Cruise's part requires him to speak lethargically, echoing other people's words. One knock-on effect of the sluggish pace is that it gives the spectator time to observe, to register the film's uneasy feeling-tone and recognise that the dilemmas it sets have to be engaged with both rationally and emotionally if the film is to be well understood.

The film's story world taps into both old and new concerns. It works with ancient narrative themes in, for example, the journey of the would-be hero and the corruption inflicted by great wealth. And it presents myth-charged images from times past such as the Gothic mansion and the Venetian masks of the commedia dell'arte. However, it also features today's obsessions – in particular, desire manifested in various modes from pornographic degradations to the (potential) fulfilments of marriage.

Establishing the register

For a film which for the most part progresses with measured solemnity (like several other Kubrick movies including *2001* and *Barry Lyndon*), *Eyes Wide*

1 An earlier version of this chapter was written with Jana Branch.

Shut starts at a driving pace, with Dmitri Shostakovitch's 'Jazz Suite, Waltz 2' playing over the titles. Heard while the protagonists are at the height of their fortunes, the piece has a smooth energy that signals a sense of the confidence of Bill and Alice Harford's lives. When we first see them, they are doing nothing more than dressing before going out to a formal Christmas dance. But the music combines with what we can see of their apartment (expensive furnishings, spacious rooms, brilliantly-coloured paintings) and overrides suavely the petty distractions of getting ready for a night out – the mislaid wallet, the husband who does not look at his wife before telling her that she looks great and the sense that they are running late.

Kubrick's use of Shostakovitch's Jazz Waltz can be compared with the way he placed Johann Strauss's 'The Blue Danube' in *2001*. In both cases the music was radically new when originally composed but then had become clichéd through overuse. In Kubrick's hands, however, each piece gains new freshness through its positioning in the film's narrative.[2] This confirms something about the way music functions in films in general; and with reference to *Eyes Wide Shut* in particular it shows how music does much to construct this film's distinctive register.

It is a commonplace of film theory that music on the soundtrack affects the way an audience perceives the narrative: it alters the spectator's perception of the action's rhythm, inflects the emotional impact of on-screen events and directs attention toward preferred meanings. This formulation, however, does not explain the flow of influence in the contrary direction – does not speak of the way, when Kubrick dubs in a clichéd piece, that the scene's images and action refresh the music. Nicholas Cook (2000: 70–1) has dealt with this in describing cross-media interaction as comparable to the way metaphor functions. He argues that a transfer of attributes from one medium to the other occurs where an 'enabling similarity' is found between aspects of the music and the visual, narrative or linguistic content. The process is complex in the case of film since several media are involved. As with metaphor, such interaction between media is not restricted merely to augmenting a pre-existing sense but can cause new meaning to emerge. The transferred attributes are more striking the more actively they construct meaning.

Cook's observations are vindicated when the Jazz Waltz is reprised the morning after the party as Bill starts a mundane working day in his surgery and Alice begins the tender (but less than glamorous) routine of looking after their daughter Helena. The smooth energy of this couple's social confidence is still present; but by this time the Harfords' love has been tested by their flirtations with extramarital sexual adventures, and fissures are already opening in their self-assurance. Memories of the previous

2 Thanks are due to Jane Ryan for guidance on this point.

night combine with the tedium of the day's business to lessen the suavity of the music.

By the end of the film, the former exuberance of the Jazz Waltz has dissipated. At this point both the pain that has come into the Harfords' lives and repetition of the music colour our perceptions so that it takes on a quality that is almost mechanical. Leaving no space for invention and improvisation, it sounds more like a pompous repression of jazz and appears, through the suffering of the characters, to have taken on the lugubrious qualities of a Valse Triste.

Kubrick's deployment of the Jazz Waltz makes the point that music plays a key role not merely in accompanying narrative action, but in setting the register of *Eyes Wide Shut*. Events impacting on the characters influence the way we hear the music, which in turn tends to detach narrative events from social realism.

As Janet Maslin (1999) noticed, another aspect of the film's subliminal manipulation, a 'kind of sly foreshadowing' also operates through its use of colours. Reds and blues are juxtaposed uncomfortably in many of the scenes, the warmth of the former jarring against the coldness of the latter. Where they blend, they produce a sombre precognition: for example, the purple dress worn by a prostitute signals not only her moral nobility (purple as the royal colour) but also foreshadows her funeral because, a day after wearing it, she learns she has tested HIV positive.

Music and colour are not the only elements that distance the surface representations of the film from everyday normality. The doubling of dialogue lines has a similar effect. Bill Harford, for example, often repeats what another character has just said to him, turning the echoed words into a question. The recurrence of this verbal pattern produces an obsessive feeling-tone suggesting that the doctor's mental habit has become a defence mechanism allowing him to avoid expressing his own spontaneous opinions and thus hide his desires from himself. It recalls Jung's experimental observation that a delay in a patient's verbal response was evidence that the stimulus word uttered by the analyst had touched on an active feeling-toned complex (1907: 52–3). This being the case, Harford is not the only character masking a complex: ponderous speech patterns are common throughout the New York upper class to which he aspires.

Then there is the location. Peter Wollen distinguishes between films that represent New York City by shooting on location and others that are studio-based. Of the latter he says that 'The city is perceived as a kind of dream space, a delirious world of psychic projection rather than sociological delineation' (1992: 25). He finds that studio-based films often confirm Rem Koolhaas's vision in which New York becomes a place where unconscious desires, fears and fantasies break through the urban strait-jacket of rational order that its grid layout imposes and express a residue of madness in weird architectural visions. In its vision of the city, *Eyes Wide*

Shut adds to our sense of the familiar made strange by mixing the two modes, location and studio shooting. Its art direction (by Kevin Phipps and John Fenner), its sets, lighting, colour, perspective and the gliding Steadicam create Kubrick's New York as simultaneously the recognisable architectural and sociological city and Bill Harford's waking nightmare. Given that Wollen shows how one of the perennial attractions of New York for filmmakers has been its skyscrapers, Kubrick's disregard of the city's vertical dimension is striking. In *Eyes Wide Shut* the camera never tilts up to look at the buildings towering overhead. Its gaze remains locked on existence at street level. In this it is like Bill Harford's eyes. Noticeably (when driving, for instance) he has tunnel vision as if only capable of focusing along the axis of his conscious will, seeing nothing happening on either side.

Our take on the New York world fluctuates, dissolving back and forth between expressionist fantasy and observed reality. In this respect it brings to mind Orson Welles's de-realised ghost city Macao in *The Immortal Story* (1968). And the cumulative effect of the shifting aesthetic register recalls a similar impression in *Heart of Darkness* (1993). In Nicolas Roeg's film version of Conrad's novella, we discover to our discomfort that, somewhere on the river journey, without knowing exactly when or how it happened, we have fallen through the surface of the known, safe world. Beneath it, in the mind's dark Congo, everything is confusing and dangerous. Much the same happens to Bill and Alice Harford. Though comfortably placed on the fringes of New York's upper crust, they will enter places in the mind that are confusing and dangerous to them. The aesthetics of *Eyes Wide Shut* contribute to our sense of looking at a material actuality which is an arduously cultivated but permeable reflection that most of the characters mistake for reality in its entirety.

The register of *Eyes Wide Shut*, subtly different from that of most mainline movies in the way it eschews some of the properties of formal realism and distorts those it does play with, ensures that the audience, like the characters, experiences an estrangement from the daily life depicted. The film's New York – both the city streets and the interiors – can be compared with the impossible hotel suite in *2001*. The latter can be read as a metaphor for what we make consciously of our lives – the 'room' that gives Dave's life its shape (Izod 2001: 195). As a frame around the lives that pass within it, the city in similar manner puts quote marks on the sentence of time which frames the existence of the characters.

Working in the register

If *Eyes Wide Shut* can properly be described as symbolic, it must be in such a way as takes account of its subtle register, shimmying between the rational and the fantastic. I propose therefore that the whole film as well as its parts constitute symbols in the special sense of the term derived by Jung: 'The true symbol . . . should be understood as an expression of an intuitive idea that cannot yet be formulated in any other or better way' (1931a: 70) and '[it] is the best possible expression for an unconscious content whose nature can only be guessed, because it is still unknown' (1954a: 6n). The symbol forms the crux of Jungian methods of analysing screen narrative by supplying a strong and supple link carrying two-way traffic between the psyche and the text. It forms in the mind of the filmmakers when the stirring of unconscious energies provides the stimulus that generates the symbol. In *Eyes Wide Shut*, images, characters, narrative and music fuse together in just such a clandestine, deep-level manner.

The symbol-forming activity of filmmakers has its counterpart when members of the audience respond to the same figure. If their emotions are aroused on receiving it from the screen, they may introject it and make it part of their inner world. Thus Jungian symbols are stimuli distinguished by their capacity to channel unconscious energies and affects which they make available for eventual recognition. That recognition in turn can awaken the conscious mind to new understanding.

Eyes Wide Shut provides promising grounds for a Jungian reading because it plumbs with the lead protagonists the phantasmagoria that populate their own under-explored personalities. It illuminates experience that stems from but goes beyond the Harfords' social activities, fluctuating across their inner and outer lives, seldom marking the boundaries between them. And because each of the minor characters either darkens or illuminates the lives of the two main protagonists, these other characters can be read as embodying features of the principals' inner landscapes.

Through the looking glass

The host of the Christmas party to which Bill and Alice (Tom Cruise and Nicole Kidman) have been invited is Victor Ziegler (Sydney Pollack). A wealthy patient in Bill's prosperous medical practice, he pays his social debts in this way every year. The extravagance of his grand rooms (walls and stairway sheathed in lights) reeks of moneyed propriety. The guests' formal dress and the band playing Victor Sylvester's foxtrots add to the deadening impact. Although Kubrick offers a wry authorial comment on the seduction scenes by backing them with numbers such as 'It had to be You' and 'I Only Have Eyes for You', here, rather than being refreshed by the cinematic context, music so clichéd that it was consigned to middle-aged parties in the 1950s anneals the scene's bland surface. In this staid milieu the Harfords are outsiders, but actually nobody other than Ziegler and his wife appears to recognise anyone else. Bill accepts the dull evening as one of the dues of his professional life, but Alice hits the champagne hoping to free herself from boredom.

When libido stirs, however, nothing can withstand its flux for long. Alice is first to be surprised by it. Waiting languidly at the bar for her husband, she becomes aware that an elegant middle-aged man is drinking her champagne – his opening gambit in a morbidly practised seduction routine. This is an early scene where the heightening of aesthetic effect suggests that we have fallen through the looking glass into a nightmare world which both informs and hides behind the images on screen. Philip French described Sandor Szavost (Sky Dumont) as 'a suave, somewhat ludicrous Hungarian roué' (1999). Fair enough so far as it goes, but Kubrick's presentation of the scene and Dumont's embodiment of the role imply more than an attempt at sexual conquest. As Szavost leads Alice circling the dance floor, the peachy tones of the Zieglers' ballroom become warmer than when she was dancing with Bill, the diffused light (the Vaseline lens effect) becomes smokier still and the gliding Steadicam embellishes their serpentine path.

Meanwhile Szavost (for American viewers, a clichéd representation of the sophisticated European) tries to disarm Alice with the thought that deception rather than lust gives extramarital sex its zest. Prompting us to recall the human potential for betrayal, he has the archetypal quality associated with the dark shadows of the mind. Framed constantly in profile, Dumont emphasises Szavost's Nosferatu-like hunched back. His intense gaze and insistent, absurdly overwrought words are replete with guile of the oldest seducer of all. Not that the Hungarian is Satan, but his presence bears the lineaments of that ancient figure whose provenance reaches back far beyond both Murnau and Milton.

Arguably it is just this exaggerated quality which guarantees his failure. Alice plays with him, amused by a temptation that she will not let succeed. Her engagement in the dalliance suggests that the situation rather than the man flatters her. Despite her drunkenness, she exacts a nice revenge (and perhaps justifies the flirtation to herself) by cock-teasing the would-be ravisher.

Why does she resist the seducer? To answer that she loves her husband, though true, does not exhaust the matter. Szavost's links to the shadow archetype make him a figure who represents to the conscious mind those aspects of the personality that are repressed or feared. However, in the vengeful and overblown form in which Szavost embodies Alice's shadow, he is easy for her to dismiss: she has already been tried by a much sharper temptation.

Alice's dancing with the Hungarian is observed by her husband from across the ballroom. Szavost gives Bill a preposterous advance glimpse of the jealous shadow that will soon haunt him. But in the meantime he too is tasting sexual temptation. Two beautiful models, as single-minded and empty-headed as Szavost, lead him away from the throng. They nudge him onward with sensual bodies that move lasciviously within the sheath of their frocks (one girl's dress is cut from a fabric like snake skin, another nod toward loss of an Eden). Fascinated, Bill enquires where they are going. The women say they are taking him where the rainbow ends and Bill leers, savouring the prospect of discovering their offered treasure.

Bill's adventure differs from Alice's. She is tempted by a single shadow figure; he by two women. In a Jungian scheme, this suggests anima splitting. The anima (like the animus, of which Szavost is a variant) is one of the contrasexual archetypes. A simplified version of Jung's theory sufficient for our needs posits that, just as the animus symbolises the concealed masculine in women, men's experience of the anima presents them with the hidden feminine aspects of their personalities. The contrasexual archetypes mediate between the ego and the unconscious and can lead individuals to a measure of knowledge of their inner world. They thus counterbalance the persona, which mediates between ego and the social world.

Married men often locate their anima in the guise of their wives. In Bill's case, a disruptive inner complex is forming, signified by the mental imprint of his anima beginning to detach itself from Alice. However, although Bill is tempted, matters do not advance further at present because the sirens' seduction is interrupted. Uncertainty about the outcome of this first temptation matches the hesitancy of Bill's anima shift, conflicted and in denial as he is over his libido: while the models try to seduce him, he fiddles with his wedding ring.

Stuart McDougal has remarked that *coitus interruptus* is a governing metaphor for the narrative. Intrusions disrupt every attempted seduction and several meetings (2001). Characters immediately answer the demands of faceless notes and messages, abandoning their more personal and emotionally-charged interactions. The effect is the interruption of every moment edging toward authenticity: just when they might be opened, eyes wide – shut.

The models' seduction is interrupted when Ziegler summons the doctor to an upstairs bathroom. He has taken time out from his party to fuck a hooker. Mandy (Julienne Davis), a former beauty queen, has overdosed on a speedball (*coitus interruptus* again). The set up, with the naked body of the unconscious woman splayed in an armchair, is strikingly out of kilter. It's not just that Ziegler's power is so great he need not pretend innocence. The scene in the palatial bathroom gleams the more weirdly because 'preternaturally vibrant' (Maslin 1999), a vast painting of a spread nude almost exactly like Mandy hangs over them. What can this doubling mean? Ziegler's coldness toward Mandy suggests that he has not consciously been trying to replicate the painted scene – not least because the woman pictured is massively pregnant. Rather than bring the painting to life (let alone new life to the world through Mandy's womb), he seems more interested, albeit unconsciously (eyes wide – shut), in inflicting a symbolic death on the living woman. So there's bitter irony, which will deepen nastily before her life plays out, in Bill solemnly assuring Mandy when he has brought her round, 'You are a very, very lucky girl.'

Jung claimed that the anima and the woman's corresponding animus are, because of their suggestively magical power, the archetypal bases for all masculine and feminine divinities both negative and positive: 'As numina, anima and animus work now for good, now for evil' (1950b: 268). Alice's animus reveals its (albeit easily dismissed) Satanic aspect; Bill's anima is at risk of splitting; but Ziegler has virtually killed his anima. His wife is nothing more than an elegant co-host; his whore arouses no emotions in him other than, perhaps, the greed for sexual sensation. He possesses power without potency and uses his abundant though infertile vitality to manipulate rather than rejuvenate those around him.

Ziegler had escaped upstairs from his peers to his well-lit private bathroom (notably more palatial than the family facility the Harfords share). In both myths and dreams, descent to some dank lower place, be it basement, cave or underworld, is a trope which often signals entry into the unconscious. Conversely, ascent can signify movement into consciousness and away from the unconscious. Ziegler's 'ascent', however, is better illuminated by the terms with which Jung described an over-inflated consciousness. A pathological shift of this kind fits with Ziegler's fascination with, yet paradoxical coldness toward, the anima, which ordinarily stirs emotional heat when it constellates in a man's mind. Inflation also characterises the threat Ziegler poses to the people he tries to control (see Samuels *et al.* 1986: 81–2):

> An inflated consciousness is always egocentric and conscious of nothing but its own existence . . . Paradoxically enough, inflation is a regression of consciousness into unconsciousness. This always happens when consciousness takes too many unconscious contents upon itself and loses the faculty of discrimination, the *sine qua non* of all consciousness.
>
> (Jung 1952a: 480–1)

Jung observed that activated archetypal images may be so charged with their specific energy that they can appear to behave with the autonomous nature of characters and exercise an overwhelming compulsion on the individual, never more so than when actively repressed (1952b: 178). When such an image seizes hold of the psyche in an inflationary manner, it does so 'with a kind of primeval force and compels it to transgress the bounds of humanity. It causes exaggeration, a puffed-up attitude (inflation), loss of free will, delusion, and enthusiasm in good and evil alike. This is the reason why men have always needed demons and cannot live without gods . . .' (Jung 1942: 70–1).

Ziegler, corrupted by his willing enslavement to power, serves his demons through rituals of control. Money, sex, information and eventually even life and death are all game pieces in his hand. Ziegler's every move attempts to constellate the people around him into the creations of his own psyche: both his names mean 'conqueror'. The women reflect his own lifeless anima – were it to thrive, its influence would inhibit his relentless, dehumanising drive to control. So he preserves his worldly power at the cost of a hubristic attack on his anima's vitality. Meanwhile the men whom he injures (and Bill will be one of them) fall victim to his rampant shadow.

During the Christmas party, as Larry Gross has remarked, 'the scenes of Bill and Alice "playing" at flirtation downstairs have no literal connection with the perversions going on upstairs, yet their temporal proximity makes them feel linked'. The correspondences between the callous fucking upstairs and 'the barely restrained sexual decorum maintained downstairs' are pointed enough to raise the question (1999: 20). Bill, meanwhile, is tainted by the obligation to keep Ziegler's nasty secret.

Refracted vision/precipitation of the soul

Bill, who had no eyes for Alice while they were still at home, only sees her as sexy when aware she might be someone else's lover (Whitehouse 1999: 39). Sure enough, back home, gazing into a looking glass, he finds her naked reflection arousing and begins to make love. Their evasive eyes (Alice still drunk, Bill trying to maintain control) and Chris Isaak's 'Baby Did a Bad, Bad Thing' accompanying the scene, give away their secret guilt; but both Bill and Alice are so preoccupied with dissimulating that neither is yet ready to challenge the other.

The next night, wanting to tackle the awkward fall-out from the party, Alice brings out some dope, taking deep tokes on the joint so that she can say what she needs to.[3] She and Bill admit for the first time that they were watching each other and talk about their adventures. Bill smokes very little and remains in control of the dope: he denies any sexual interest in the models. By contrast, Alice says frankly that the Hungarian wanted sex.

The matter might have ended there had Bill not started plugging crass patriarchal notions. He insists he is not jealous of Alice because, firstly, he knows she would never be unfaithful; secondly, the male constitution makes all men sexual hunters (except, flying in the face of what Alice saw the previous evening, for him); and thirdly, women don't think like men about sex. Alice is offended and interprets Bill's assertions to mean that a man would only want to talk to her because of her beauty. Intended as a

3 It is hidden in a Band Aid box, but sticking plaster will not repair the injuries in question.

compliment, Bill's comment instead bares Alice's lurking self-doubt. The art gallery she managed has failed, leaving her at home to raise their daughter (a perfect fit for a doctor's wife on the Upper West Side). But her husband's slighting patronage and the lack of intelligent challenge reveal the trap in which Alice is caught.

If we had not noticed before, we cannot now fail to see that the Harfords' marriage is, in the way Bill sets the agenda, deeply patriarchal and hence politicised. As such it is dangerously close to mirroring in miniature the sexual politics of the New York world in *Eyes Wide Shut* – Ziegler's callous control over women gains him political advantage over men.

Weed-fuelled rage freeing her tongue, Alice pushes Bill into a row by mocking his work with patients. Then she disinters a lustrous, hurtful secret, recalling an incident from a family holiday when a naval officer sat near them in the dining room of their hotel. The man only glanced at her once, and Bill was never aware of him. However, Alice was overwhelmed by his presence: 'If he'd wanted me even for one night, I was ready to give up everything: you, Helena, my whole fucking future.' Her disproportionate reaction to this man reveals that he entered Alice's consciousness like an annunciation. As a vision of her animus endowed with a godlike, magical aura, his presence made her feel the potential for completeness. But, typically of animus and anima at their most intense, the figure soon vanished, leaving a knowledge of glory that still resonates through her whole being. Yet even while the man was still in the hotel and emotion was battering her, Alice was conscious that paradoxically Bill was dearer to her than ever. When she realised that the officer had left, she felt relief.

This episode, and her ability to speak about it, have initiated Alice from a state of untried innocence to fuller experience. She has found the beginnings of an understanding that her unruly emotions were of her own begetting, and to that extent natural. However, her newfound insight is not perfect, her confession being tainted by the desire to take revenge for Bill's blatant hypocrisy. This darker side to her motivation is also typical of the contrasexual archetype whose associations with the shadow always make themselves felt eventually.

The row is interrupted by a phone call which brings Bill word that one of his wealthy patients has died. Instead of resolving the quarrel (did Alice have more to say?), he rushes off post-haste to make a call on a dead man.

Micro-odyssey of an astigmatic antihero

Bill leaves home with no inkling that, whether he likes it or not, he too must suffer loss of innocence. Torment overwhelms him whenever the intensity of his conscious focus diminishes; visions of Alice fucking a naval officer plague him. He cannot digest the fact that Alice has not had an actual affair, but rather a craving for a deeper passion; but by denying his own extramarital sexual itches, he has damaged his ability to differentiate fantasy from deed. As will be revealed, this lack of differentiation extends into other areas: Bill's reactions show that he can't distinguish the nature of life and death, reality and fantasy, love and betrayal, truth and lies.

Arriving at the Nathansons' apartment, Bill is shown to the body. After putting his hand to the corpse's forehead, he turns away, leaving the dead man's face uncovered. This indifference to a dignity routinely accorded the dead grows in its callousness as Bill and Marion, the dead man's daughter, sit nearby exchanging tearful but trite consolations. (Later, his emotionally absorbed viewing of Mandy's corpse will, in contrast to his perfunctory glance at Nathanson, mark a breakthrough.)

His indifference is partly a consequence of emotional shock but it also reveals a psychological orientation. As a medical practitioner, Bill's mythological ancestor could be Asklepios, whose concern was the well-being of the whole person. Until his collapse at the film's climax, however, Bill shows no sign of following the wounded healer by acting as a practitioner who makes use of a variety of techniques including (like a psychoanalyst) insight into himself as well as his patient. Rather, as a modern medic, his forebear is Hippocrates, whose heirs concentrate on physical healing. But Bill takes this practice to extremes, focusing on the physical to the point of ignoring the inner life. In actuality, far from being the healer as hero, to use Hillman's phrase (1988: 119–26), Bill never really comforts anyone.

Read as a reflection of Bill's psyche, his treatment of Nathanson's corpse (the name links him to a Biblical prophet) suggests a disconnection from the archetypal figure of the Old Man – a potential source of wisdom. In the absence of the Old Man, it is the nightmarish image of Alice fucking the naval officer that compels Bill. This imagined figure, who mirrors Bill's unacknowledged desire for extramarital action, presents him with his shadow. I mentioned earlier that the shadow embodies those unrecognised aspects of the personality which the individual fears acknowledging. While Bill focuses obsessively on his shadow, jealousy urges him to discard his old anima image. Soon he meets a series of women offering themselves as if to usurp Alice – a sure sign of the anima running amok and inciting him to sexual adventure while blocking insight into his psyche. Were the anima functioning steadily (were Alice still the constant object of his libido), she could guide him toward the better understanding of his soul that he so badly needs (Samuels *et al.* 1986: 23).

The first, wholly unexpected temptress is Marion (Marie Richardson). Desperate for reassurance, she blurts out her love for Bill. Her shocking invitation mirrors bizarrely the Hungarian's sexual overture to Alice, her Scandinavian accent hinting at a second instance of American seduction by supposed European sophistication. But whilst Alice's interlude enriched her subtle complexity, Marion is debased by the act of declaring her love and begs Bill not to despise her. Bill backs off because her kiss conveys less the tender invitation of a lover than the urgency of a succubus who needs to drink his soul to live. However, as a twisted reflection of his own libido, Marion's temptation suggests the attraction of a kind of emotional death, the chill sexual revenge he wants to wreak on Alice. Moreover, whereas Alice dismissed the Hungarian once and for all, Bill's interest in Marion will revive in 24 hours' time.

Bill's male self-image takes yet another blow when, walking through the wintry streets after leaving the Nathansons, he is knocked off the sidewalk by a group of yobs who bait him as an effeminate homosexual. His need to reclaim his heterosexual confidence grows so, despite hesitations, he lets the chance invitation of a prostitute (Vinessa Shaw) steer him. This young woman has an authentic personality, as lived in as the warmly chaotic shared bathroom and kitchen in her cramped apartment. Her bedroom, with its plethora of books and African masks, confirms her intelligence and implies some understanding of sacred ritual. In these respects she resembles Alice, who is equally authentic in her frank embodied nature (for example, using the toilet with her husband in the bathroom or smelling her armpits as she dresses). However, the prostitute's life on the economic edge of society is remote from the Harfords' – let alone Ziegler's – wealth. Ziegler is implicated here because (though gorgeous to look at in purple and tender with the nervous Bill) this woman looks disconcertingly like Ziegler's drug-dependent hooker Mandy. But unlike Mandy, this sensual anima figure appears to own her life.

Bill's desire for sexual revenge sits uneasily with timidity. No sooner have he and the prostitute tried a first kiss (the intimacy of which suggests her warmth) than Alice calls his mobile. *Coitus interruptus* again. Bill does not know what to do. Some men might switch off the phone and slake their anger by fucking the generous hooker with all the greater pleasure. But Alice's call intrudes her presence not as a one-dimensional figure (which is all Bill allows the willing prostitute to be) but as a complex woman with whom Bill shares a history. She has been waiting through the night for her husband in order to resolve the unfinished row that might wreck their marriage. He leaves the prostitute regretfully, but (though she demurs) insists on paying. It both eases his guilt and indicates a developing pathology as he begins to spend freely. 'To spend' once meant to reach orgasm. The echo of the old meaning invokes the warmth of Eros ironically, and paying may be Bill's way of telling himself that he has had the girl. However, money has always had ambivalent associations through its links with the gold hoarded by Mammon, and hence with anal retention. There is therefore something infantile in Bill's spending wads of cash, but (despite his mistaken self-perception) little truly erotic libidinous energy. While Bill hasn't begun to reach the end of the rainbow, giving over some cash comforts him that he is at least in touch with its magic.

Secret passage to the dark

Back on the streets, another chance encounter overturns Bill's conflicted intention to return home. He is in Greenwich Village, topographically a descent from his apartment on Central Park West. Finding himself in front of the Sonata Cafe, a jazz club where an old acquaintance is playing, he goes in.[4] In this setting red and blue again clash oppressively. The guest pianist is Nick Nightingale (Todd Field). He and Bill were medical students together and had lost contact after Nick dropped out of his degree course, until Bill spotted him playing at Ziegler's party. Here Nick, a jobbing musician, leads a bland jazz quartet. His second name, given the banality of his music, may allude ironically to Keats's bird pouring forth its soul in ecstasy (McDougal 2001). However, his first name links him with Old Nick; and the way he is lit from below adds to the sense of spiritual darkness. Nightingale is not an evil figure himself but, as he says, enjoys walking away from things. In mythological terms he is an ambivalent psychopomp, a guide to the underworld. In psychoanalytic terms, the psychopomp can guide individuals to fuller understanding of their psyches. Paradoxically, Nightingale leads an all too eager Bill into darkness rather than the light. He fits the type of the *puer aeternus*, the eternal boy with a narcissistic borderline personality, who avoids work and never grows up (Tacey 1997: 80). His unsettled life, moving from one short-term job to another, not to mention his pack of four boys back in Seattle with their mother, underscore the allusion to Peter Pan. So his re-entry into Bill's life at this time of crisis confirms that the latter is regressing to a similarly immature state of mind – witness the moment when he and Bill discover each other at Ziegler's ball, and instantly revert to college-boy joshing and back slapping.

Further evidence that Bill is drawn toward the *puer* comes when a phone call interrupts their conversation. Nick has to leave for a late-night engagement and drops lubricious hints that he is providing music for an orgy. Bill is instantly sold on gate-crashing the masked revels. This is the first energetic decision we have seen him make, his face (lit like Nick's from below) taking on a devilish leer. He seems interested not only in the sex itself, but also in college-boy daring to restore his manhood among men.

In the dead of night Bill awakens the owner of the Rainbow costume shop. Its name both signals danger by recalling the rainbow's end where Ziegler's models wanted to lead Bill, and has a thematic function. In many scenes, colours other than the blue-red pairing are drab. Here the theatrical

4 McDougal (2001) noted that the club's name draws attention to the film's three-part sonata structure over three days (exposition, development and recapitulation), a form which also shapes each of the three days.

store and the self-dramatising personality of its owner serve as a marker that life can be lived across a fuller spectrum of moral colours than Bill has ever allowed himself to see.

The owner, Milich (Rade Sherbedgia) declines to serve him at so late an hour until offered a hefty bribe, whereupon he opens up with alacrity. An unpredictable figure, he switches at will between roles – haughty shopkeeper, master of ceremonies and doctor's humble patient. As impresario, renting Bill a black cloak, hood and mask bores him: perhaps he has hired identical costumes to other guests at the orgy. Milich is a shape-shifter who has only one constant role – the trickster. As such he belongs to a tradition far more dangerous than the middle-aged playboys in their orgy. The roots of the archetypal figure of the trickster were traced by Jung to twelfth-century Fools' feasts with their grotesque masquerades and frenzied days of misrule. In the sixteenth century, the masquerades were adopted by the commedia dell'arte (Jung 1954b: 257–60). Venetian masks worn by the orgiasts confirm the link.

Milich soon displays a main characteristic of the trickster – that he is capable of anything, whether admirable or vile. While serving Bill, the shopkeeper discovers two middle-aged men hidden behind costume racks. Stripped to their underwear, their faces whitened (the clown's mask of misrule), they have been toying with his daughter, a nymphet who looks 12 years old. Milich, the outraged father, threatens the men with the police and locks them up. Meanwhile the nymphet (LeeLee Sobieski) hides behind Bill's back and secretly flirts with him. But when Bill returns the costume next day, he finds to his astonishment the same two men taking their leave escorted to the door by the nymphet (still in her underwear) and unctuously thanked by the shopkeeper. Milich explains that they have come to a satisfactory arrangement. What is more, he adds, if there is anything, anything at all, that his daughter can do for Bill, it will be a pleasure to arrange. Once again, the girl flashes Bill her jailbait smile.

With the father openly acting as pimp, Kubrick's return to the Lolita theme carries a much darker vision than his 1961 film. Milich's black trade in his child's services pushes sexual licence to a reach far beyond anything either imagined or desired by Bill. Thus Milich fulfils one of the trickster's functions: anamnesis of humankind's atavistic animal nature. He brings back to mind an older, lower level of consciousness covered up by its later and higher developments. That earlier state of being continues, however, to fascinate the mind for its frank engagement with immorality and evil, an access subsequently repressed by the parallel development of consciousness and the more restrictive moral norms that went with it (Jung 1954b: 265–6). Milich as trickster has the power to awaken Bill's consciousness by showing him, through a more evil sexuality than that with which he has been toying, how black the shadow can become. Understanding that would help Bill recognise his shadow and integrate it before disaster strikes.

Masquerade of pale desire

With the cynical password 'Fidelio' learned from Nick, Bill gains entry to the vast stone chambers of a mansion in Glen Cove. Somerton fits the stereotype of the house in Gothic fiction – a mode of fantasy known for its blurring of reality and imagination.[5] It also fits the register of this scene, which is closer to dream than the kind of reality Bill experiences at home. Kubrick plays on our expectations by hooking us with the Gothic aesthetics of the setting and then distracting us with the pornographic (if cold) action inside. So Somerton presents the shadow side of Ziegler's house, and the orgy shadows his party. This is gloomy where the other had been brilliantly lit, and devoted to illicit pleasures where the earlier event had on the surface been decorous in the extreme.

Like Bill, all the guests wear black cloaks and hoods. Distinguished only by the masks that cover their faces, they encircle an inner ring of model-perfect women, also cloaked and masked. The orgy (which, as in a dream, appears to have attended the hero's arrival) begins when Nightingale fills the Great Hall with the pompous notes of a synthesised organ. It leads into a parody of Russian Orthodox chant, the singers vocalising gibberish. The music complements the actions of a crimson-robed mock cardinal wearing a brutal mask who officiates with a censer in the middle of the circle.[6] As a parody of religious ritual, the orgy might be likened to Szavost trying to justify the unjustifiable, blessing what is clearly not remotely sacred. Alternatively it could be read as a black mass deliberately challenging a moral God whose rituals it mocks – except that this ceremonial is staid and lacks the rebarbative energy usually associated with diabolism. These celebrants are not religious iconoclasts; they have other fixations.

At the mock cardinal's command, the women let fall their cloaks and, strutting like models on the catwalk, move into the crowd to lead off their first partners of the night. As indentured women whose only function is sexual service, they are remarkable in their identical representation of a

5 'The fantastic requires the fulfilment of three conditions. First, the text must oblige the reader to consider the world of the characters as a world of living persons and to hesitate between a natural and a supernatural explanation of the events described. Second, this hesitation may also be experienced by a character; thus the reader's role is so to speak entrusted to a character, and at the same time the hesitation is represented, it becomes one of the themes of the work – in the case of naive reading, the actual reader identifies himself with the character. Third, the reader must adopt a certain attitude with regard to the text: he will reject allegorical as well as "poetic" interpretations . . .' (Todorov 1973: 33).

6 The women are actually standing on a square red carpet; but it is the bright inner circle on whose circumference they are placed that we notice. Squaring the circle is a time-honoured motif for reconciling the physical with the spiritual, a sacred motif reversed in its implications here.

male pornographic ideal: centrefold figures, shaved pubic hair, 'fuck-me' stiletto shoes, depersonalising masks. The fetishised presentation of their bodies objectifies both the gazers and those gazed upon. Authenticity and individuality are erased on both sides of the exchange. And as voyeurs ourselves, we too are aroused by the women's sexuality while noticing their resemblance not only to each other but also Mandy and the young prostitute. The orgy's presentation deploys the principles of anonymity, nudity, fetishism and objectification that characterise pornography, projecting them forward to their absurd (idealised and chilly) conclusion.

As we tour the house with Bill, we scan room after room. Bizarrely, all the guests observe a tacit decorum not unlike that of upper-crust New York society. Again the orgy shadows Ziegler's seemingly staid Christmas party, and there is little sign of real pleasure amid the sexual activity. Some couples bang away like piston-driven machines, observed idly by strolling onlookers, and others solemnly awaiting their turn. Their copulation is as mechanical as a workout. Without words or the sounds of lovers' ecstasy, the masked participants seem isolated, as if masturbating. The scene resembles an Hieronymous Bosch painting, with all present, including Bill, caught in a cold hell.

As mentioned, the only features which distinguish those present are the full-face masks with their long cultural history. Whether donned for religious ritual, the drama or a ball, masks disguise their wearers and license them to play roles remote from daily life. At one extreme, masks can empower the religious celebrant to take on not only the appearance but also the nature of a god by hiding the frailties of the human face. At another extreme, they can allow the wearer undetected release for barbaric instincts, as implied by the mock cardinal's brutish visage (Sorell 1973: 11–12). Many at the orgy have chosen masks from past epochs (the commedia dell'arte principal among them) that have emblematic associations with perverted lust, moral hazard and deceit.

The commedia dell'arte borrowed many of its emblems from Dionysian rites. The principal themes of those rites were drunkenness, inspiration and fecundity linked (as here) to parody of religious ceremony. They were celebrations of wild, animalistic misrule which had the effect, contrary to appearances, of reinforcing the social status quo by allowing people periodically to break out from its moral constraints (Grimal 1991: 128–9). In this orgy, however, wildness is suppressed. The masks muffle the voices, which further distances the characters. Instead of abandoning restraint and overthrowing Apollonian intellect, the participants keep their Dionysian impulses leashed. Let alone fecundity (which would be truly unwelcome to these elite party-goers), there is no sign of their enjoying release, but much evidence of brutality evident in the cold rituals of sexual subjugation through which these wealthy men confirm to themselves their authority.

The wildness of Dionysian orgy, seen from a Jungian perspective, allows the expression of 'emotions and affects which have found no suitable religious outlets in the predominantly Apollonian cult and ethos of Christianity' (Jung 1952a: 143). But although, as Jung reminds us, drunken ecstasy found a place in pagan religions when Christianity grew too severe to host inflamed celebration, this orgy shows no sign of people searching for the divine through excess's wild intoxications. These simply want exhibitionist sex to slake an almost emotionless physical appetite. More accurately, that is what the men want, most of the women having been hired to serve their gratification.

The dominance of the event by men means that the orgy does not comfortably map (as it might otherwise have done) onto the *coniunctio oppositorum*. This concept, which Jung drew from intensive reading of alchemists' texts, has one of its primary expressions in an image cluster centred on male-female sexual coupling – the royal marriage of king and queen. The marriage symbolises a union of body (the male) and spirit (the female), their intercourse having the potential to bring forth new life (often symbolised by the child) in the soul (Jung 1952a: 330; 1956b: 166–7; Samuels *et al.* 1986: 35–6). I have already referred to the sterile nature of the orgiastic coupling in *Eyes Wide Shut*; it is also apparent that the imbalance between the participating men and women differs markedly from the equality of the royal couple. Here, the body dominates, seeking to enslave the spirit to its will: no rebirth for the psyche is signalled.

Despite Bill's resemblance (apart from his mask) to all the other men, cult members have no trouble recognising that he does not belong. Mandy (although unrecognised by him) identifies him immediately; a couple in the crowd – perhaps the Zieglers – bow to him. Like us, they may have noticed that his mask (pale as death) looks rather like him and reveals his state of mind. Its superficial prettiness, emblazoned with gilded motifs, recalls his links with the *puer aeternus*, but in some lights these motifs are sinister, looking more like human guts than pleasing decorations.[7] It may be inferred that Bill's psychological orientation is comparable but not identical to that of the others present. While he might have hoped that participating in the orgy would relieve the pain caused by Alice's confession, he finds, as he ogles the pornographic scene, only the deathliness of his own solipsistic needs reflected in those around him.

Appropriately, given the Gothic aesthetic, a strong undertow of anxiety runs beneath the orgy's activities. While, unaware that arraignment awaits him, Bill is led by a strongman back to the Great Hall, the blindfolded Nick (found guilty of betraying the orgy to his friend) is being escorted out of the

7 The mask reinforces an aspect of Bill's psychology already mentioned by replicating his fixed stare.

building by another heavy. Nick passes through an outer chamber where, in a further nightmarish inversion of the Zieglers' party, couples (one partner masked, the other not) dance a sedate foxtrot to 'Strangers in the Night'. But the couples are woman/woman and man/man. These same-sex pairings recall the homoerotic threat Bill encountered (being called a faggot and 'Mary' on the street) that helped fuel his micro-odyssey. Having assumed that the orgy would give him a chance to affirm his sexual prowess and reinforce his masculinity, Bill is now about to be humbled into a more complex idea of manhood. His crude sense of power, heretofore mapped neatly into dualities of dominance/submission, masculine/feminine and male/female, will not hold.

I said when discussing *Barry Lyndon* that in Jungian thought the mask is associated with the persona as the face that the individual turns to the world for public consumption. As a twentieth-century figure, Bill allows us to see that persona comprises not only the individual's appearance, but his or her response to how others regard that appearance; not just visible appearance but the public face of the personality shaped by the way people react to it. We work to detect in the minutiae of every social situation other people's impressions of us, and try in turn to control those opinions, developing important parts of our identity (and seeking to recognise the identities of others) through exterior appearance (Finkelstein 1991: 155–6, 185).

It is characteristic of our present-day obsession with signs created from surface appearances that we use external identity as a sign which we tell ourselves is the self. In so doing we ignore the fact that this exterior identity, in large part socially constructed, can be false to inner reality. Just such falsity lies at the root of Bill's problems in his relations with the outer world. He has identified himself with the persona of the successful and unimpeachable professional, but this persona overwhelms his role as a caring doctor and overlays a lack of confidence. When, during Bill's arraignment, the mock cardinal insists he strip, the role reversal required humiliates him because women are (patients excepted) the only 'proper' people to be stripped (Baum 2001). Worse, however, he has to expose his face and allow his peers to see the scared *puer* behind his mask. At the Zieglers' party, he was The Doctor, his mask firmly in place. Now, at the orgy, where conscious identities don't matter, he is powerless. This is the first of a number of occasions when Bill's mask will fail: his persona has begun to crumble, exposing the fissure between his outer and inner worlds.

Jung thought each person's ego-consciousness was at first identical with the persona.[8] As we said when characterising Barry Lyndon, prolonged

8 Jung's idea is contentious if applied universally. Women, for example, often have more flexible personae than men because of the variety of social roles they have to play full-time, as Alice's careers show. She is trophy wife, mother, lover, housekeeper and former businesswoman.

identification with one's persona is dangerous because 'it leads to a life based on something false and partial, leading one's unconscious to compensate too bright a persona with sometimes truly horrendous private behavior' (Hopcke 1995: 16–17). This is Bill's condition before his exposure begins to change things. Psychological development arises because 'the unconscious self cannot be repressed to the point of extinction' (Jung 1935: 158), which it might be were ego, shaped by the persona's strong identification with its social role, to dominate the individual. In reacting to compensate for the overwhelming bias of consciousness, the unconscious produces collective fantasies, and these become the seeds of the individual's inner development (Jung 1935: 158, 194). This dynamic process of homeostasis (the system regulating its own balance) accounts for the changes just beginning in Bill despite his relentless attempts to control his inner no less than outer life.

Like the whole film, the sequences in the mansion both observe events and give the sense that they are tempered by the characters' psychological state. The gap between these two perspectives frees spectators to inflect interpretation of the scenes with their own sense of irony. When Bill is called back to the Great Hall to account for his trespass, it fits this register that the masks of the participants circling him include, as in a nightmare, many more distorted by cruelty, hatred and morally diseased appetites than in earlier scenes. They are like collective fantasies produced by his unconscious. Some wear Venetian masks representing the cardinal sins; others recall the torments of Bosch's visions; there is a Janus face, a Cubist face and a nightmarish Picasso.

Jung held that the persona and anima were in compensatory relationship. While the former mediates between a man and the public world, the latter relates him to that which is interior. Alteration in either leads one to expect change in the other (Jung 1935: 177, 192–5; Samuels *et al.* 1986: 107–8). So when the mock cardinal judges Bill before the community and robs him of his mask, the anima steps in to redeem him: incognito, Mandy (the latest manifestation of his troubled contrasexual archetype) volunteers to take his punishment on herself. She is immediately led away by a man masked with an immense curved beak like a sacred ibis. This doom-laden image and Mandy's fear that she might be suspected of having arranged Bill's admission to the orgy arouse both his and our fear for her life.

That Bill's anima is indeed at risk of serious harm is confirmed by the red cardinal's warning that dire consequences will follow for Bill and his family if he tries to find out more about the orgy. The danger is not now his alone and thus mirrors Alice being willing to give up everything, both family and future, for one night with the naval officer. Yet there are small hopeful signs too: Mandy intervenes just after Bill has shown interest in her as a person by asking who she is rather than, as the party's decorum requires, penetrating her naked body wordlessly. Although he does not know it yet, Bill has started on the painful process of self-discovery.

Loss of Eden

When Bill creeps home at 4 a.m., Alice is in the throes of a nightmare. He awakens her and she recounts her dream, the themes of which pick up where their unfinished argument had left off. The first scene places her with Bill naked and afraid in a deserted city. Plainly it expresses her feeling of exposure and abandonment (Paradise Lost?) for which, in the dream, she blames Bill.

The scene changes and she finds herself in a beautiful sunlit garden, feeling wonderful, naked and alone. The dream has brought her to the *hortus conclusus*, the enclosed garden where both profane and sacred love attain perfection, a blessed place where the self can be discovered in its wholeness (twentieth-century Paradise Regained?). However, the naval officer comes out of the woods and mocks her. In contrast to the garden, the woods from which her phantom lover emerges have long-standing associations with the wild, and hence with the untamed unconscious. Alice's animus in its god-like form has returned to violate the illusion of a perfect self-realisation for which she is not yet prepared (Paradise Lost once again). She gives herself to him and they make love.

The final part of the dream mirrors Bill's night askew. Around herself and the naval officer Alice sees other people fucking. But, unlike her hesitant spouse who, despite temptation, balked at Dionysian excesses in the flesh, she takes part in this wild orgy, in her mind's arena fucking many men. She knows that Bill in the dream can see her and mimics the contempt of her god-lover for timid mortals by laughing at him.

Ann Belford Ulanov hypothesises a stage in a woman's development when she may be invaded by the animus springing from the transpersonal (or collective) unconscious. When this happens the animus is experienced as an overpowering archetypal image charged with numinous energy. The mythological representations of such animus figures include the phallic gods (Dionysus among them). Often dressed in the image of an impersonal male divinity (sometimes a ravishing penetrator who breaks into her consciousness), this figure, if she can accept it, connects a woman to her own instinctual nature (1971: 246–7). However, this invasion is not without its dangers, and where ego and animus are not separated (as with the dream naval officer fucking Alice), inflation may occur. Indeed, Alice has experienced a vision of the royal marriage. One of the dangers to which it can expose the dreamer eventuates where her body seems to take on spiritual form, resulting in just such an inflation (Samuels *et al.* 1986: 36). Then the ego is in thrall to the animus, and that can lead to a ruthless power drive (Ulanov 1971: 42–3). In her dreamscape Alice succumbs to this danger in viciously mocking Bill (an echo of the scorn with which she addressed his professional conduct during their row).

Once awake, however, she pulls away from identification with the animus and shows greater maturity. When talking Bill through the nightmare, she cradles him to bring them mutual comfort in their sorrow. The recognition that her animus is so dangerously seductive has alarmed her, and she has reasserted a measure of conscious control. Bill, however, does not reciprocate, in his shock blocking any further movement toward self-discovery by failing to divulge the way her dream mirrors the events of his night.

Intermission – and about time!

When Bill woke Alice from her dream, she asked, 'What time is it?' This is just one of several instances when Bill is either asked the time or expresses anxiety about the lateness of the hour (when we first see him he tells Alice that they're running late). Bill invariably knows the time, but he doesn't know what significance the moment has.

Cumulatively these references suggest that moral time is the issue, although Bill is not aware of it. The young prostitute's opening gambit is to ask Bill the time, curiously following up later to say she doesn't keep track of the time. It's as though her enquiry may be more for *his* benefit than hers, a tactic culled from the Garden of Eden and a much earlier moral awakening.[9] Similarly, the prostitute's question is like Bill's own conscience to whose prompting he is not yet attending.

The concept of moral time maps sweetly onto Jungian theory. Its crux is that epoch when individuals find themselves called to respond to the archetypes' dominion over their lives. Jung recognised this when he asserted that the integration of the shadow was not only a psychological problem but a moral issue:

> In working out a difficult [psychological] problem the moral aspect of it has to be considered if one is to avoid a repression or a deception. He who deceives others deceives himself, and vice versa. Nothing is gained by that, least of all the integration of the shadow. Indeed, its integration makes the highest demands on an individual's morality, for the 'acceptance of evil' means nothing less than that his whole moral existence is put in question. Decisions of the most momentous kind are called for.
>
> (Jung 1949: 619)

9 After Adam senses his nakedness and hides, God as provocateur asks him, 'Where are you?', an opening for Adam to locate himself in his new moral universe. An omniscient being, after all, could not fail to know where his creature is.

These words pinpoint Bill's moral predicament. As a doctor, his meagre understanding of time is especially ironic since healing and being pressed for time are incompatible. The healing process takes time, but (both morally and psychologically an invalid himself) Bill does not grasp this. Given that he chose to leave home in the first place, he has returned prematurely.

The micro-odyssey resumes: the astigmatic hero retraces his steps

Bill's original search can be compared with the classic quest of the hero which, if it succeeds, entails some or all of these phases: separation; a journey across borders; a test or trial; conflict; exposure to injury; gaining a trophy; and triumphant return home.

Bill's quest began after the row with Alice, with his separation from the familiar. Then followed a significant journey through various kinds of moral darkness while he struggled to decide just how married he really felt (Alice's struggle too), and that brought him to his present borderline condition. Tested several times (at the Nathansons, by the prostitute and at the orgy), he has been confronted with some troubling questions. How much do the circumstances of life bind us, and how much freedom do we have to change those circumstances in order to follow a fantasy? How do we find our way between the worlds of social custom (which in his and Alice's case have boxed in any truly creative ambition they might have had) and the drive toward personal fulfilment (which tends to work against social custom)? Having failed to acknowledge these conflicts for himself, Bill has suffered injury not only to his self-regard but also his persona. He has returned home too soon, far from triumphant. The only trophies he brought back he has stashed secretly – his deathly mask and a cloak of guilt.

Since, self-deluded though he be, Bill can hardly conceal from himself that he has not lived up to the hero myth (the model for so many men caught in a competitive culture), it is no surprise that he sets out on the third day to retrace the previous night's moves. He has dangerously mixed motives. In part he is attempting to find out more about what he experienced the previous night. But throughout the long day he is visited by jealous waking nightmares of Alice fucking the naval officer – so in part he continues to seek revenge.

The lost guide and the gatekeepers

First Bill traces Nick Nightingale to his hotel, only to find he has checked out. His disappearance deprives Bill of his only possible source of information about the fate of the girl who saved him at the orgy. The desk clerk

(Alan Cumming) triggers his suspicion when he tells Bill that a bruised Nightingale was strong-armed out of the hotel in the middle of the night. Since Bill is acting the bumbling amateur detective and our knowledge of that genre assures us that the detective's doubts are usually justified, his anxiety gets to us. Bill accepts the tale of skullduggery at face value. It increases his fear that those who organised the orgy are carrying out their threats. However, it is possible that the clerk's story is designed to scare Bill off. And a man who passes through the lobby may be observing Bill. Such speculation will gain weight later from Ziegler's admission that he was one of those behind the orgy and has had Bill followed.

The clerk is all persona, an amusing Harlequin who presents Bill with a bizarre masquerade as he tries on a swift succession of personae. His mincing speech may signify only that he is a scene gay letting Bill know he is interested. However, he could also be a fantasist who relishes fabricating airy notions of conspiracy. A bystander to the main plot, he directs attention to the eccentricity of everybody's mask and the element of fantasy in it, no matter how normal its appearance. I mentioned Jung's idea that the bond between persona and ego-consciousness is loosened by collective fantasies (1935: 158). The observation will help us understand the clerk's function since fantasy turns out to be a key theme of *Eyes Wide Shut*.

Bill moves on to return his costume to Milich. We have seen how barbarism flourishes in the Rainbow fantasy shop of many coloured masks. Paradoxically, when the trickster proffers his daughter's services, his vileness helps Bill see to what evil unchecked sexual desire can lead. Milich is Bill's guide despite his worst intentions. Meanwhile Bill has lost his mask, unwittingly revealing that his rigid persona is not holding.

Not every minor character whom Bill meets has a helpful function. All the rich families in *Eyes Wide Shut* have servants. Bill himself resembles them in being, bottom line, little more than a servant of the rich. Some (the Nathansons' maid, for example) are almost invisible to their employers. Others, their faces marked by self-interest (like Ziegler's assistants and the strongmen at the orgy), relish their masters' reflected power while exuding a sense that there is real danger, difficult to control.

Yet others are more sinister. Bill cancels his afternoon appointments and returns to Somerton, the Glen Cove mansion he gatecrashed the previous night. High gates bar his way and a security camera examines him. While he waits, the forbidding hammer notes of Ligeti's 'Musica Ricercata II' (first heard during Bill's arraignment at the orgy) add to the chill. A black-coated flunky arrives from the house in a Rolls-Royce and hands Bill an unsigned note reiterating the warnings of the previous night. These funereal gatekeepers, when read as factors in Bill's psychological profile, function like ravelled complexes that obstruct entry into the psyche. Their role is quite contrary to Nightingale's and Milich's who as psychopompi lead Bill, albeit riskily, into the deeper levels of his unconscious.

The sick anima

The severity of that risk is seen after Bill returns home in the early evening. Alice's affectionate smile still seems to him wreathed in treachery, and his secret rage drives him out again. Still tormented by involuntary images of Alice fucking the naval officer, he phones Marion Nathanson. Her fiancé answers and Bill hangs up. It's another failed connection but, though he has used his standing as a family doctor dishonestly before, this time he has sidled toward taking sexual advantage of a patient whose judgement he knows to be impaired by desperation – a perversion of love and duty as black as Milich's. Bill returns to the prostitute's door, bizarrely bringing her a box of pastries. The gift is perhaps a foil to put an innocent mask on his visit to a whore. For the first time he uses her name, Domino. It winds her right into the film's themes. 'Domina', shorthand in sex ads for 'dominatrix', refers directly to her trade. But a domino once was the hood worn by priests in winter. In the seventeenth century the word transferred to the hooded cloak and mask worn at a masquerade ball. Her name and business underscore the young woman's role in bringing fantasies to life and hint that she might have had a sacerdotal function had Bill sought it. Finally, from the game comes the idea of the domino pieces falling – as the girl will now do (French 1999).

Domino is not at home, but her flatmate Sally (Fay Masterson) makes him welcome and at first seems to be (like Domino) the perfect anima fantasy, a woman warmly willing to fuck him on sight. But Sally pulls back from intimacy to tell him that Domino has left because she has tested HIV positive. The counterpoint of sex and death intensifies as we recall the lovely young woman in prophetic royal purple, her sickness a further sign of the state of Bill's wayward anima. However, Bill himself, still centred on his wounded ego, is not capable of registering anyone else's pain. Transfixed by his own narrow escape from infection, he cannot even see Sally's concern for him. Muttering with no sign of feeling a few formal words of regret, he exits into the night. But the news of Domino's condition shatters the illusion of romantic sex, free of responsibility, a rupture soon to be confirmed by Mandy's fate. Now he can no longer dodge the crisis which has been threatening for 24 hours.

Stumbling along cold, empty streets, he becomes aware he is being tailed. The warning note handed him at the mansion implied he was being watched, but this is the first time Bill has observed his shadow. As in a nightmare, he tries futilely to escape his pursuer. The man follows without pretence, boldly returning Bill's fearful gaze. Throughout his reckless pursuit of the anima in its increasingly distressed forms, Bill has remained blind to the dark side of his motivation. Now the shadow (both the private eye and the fearful, concealed aspects of his personality) presents itself openly to him. It behaves like a classic instance of a repressed archetype, the phenomenon mentioned earlier. Appearing to have autonomous being, it becomes more menacing the longer Bill ignores it, and shortly will insist on being dealt with.

Distressed by the relentless gaze of the private eye, Bill buys a newspaper and escapes into a decorous coffee shop. However, the atmosphere of even this safe retreat is out of joint in that the Mozart on its sound system is not a seasonally appropriate Christmas oratorio but the *Requiem* – unremarked precognition once again. The banner headline of Bill's paper screams an echo of his words at Ziegler's party: 'Lucky to be alive'. Bill misses the irony because his eye is caught by an article reporting the admission to hospital of Mandy (the very woman to whom he addressed those words) after another drugs overdose. Mozart is wiped out by the hammer notes of the 'Musica Ricercata'.

By the time he reaches the hospital, Mandy is dead. In the mortuary he bends long and low over her corpse, almost kissing her death mask. It is the first time he has understood death, and his grieving gesture of farewell shows him at last in touch with emotions other than defensive rage. He recalls her warning that his presence at the orgy could cost her life and perhaps his own. Bill recognises that, whatever the circumstances of her death, she was due more than he gave her. Her death is the sacrifice that kick-starts the rediscovery of his own feelings.

Encountering the shadow

Before Bill can get his emotions under control, the shadow in its most intense manifestation demands its dues. Ziegler summons him and they meet in his enormous pool room with its 'jarringly red' table (Maslin 1999). The room reverberates with Ziegler's ostentatious power, the table adding to the effect. Its vulgarity goes with his coarse language and undermines the show of cold rationality he puts on. At the same time, wide-angle shots of the room recall Charles Foster Kane's vacant halls and underline the emptiness of his power. The absurd scarlet table also implies the intervention of fantasy. Power and fantasy blend to motivate Ziegler with the illusion of omnipotence.

Ziegler reveals that, as one of its organisers, he saw Bill at the orgy. Charged with sorting out the mess caused by Bill's gatecrashing, he has had him followed all day. While admitting that the masked woman who warned Bill was indeed Mandy, Ziegler turns that fact against Bill by insisting that the doctor has leapt to the wrong conclusion about her fate. Although he pretends to use reason, he is actually flaunting his power over Bill to cow him into silence. His argument is equally revealing considered in the context of fantasy. He refers to the immense clout of the unknown men for whom he is covering in order to persuade Bill that things are not as they seem. In effect Ziegler denies one fantasy (Bill's suspicion that Mandy was murdered) by affirming another: he suggests the threats made to Bill at the orgy and Mandy's offer to sacrifice herself in his place were a charade designed to silence him.

Jungians describe fantasy as 'the flow or aggregate of images and ideas in the unconscious psyche, constituting its most characteristic activity' (Samuels *et al.* 1986: 58). Even when the raw material for fantasy derives from conscious elements, fantasising takes place independently of ego-consciousness. One of its prime characteristics is that what at first sight may appear to be the free play of images and ideas will have been shaped by the individual's pre-existing unconscious dispositions. Fantasy, therefore, is the bridge between the archetypal inner world and external reality (Samuels *et al.* 1986: 58–9). With the world of many characters tinted by their unacknowledged impulses, this is fantasy's role throughout *Eyes Wide Shut*, nowhere more nakedly than in this scene. Emotion-fuelled fantasy has dominated Bill's mind for the past 24 hours and is now closer to the surface than ever. In particular, Ziegler's urge to spin out fantasy scenarios in an obsessively self-satisfying exercise of power is the concentrated, black reflection of the same impulse in Bill. For the latter, it makes their meeting the climactic confrontation with his own shadow-side.

Bill is caught between horrible alternatives, neither of which is tolerable to a caring person. The first is that Mandy may have been murdered. The second is Ziegler's brutal rationalisation (the fantasy bedrock on which its participants excuse the orgy) that nothing happened to Mandy of any significance: 'She got her brains fucked out. Period.' Ziegler sees no link between the unfeeling sexual use of Mandy and her fatal addiction, but Bill seems finally to be getting the connection.

As a power broker, Ziegler secures his goal – Bill is frightened off. However, as Bill's fantastic shadow, his brutality has a salvific effect. Knowing more about Bill's negative side than the doctor himself, Ziegler helps, through their confrontation, to wreck Bill's picture of himself as the pitiable, injured spouse. Bill has for the first time to recognise his own personality's cold, self-serving side, manifested in his dealings with Mandy and the inadequacy of his care for her. In the excruciating moment when he faces his failings and apologises to Ziegler, we see above his shoulder a mud-coloured painting of a long-dead woman. The contrast of this dour ancestral portrait (whose drabness augments the anguish of Bill's drained face) with the vividly painted pregnant nude in Ziegler's bathroom could not be more decisive. Once again, the death of the anima is indicated.

The ghost of Christmas Past

Christmas trees have been seen everywhere including the Zieglers', Bill's surgery, the Nathansons', Domino's, the Sonata Cafe and the lobby of Nick's hotel. The phallic connotation of such trees recalls their place in

Dionysian rituals of sacrifice celebrated to reawaken the earth's fertility (Baum 2001). The Christmas tree has links with the Christian cross in a vivid, ancient chain of meaningful images – first the Tree of Life, second the Tree of Death that ultimately transforms through resurrection into a third, the eternal Tree of Life. But these fake, manufactured trees, draped in glare and glitter, have been divorced from their deeper ritual meanings. In the same way that the orgy's models are a parody of fecund womanhood, the multiple Christmas trees decorate with a cold light that has no ability to warm or transform.

The potential for transformative vitality, however, is irrepressible, though just beyond Bill's awareness. When he fantasises Alice fucking the navy man, the bed he imagines is covered with a quilt in a traditional pattern known as 'tree of life'. Domino's bed cover has an appliqué tree whose branches are populated with colourful birds. He sees neither design. Alice, however, has decorated their apartment with indoor greenery and vivid landscape paintings, a reflection of her art gallery background and an indication that she is closer than her husband to inner reality.

At the end of his second micro-odyssey Bill returns home during the still hours before dawn. Before going to bed, he turns out the lights on the family tree, signalling the collapse of meaningless public displays and the end of hollow ritual.

Unmasking the soul

A reprise of the icy 'Musica Ricercata' intensifies the ghastly blue light in the bedroom where Alice lies like another dead anima on sheets of royal purple, her face turned toward the pillow where Bill's head should be. Beside her, pale as death, its jewelled curlicues looking like a frightful skin disease, lies the missing costume mask. Metaphorically speaking, all Alice possesses of Bill is his public face, the dead persona.

The painful irony for Bill is that Ziegler has just ripped his persona to shreds; but paradoxically that injury triggers his psychological recovery, for the real threat of Ziegler was always that Bill would take him as a role model and become callous like him. Injury transforms Bill into a wounded healer, though in the first instance a healer only of himself. Already aware that Alice's dreams have crisscrossed his wanderings, he fears from what she has intuited that she may know everything. For the first time he unmasks himself voluntarily as his emotions break through the persona which has concealed them from his wife. Overwhelmed by guilt, he seeks redemption through confession.

Something does die in the marriage bed's asphyxiating purple – the couple's innocent belief in the deadened convention of their lives. Alice's own disclosure first injured it and now Bill's confession hammers nails into its coffin: the tears they shed in the early morning bear witness to the destruction they have wreaked on each other. But out of this death something is arising. New tenderness is the prize they can bring back from their suffering.

This possibility dawns on Alice while they shepherd their daughter on a Christmas shopping trip. While the child explores, Bill asks Alice what they should do. She feels her way from pain-filled uncertainty toward a wise proposal. Though she phrases it indirectly ('The important thing is we're awake now'), she wants them to stay together by integrating the mutually hurtful knowledge of their misadventures into understanding of themselves.

Bill and Alice have been influenced by complementary archetypes. His ego having become over-identified with his persona, while her ego has been threatened by invasion from the animus, their tendencies to inflation (the former through consciousness, the latter through the unconscious) are in counterpoint. However, those tendencies can actively counterbalance each other only when the couple open their fantasies and dreams to one other. Doing so enables each to start the painful process of comprehending and accepting the desires that erupted so disturbingly in their partner and themselves.

Having said this, Alice as usual shows the better equilibrium, whereas Bill is at risk of renewed inflation. Although her memories and dreams were spontaneous visitations, she has reflected with increasing understanding on the distressing revelations they brought. But Bill has always acted as if his life depended on complete control of his feelings. In a wild swerve to the polar opposite typical of recent converts, he assumes that the emotions released by his confession show him how to resolve all his and Alice's problems. Reaching for absolutes, he asks her to agree that they will be together forever; but Alice, while reaffirming her love for him, reminds him that lived truth is complex. She offers instead a commitment more cautious than eternity but better grounded in their present needs.

Alice's wise words provide a bookend to the brief image that opens *Eyes Wide Shut*. We saw her then from the back, stepping out of a black gown that she has just let slide off her. Naked except for black stiletto shoes, and caught in the moment between one rejected garment and the next possibility, Alice casually ponders her choice of dress, while we are transfixed by what has just been revealed. The unfolding drama shows that if we've fallen for this sleight of hand, we should now know better: the gowns, uniforms, shoes etc. the characters choose to put on reveal more than their mere nakedness ever could. The acts of baring and dressing oneself (as well as being bared and dressed by others) reveal inner orientations, beliefs about the self and others, and act as catalysts for transformation. Shared revelations for Alice and Bill lie in the simplifying movement of stripping their defences and being stripped of them – and even more potently in the hard knowledge that they must learn to see the multiple, shifting layers each puts on.

I have said that archetypal energies do not die even when recognised. Should they be suppressed, they can eventually return from the unconscious more potent than before. How can the Harfords dissociate themselves from images which have done them so much harm? Alice intuitively finds the answer in telling Bill they must fuck as soon as possible. Her idea may work, given that sex between conscious human beings creates, in the seduction, a subjective image of the other (Carotenuto 1989: 43). These newly-shaped images will enable the Harfords to revitalise their contrasexual images in a wiser form: Bill will draw Alice's animus away from Szavost and the naval officer back onto himself. Alice as Bill's enlivened anima will help reshape his persona. As for the machinery of Bill's restoration, Jung understood that the problem stirred up by the trickster and constellated by the shadow would be answered on the plane of the anima through relatedness (Jung 1954b: 271). So it is Alice who has the power to redeem Bill from the darkness stirred by Milich and Ziegler.

Alice's proposing lovemaking invokes for one last time the bewitching idea of the *coniunctio oppositorum*, the royal marriage – here finally to be the egalitarian pairing of a loving couple. She does so within a marriage in which a new child could yet be conceived. And she does so within a world where daily life must go on. Pertinently, Samuels *et al.* (1986: 36) have argued that *coniunctio* should not be mistaken for an actual goal to be realised lest psychological inflation follow, or unbridled sexuality be licensed in an attempt to embody it. Rather it is a symbolic guideline to encourage the balance of male and female, body and spirit, for those who find the idea occupying their dreams. This time the milieu in which Kubrick has set the Harfords suggests that they are secure from both inflation and licence.

Though the Harfords' final exchange is both adult and serious, they are discussing their future in a toy shop where their daughter is seeking out what she would like for Christmas. The behaviour of their child (Helena's name means 'light'), were Alice and Bill only watching her more closely, might ease them toward another productive therapy. They are moving through a world of costume, mask, theatre and (as the flights of bubbles remind us) fantasy. Through her unrestrained delight the 7-year-old shows that, rather than be afraid of fantasy, her parents could enjoy it and the delightful opportunities for play and growth that it brings. Thus the enthusiastic presence of the child, untouched by the savage traumas that have rocked her parents, re-emphasises the idea of rebirth, as does the season's reminder of the birth of the Christian human-god.

All the same, Kubrick's ironic view of late twentieth-century humanity never deserted him. The Harfords' initiation into new growth is celebrated in a cathedral spilling over with tacky toy icons and devoted to an impersonal commercial culture. Helena would like a Barbie doll for Christmas; but Barbie is like the naked model women at the orgy (indeed, the origin of Barbie's design lies in German dominatrix dolls). Alice has tried to play the housewife's version of this role (as her spiked shoes and nudity showed when she stepped out of her dress in the first shot), but it failed her. When fantasy gels into stereotypes that regulate culture (Alice as Barbie housewife, Bill as complacently successful medic), it eventually deadens. Stereotypes cannot help individuals realise the fullness of their lives.

The question for Bill and Alice is how can the dialogue between two people essential for a living marriage be enlivened on an ongoing basis, especially in a world where everything conspires to deaden relationships. Locking onto culturally ossified fantasies failed them. Rather, they resolved their anguish by first becoming aware of, and then discovering how to deal with, the currents of fantasy that surfaced from their unconscious. Renewal came from shunning stereotypes and responding to archetypes. A final question left open by the film is whether they will continue in their new awareness of themselves or settle back into the old, deadening patterns of the *senex* culture that has dominated them.

In *2001* Kubrick's ironic view of the dessicating potential of human society to reduce people to stereotypes was equally sardonic, despite the momentous optimism of the overall project. That film created an odyssey in which the spirituality of our species was tested at its furthest resolve. It represented an adventure of the soul, a quest to bring to light barely apprehensible significance caught on the wing from the unknown. *Eyes Wide Shut*, presenting a micro-odyssey set close to home, counterbalances the earlier film. It features an unacknowledged, resisted search to find wholeness in both marriage and the soul. But although comparatively muted, it is no less optimistic a film in that it shows how the unconscious can actuate to embark upon a redemptive process two people whose most remarkable quality is that, in the outturn, they are perfectibly ordinary.

I said at the start of this chapter that the minor characters have qualities that illustrate archetypal aspects of the principal figures' personalities. That factor alone would suggest that the psychological nature of the main protagonists mirrors and is in turn reflected by the culture of the on-screen society. This is clearly true of the smallest social unit, the family. The patriarchal structure of the marriage and the psychological dispositions of Alice and Bill are closely connected. The link is so tight that the marriage and the characters' psychology alter together when both come under pressure. Lives outside the family circle are also integrated with the mental disposition of the characters. Bill's abuse of his power as a medic reveals this as does Nick's role as a musician. Even the absence of such a role – Alice's suffering from the lack of a life outside the family – has its psychological consequences. Power structures of a quasi-political kind in the film's society at large are equally bonded to the characters' inner personality types. One example stands for all when we reflect on Ziegler's psychology. Aside from his dominion over and impact on Bill's mental state, he demeans almost all the women he has dealings with. A symbolic death-giver, he renders those to whom he is closest (his wife and his whore) psychologically inert.

After taking this long journey through an oblique and complex film, can I say whether the psychological power it taps and the interlocking of characters' fantasies activates a commensurate psychological response in the audience? Although this reading indicates how it might have, it almost certainly did not. Whilst the film drew good numbers to the box office, the main attractions were its three stars – Cruise, Kidman and Kubrick – and a certain notoriety stemming from rumours about disputes on the set and the director's untimely death hours after the arduous completion of this last great project. *Eyes Wide Shut*, given the difficulty of its subject and its aesthetic distance was probably on the surface (though not at all beneath it) too typically cool a Kubrick project to generate a strong collective response on its release. There remains the possibility that it may do so, like several of the director's earlier films, in later years.

Chapter 3

What the camera took: Bernardo Bertolucci's *Stealing Beauty*

Introduction: Politics and psychology

Ever since Bernardo Bertolucci released *Prima della Rivoluzione* in 1964, three themes have dominated discussion of his films: politics, aesthetics and the director's experience of psychoanalysis. He himself has frequently spoken of these interests in interview. During his early period as a director, his convictions were predominantly Marxist. His beliefs shaped both the form and content of his work in harmony with the ideologies of those New Wave directors who influenced his first films, Pasolini and Godard in particular. At the end of the 1960s, however, he entered Freudian analysis, wanting to counter the depression which he believed public hostility to *Partner* (1968) had caused (Wagstaff 1994: 19). From this experience there developed a fascination with dreams and their resemblance to cinematic sequences.

Analysis also seems to have caused Bertolucci to doubt whether a film that failed to engage an audience was fully achieved. His concern distanced him from Godard's influence, the latter continuing to make films that conceded little to audience preferences. Bertolucci now took the view that the deconstructive aestheticism of the New Wave, revolutionary in its innovatory practices a decade earlier, had itself become an established form. It had the drawback, contrary to American movie rhetoric, that it locked the audience out from 'a first level of reading' (Vogel, 1971: 28). Starting with *The Conformist* (1970), Bertolucci rendered his films more accessible by making that entry level easily readable. But he noted with wry amusement that, underneath its simple exterior, *The Conformist* was actually his most difficult film yet (Vogel 1971: 28–9; Wagstaff 1994: 19). *Stealing Beauty* (1996) also has a limpid surface covering a rich weave of themes.

Although politics, psychology and aesthetics have often featured in analyses of Bertolucci's work, with rare exceptions all three themes have not been scrutinised together. Bertolucci himself is partly responsible for this state of affairs. Bill Nichols, for example, once commented perceptively that the overall style and structure of *The Conformist* were the very means by which its director dealt with his responses to the phenomenon of fascism

(1971: 19). However, in an interview given that same year, Bertolucci himself denied the link: 'For me it's very difficult to succeed in mixing together the idea of beauty that I have as a moral fact and a reduction of reality in political terms, exactly because I think they are two irreconcilable things' (Bertolucci cited by Purdon 1971: 7).

In the past, psychological analysis of the dealings between his characters often concentrated on father-son relationships, a focus justified by Bertolucci's repeated assertions of the significance of that axis in his own life. He has often mentioned the awe in which he holds his father's poetry. There's an obvious Oedipal disproportion here, seductive to any dollar-book Freudian – the major filmmaker transfixed and labouring for decades to outdo a poet unknown to his international audience. We shall see that other themes can be found in a fuller psychoanalytical reading of Bertolucci's films. Nonetheless, the relationship he had with his father is clearly the source of recurring motifs in many of the films. He even said of *Stealing Beauty* (its main protagonist a girl) that it has a theme 'rather like the leitmotif of all my films: losing the father, rediscovering the father, killing the father' (1996: 33). Thirty years after analysis uncovered this complex for Bertolucci, it appeared to retain a measure of power to shape his work. But perhaps now it had become more a trope than a corrosive anguish, a softening notable in the heroine's discretion in *Stealing Beauty* when she discovers her true father. Her reaction is one of love for him and the family rather than hostility.

Bertolucci has long recognised the connection between the life of the psyche and political action.[1] The question which I shall explore in this and the following two chapters, using *Stealing Beauty*, *Besieged* and *The Dreamers* for illustration, is whether in his later films films psyche, style and politics are parallel but independent currents in his work, or whether they entwine at a deep level and embellish each other.

During the 1980s and early 1990s Bertolucci had refrained from making films in Italy because the political corruption in his home country dismayed him. *Stealing Beauty* represented a change of direction. Yet, as he said, this was not the explicitly political film on the renaissance of the Italian right, on Berlusconi, or even on the realities of Italian life that might have been expected of him. Rather, he thought of this intimate film as a first speculative exploration marking his return after 15 years to a land which during the 1980s he had found hostile (Bertolucci 1996: 22–3). Although macro

1 He said as much when interpreting a dream he had shortly before shooting *The Last Emperor* in 1986. The dream presented him with an analogy between the political life of the emperor Pu Yi and the domestic life of every family – where all children are emperors, believing that life or death should follow their every whim (Bertolucci in Sklarew *et al.* 1998: 13–16).

politics are not emphasised, the micro politics of personal relationships are in plain focus.

Deliquescent vistas

After the death of her mother, 19-year-old Lucy Harmon (Liv Tyler) is sent on holiday by her American father to friends in Tuscany. She wants to do two things in particular – to find her natural father and to lose her virginity, preferably to Niccolò Donati, a boy she met on a previous visit. When she reaches the Graysons' home after the long flight from America, Bertolucci presents her arrival in a manner both tranquil and exuberant. As the taxi from Sienna drops her off, we find ourselves looking at the front of a traditional rural dwelling. In the quiet that follows the car's departure, the camera tracks across the forecourt and picks up Lucy carrying her bags to the front door. She pauses to peer through the glass and, seeing no one, enters. The camera pans as if attached to the door hinge, a distinctive shot that implies Lucy's position whilst plainly being detached from it. It initiates a tantalising play with point of view. As she walks through a workshop to gain entrance to the house, the camera trails behind, partially dissociated from her path and weaving quietly across unfinished carvings and sculptures on the floor. The languor of the moment is enriched by the limpid clarinet from the slow movement of Mozart's concerto. Its notes hang in the air leaving us unable to discern whether someone in the house is playing a disc or Bertolucci has laid a non-diegetic track to accompany the scene: the aural 'point of view' is also deliberately ambivalent.

When Lucy goes out to the patio and takes in the scene outdoors, the camera once again partially detaches itself from her point of view as it too looks around. While the clarinet's cool notes bring tranquillity to the glorious afternoon, the camera does what Lucy cannot (unless in spirit) and embarks on a circular aerial tour. It meanders above emerald grass and glides over the recumbent bodies of both sleeping diners and life-size terracotta figures. Then it rises to open the vista across garden, outbuildings and distant hills, continuing a marvellous sweep above the landscape before turning back across the house's front to descend beneath the pergola. There it rejoins Lucy as she wakens her hostess Diana Grayson (Sinead Cusack).

The trajectory and narrative setting of this crane shot make a striking impact on the spectator through its bravura movement. It constructs a perspective on the action that departs from the privileged points of view familiar in mainstream cinema. We might describe it and the other travelling shots in the sequence as producing psychologically motivating points of view: they augment for spectators the feelings that the storyline generates. However, this is not a sufficient explanation, not least because mainstream cinema routinely constructs points of view that help deepen spectators' emotional responses to the action on the screen.

Further insight into Bertolucci's style is found in the welcome Lucy receives from Diana's husband. Ian comes forward hesitantly, glancing at the young woman almost furtively as he greets her. Yet moments later, when escorting Lucy to her quarters in a converted outhouse, he is self-assured. Now, however, there are suggestions of something sinister in the way the camera tracks them from behind a row of trees. The combination of Donal McCann's performance and the way this skulking shot glosses his gaze allows the spectator to wonder whether the middle-aged Ian might be sexually interested in the young woman. But as he and Lucy talk it emerges that her father has asked Ian to paint her portrait during the visit. So Ian's is the complex gaze of the artist, at once hesitant and bold, loving and louche, tender and cruel. Meanwhile, the sequence is rendered even more complex by the bewitching shimmer of notes (Richard Hartley's original music) just audible when Ian leads Lucy past his beehives. Ian takes the moment to remark reassuringly that the bees will not disturb anyone who leaves them alone. Yet seemingly unprovoked they will attack Lucy a few days later.

These various opposing motifs put us on notice that, just like the surface representations in this film, the work of artists can generate and become caught up in energies both dangerous and magical, melting and changing established perspectives. Ian's work holds the clew that binds together some of the film's main themes. He steals the *prima materia* – the raw material which he is to work with – from whatever catches his attention, and then makes it over. And Bertolucci implicates his own work with Ian's. To mention another device, when Lucy writes a few lines of verse about troubles that she cannot talk about openly, she jots down the words visiting her mind. Bertolucci superimposes her handwriting over the live-action shots, drawing attention to the film's artistry while highlighting both the pain and naïveté of her character.

Ira Konigsberg has noted that Bertolucci described his style of shooting in *La Luna* (1979) as shaped by his recollection of Freud's description of the '*fort-da*' game played by an infant repeatedly hiding an object and then pulling it back into view. Konigsberg develops Bertolucci's idea, recognising that his particular style of camera work in that film made it into a transitional object. Transitional phenomena, as we saw in the introduction, link the intensely private inner world of fantasy that first emerges in childhood to the outer world of the present day. In the case of the artist, the transitional phenomena become the work (Konigsberg 1996: 876–9). Bertolucci's use of transitional phenomena in *Stealing Beauty* will be discussed toward the end of the chapter.

Art, power and morality

As transitional objects, Ian's terracotta statues are scattered across the house and garden. Juxtaposed with the characters who live among them, they act as oblique commentators on their lives. For instance, as Ian and Lucy approach the outhouse, they pass a monumental group, an ancient council of kings and queens watching over the hilltop and those who dwell there. When these figures attract Lucy's attention we may be tempted to infer that she will find people among her hosts and their guests wise enough to play a tutelary, quasi-parental role in guiding her into adulthood. But, they do not in any direct sense; rather it is an oblique connection. The Graysons' place, though a world apart, is no Parnassus. By the end of the film the family and their friends have indeed helped. However, their relations with her are seldom simple or disinterested and they by no means always act wisely. Some of them, shackled in their own complex emotional knots, show Lucy how *not* to live rather than providing positive role models.

Throughout, Bertolucci shows human affairs as invariably entangled in the politics of family life. One way *Stealing Beauty* does this is by linking the intimate psychological observation of individuals to the power relationships that govern their interaction with other characters. This is first pointed up by the contrast between the sequence so far discussed and the film's raw opening shots which immediately precede it. The opening sequences comprise video images of Lucy *en route* to Sienna. We know only that the camera is in the hands of a middle-aged man; but his identity cannot be made out until later in the film. The disconcerting nature of the footage recorded by this clandestine observer arises from the invasion of Lucy's private space by extreme close-ups, an intrusion of which, since she is asleep, she remains unaware. In one shot she drools while in another she rests a hand on her crotch. The naked voyeurism of this amateur camera work contrasts with Darius Khondji's cinematography for the rest of the film. The former 'takes' Lucy's sexuality as if by right, with an artless and repugnant aggression which tells us more about the camera operator than the girl; the latter responds with tact and artistry to Lucy's whole being (not merely her sex) and embellishes our understanding of her nature. Through its crudity the amateur footage gives notice that the politics and psychology of sexuality and (by negative implication) of art will be the terrain of *Stealing Beauty*.

Family politics – the older generation

The Graysons' house presents a vivid politics of domestic life, the immediate family being enlarged by long-term residents, neighbours and visitors. *Stealing Beauty* puts us in the position of strangers who must observe closely if we are to learn what drives its characters. It only reveals their inner nature gradually. However, when it does finally allow us to discover them fully, we find that Bertolucci and his screenwriter Susan Minot have given the principal protagonists distinctively archetypal character traits, a factor which encourages us to look beyond their social world and show how they are linked to mythic realms.

Amusingly, Bertolucci introduces a surrogate who mirrors our curiosity. A lieutenant in the Italian army stranded by the breakdown of his car, he is enthusiastically entertained for a day by the Graysons' hilltop community. As another newcomer, he is almost as interesting to them as Lucy and, with few native Tuscans in their number, they threaten to turn the mildly bewildered man into a stranger in his own land. One cause of his initial difficulty (not to mention Lucy's and ours) arises from the number of people in the group – 15 if we include a significant ghost.

Having known each other for years, the Graysons' circle focus avidly on the newcomer. Her needs and fears are much chewed over both by herself and her friends. Meanwhile Lucy has her own reasons to find out more about them. There are four generations present, the youngest represented by Daisy (Rebecca Valpy), the Graysons' 10-year-old. Daisy's frequent demands that Lucy play with her allow the latter to slip back into childhood and provide welcome relief from the trials of adolescence. However, were she to be tempted to become stuck in childish ways, Lucy might become a *puella aeterna*, an eternal girl unable to bear the burdens of maturity. There are members of the company who are like this, and Lucy shies away from their emotional brittleness.

The oldest person in the household is M. Guillaume (Jean Marais), a retired art dealer fogged in the miasmic urges of senility – a disconcerting figure. When Lucy first meets him, he acts like a naughty boy. One night he resembles a Shakespearean night watchman, sleepwalking through the yard. On another occasion, in his cups, furious gibberish spills from his mouth. Just the once, intoning 'Beauty wounds the heart', he displays the shamanic insight of the very old. But for the most part, far from being a wise old man, he is a tragicomic figure. Yet his dementia scarcely impinges on Lucy's world because old age is a remote prospect for her.

As indicated, Lucy wants to find her natural father. Before her mother died, she had given Lucy a poem, an impressionist sketch of the night she was conceived 20 years earlier in the Graysons' olive grove. The poem does not name Sara's lover but scatters vague clues about the encounter (the man had an accent, killed a viper and gave her an olive leaf to eat). Lucy frames riddling questions from these clues which she addresses to each man who could possibly fit the bill.

Her first target is Alex Parrish (Jeremy Irons), billeted in the room next to her. A writer in his middle years suffering from leukaemia, he has come to end his days in his friends' care. Deeply preoccupied with self (a tendency which dying has intensified), his initial interaction with Lucy is self-interested. He addresses her as a beautiful (and he hopes biddable) young woman, flirting heavily, to her irritation, in the pathetic hope of making a last conquest. His mixed motives entangle the habitual seducer's desire with the half-formed hope that as an anima figure Lucy can magically renew his life. A plausibly complex character, Alex reveals himself also to be sentimental, narcissistic, greedy and irritable. Variously jealous and generous toward Lucy, he is simultaneously resigned to his fate and frustrated by it. He is also bitchy, describing Sara Harmon, for example, as 'The best dressed poet, writing transporting little verses between fashion shoots.' In psychological terms, a dominant component of Alex's personality is the *puer aeternus*, the eternal boy. Although Lucy feels compassion for his predicament and likes his sensitivity, this *puer* side of his personality repels her and perhaps fortifies her against regressing to the illusory safety of the *puella*. Yet despite this aspect, Alex is dignified in dying and, although he does use Lucy to lift his spirits, a true affection for her grows in his self-centred soul.

Lucy knows that the Graysons' neighbour Carlo Lisca (Carlo Cecchi) was close to her mother. So he is her next target, and Diana invites him over to meet her. Bertolucci leaves us to notice (but we may, like Lucy, miss it) that Carlo wears the distinctive bracelet we first saw on the wrist of the unknown amateur video cameraman. When filming, did he know who Lucy was? If so, how? We never find out. But Diana knows that he has a dark side, describing him as a good journalist damaged by seeing too much death. We see plenty of evidence for this, and Carlo knows his black side well enough to be able to tell Lucy he feels free of it only when near battle. It seems likely that he and Sara (whose own restless and tormented nature Lucy remembers with pain) were drawn together by recognising that aspect in each other. Certainly there is much in his personality that associates him with the wild, even threatening aspects of the Dionysian type (Bolen 1990: 251–78).

Questioned by Lucy, Carlo says he was Sara's friend, her lover for one night only. Lucy has no way of judging the truth of his words and postpones challenging them to another occasion. Once again it is left to us to notice that her own bracelet resembles Carlo's. Perhaps Lucy, who describes its scarab as a symbol of hope, has inherited something he first gave to Sara. Whether so or not, when we recognise his amulet it reminds us that he tossed his crude videotape down from the train for Lucy to watch: he has been playing with her innocence for some time. We cannot be sure, despite his denial, that he is not her birth father.

The two middle-aged women in the group, Noemi and Diana, complement each other's personality. Both are stirred by Lucy blossoming to recall their own youthful sexuality (Wagstaff 1996: 54–5), but there the likenesses in their attitudes to love end. Noemi (Stefania Sandrelli) is the agony aunt for an Italian newspaper and appears to move uninhibitedly from one affair to the next. She reads out a letter from a woman who cannot decide between two men, one a thrilling lover who is callous when not fucking her; the other as tender and caring as could be wished, but boring in bed. The letter is greeted with hilarity by the company, but it brings into focus the double nature of love which confronts several of the protagonists. Noemi opts for the thrill of the chase and the new adventure, Diana for the enrichment that can follow years of tender fidelity. Which form of loving to pursue is a quandary facing Diana's elder daughter Miranda and, less urgently, Lucy too.

Noemi, unlike Miranda, is not injured by her sexual appetites. She and Carlo's son Michele (Francesco Siciliano) soon become lovers despite their age difference. She is governed by the goddess Venus, young at heart, eager to fall in love, acting on desire without reckoning the consequences and living only in the present (see Bolen 1985: 254–5). She and Michele, as if struck by one of blind Cupid's random arrows, present us with the irresistible force of sexual attraction. Their icon could be the Priapic statue on the garden wall of the local grandees. Because they are peripheral to the main focus of the film, their psychology is not explored, but it is not hard to see that Michele's choice of an older woman replaces his absent mother whom Carlo presumably abandoned long ago.

Diana Grayson, a patient, loving woman with an obvious capacity for joy, takes delight in all the members of her large family. She is the quiet hero who sustains everything and everyone (including two sick men and a troubled daughter). Beneath the surface, however, unnoticed by all who depend on her, unhappiness is welling up. We are left to speculate on its source. Could it be, much though she likes Lucy, that she feels jealous of the attention which Ian and the other men lavish on her? Does the recollection of Sara's 1975 visit remind her painfully of lost youth? Is she worried because her elder daughter is having an affair with a married man? Possibly all these things concern her, but at the end of the film, after Alex worsens and is taken to hospital, she tells Ian that she wants to return to England. While Alex's impending death has triggered her distress, the fear of having to care for people for the rest of her life lies at its core.

For Diana, however, there is no escaping her caring role. No sooner has she identified the source of her wretchedness than the family drift into the house. Miranda is first back, announcing, to her mother's great relief, that she has dispatched her boorish lover. Then the others arrive, like all healthy young people, starving. Lifted by Miranda's news and the restoration of family, Diana begins to organise a meal.

Diana's psychological type has changed with the years' passage. Her name associates her with the Roman goddess of the moon and the hunt; but if she was once governed by the chaste warrior nature of that goddess, she has long since been overtaken by two other archetypes. She remembers wistfully the time 20 years earlier when Sara visited them and Diana herself had just left her first husband for Ian. She plainly was once a woman whose Venus qualities were dominant. Now, however, though the Venus woman in her comes back to life occasionally, Ceres generally dominates her personality. Jean Shinoda Bolen could be describing Diana when she says that the woman governed by Ceres will be bountiful, maternal, have a large capacity to provide for others and be unable to say no to anyone who needs her help. She has, however, to learn to choose when and how to give, or her instincts will drive her to exhaustion (1985: 189). Thus at the end of the film Diana's future hangs in the balance, but for the moment, reunited like the goddess with her daughter (though Miranda is not straightforwardly the Persephone type) she is restored to her Ceres function (Bolen 1985: 195).

Though dead, Sara Harmon remains a strong presence in the memory of all who knew her. Lucy remembers her mother in her middle years, trapped by anguish; and Carlo too knew her dark side. By contrast, most of her Tuscan friends recall the younger, blossoming woman, a restless centre of attention, then as always unable to focus her desires for long on any one person or object. Sara may have been a *puella aeterna*.

Lucy: teenager and muse

When Diana finds a gown that Sara had worn 20 years ago and adjusts it to fit Lucy for the Donatis' ball, she remarks on her likeness to her mother. But while there are these strong, not altogether comfortable bonds between Lucy and her mother, there is another no less striking link in that the ball gown resembles Flora's dress in Botticelli's *Primavera*. In allegorical terms, Lucy comes to Tuscany as a nymph – analogous to Chloris in the painting. In Ovid's version of the myth, the nymph Chloris (a comparatively plain figure in Botticelli's picture) became the gorgeous Flora (rather as Lucy is turning into a woman like her mother). As Roman goddess of everything that blooms, Flora was honoured throughout Italy in the classical era. However, Chloris was deified only after Zephyr, god of the west wind, fell in love and married her (Grimal 1991: 155). Flora is an enticing image for what Lucy has the potential to become when her soul has been enriched with experiences which she awaits but cannot yet fully apprehend. At issue for this young woman is whether she will follow her mother into a shiftlessness of soul or incarnate the Flora archetype with the promise it holds of maturing into full womanhood.

Until Lucy attains that maturity, however, she is simultaneously an adolescent troubled by a number of doubts, fears and desires, and (for the older adults in the Grayson entourage) the anima as muse dressed in the lineaments of a goddess. It is an awkward position for the young woman; and some members of the film's audience also find it uncomfortable. Bertolucci builds the tension between the two perspectives in order to use it in the film's resolution.

Family politics – the younger generation

Because the audience is offered a point of view which circulates around Lucy's in the manner previously described, we are more constantly exposed to her feelings than to those of the other young people – which is not to say that their inner lives are closed to us. Miranda (Rachel Weisz) is one of the younger generation (though about ten years Lucy's senior). We first assume her to be Ian's daughter but she is the elder child of Diana's first marriage. Her brittle personality disguises an unhappiness not uncommon in offspring injured by their parents' breakup,[2] and she too shows the signs of being governed by the *puella aeterna* archetype. Involved in an affair with a married man, a bombastic American lawyer, her emotional neediness expresses itself through what was once reciprocated lust. Now, however, with the buffoon's interest waning fast, she submits (not without troubled pleasure) to increasing sexual brutality in order to keep him. Her emotional fragility, which the arrogant Richard (D. W. Moffett) intuitively exploits, seems to be drawing her toward masochism and the risky pursuit of power through weakness.

Richard's brutishness, far from being confined to bedroom sports, is so deeply ingrained that it eventually alerts Miranda to her exposure. Hardly bothering to disguise his intention, he tries to make a sexual conquest of Lucy. Such contempt for Miranda mirrors her own for herself; but although she accepts her own self-hatred, his disdain shocks her. She throws him out, turning his contempt back on him. In rejecting him, Miranda clears the way to advance her search not only for a true partner but also a fuller understanding of her self. She and Lucy are alike in both needing to find someone onto whom the image of the male other can safely be projected. Miranda's restless disposition resembles Sara's in her youth, each having found it hard to fix her animus steadily on a decent man. However, Miranda's anger saves her, Richard having unwittingly provided her with a therapy which, though painful, she badly needs.

There are five young men in the company. Miranda's brother is Christopher (Joseph Fiennes). He might be a peripheral figure were it not for his emblematic role. Gay, wholly at ease with himself and loved for whom he is by his family, Christopher is another Dionysian figure but one, unlike Carlo, who represents the positive aspects of that archetype. This can be observed, for example, when he finds a creative outlet for his joyous nature in joining a troop of masquers at the Donatis' party. It is this, his spontaneous talent for showing others the richness of contact with the self, not his homosexuality, which makes him emblematic. Carlo Lisca's son, Michele, is also on the periphery of the drama. A heterosexual of quieter disposition than Christopher, he has a similar emblematic function. This shows when his new lover, Noemi, teases him for his idealistic passion. But Michele does not flinch from his commitment. Here is another young man

2 A successful designer of jewellery, she scorns her own past work merely because fashions have changed.

who, contrary to his father, has found his own confident moral and psychological footing in love.

This leaves the three lads who win Lucy's attention. Two are sons of the wealthy Donati family, the third a guest at their party. Visiting the Graysons four years earlier, Lucy had fallen for Niccolò Donati (Roberto Zibetti), and for a while after her return home they exchanged letters. She has come back eager to surrender her virginity to him; but when she visits his villa, he is making love to another girl. A day later, Niccolò has sent that girl away and, pleading ungovernable passion, sets about seducing Lucy. But her fear of sex intrudes, she freezes and forces him to stop. Probably she senses that Niccolò's main desire is to score with yet another girl – Bolen's Poseidon type describes him well (1990: 84–5). His selfishness and perhaps a certain reminder beneath his easy charm of Richard's voracity turn her off. Oedipal shadows must also disturb her: she cannot have forgotten her mother's poem telling her that she was conceived in the very olive grove to which Niccolò has led her.

A midsummer night's dream

Lucy is soon to meet another boy at a party given by the Donatis – a party the presentation of which pays homage to Fellini's evocations of the bewitchingly strange. The celebration begins with guests parading down the avenue that leads to the Donatis' great villa. Once again the film's style ravels delight, passion and family politics. As the guests pass us, we overhear their talk: Miranda protests Richard's inappropriate use of his mobile phone and Diana recalls parties in her youth. Then ancient M. Guillaume utters his shamanic epigraph for the event and the whole film: 'Beauty wounds the heart!'

As Lucy wanders around, exquisite in her Botticelli gown, fluid crane and Steadicam shots survey the lawns. When the camera closes in, it reveals people (several are members of the Graysons' circle) locked into their own obsessional worlds (Fellini again). They do not invite the girl into their circles. So she drifts in front of the band and finds herself facing the clarinet player whom she knows slightly because he is Niccolò's brother Osvaldo (Ignazio Oliva). He bows gravely as she applauds the music.

The mood changes as Bertolucci focuses on the sunset over the landscape beyond the villa, then racks onto the Priapus on the garden wall. The inviting sense of new possibilities infiltrates the evening. A cutaway shows Ian in his studio working on a carving of Lucy's face just as it begins to take recognisable shape. Meanwhile, at the party, Christopher and his friends perform a masque (more Fellini in this), running across the garden bearing candles and weaving them round the guests as if to unite the company. Their flowing movements express both the magical way the arts free the imagination and the diverse forms through which loving sexuality can find expression.

Irony suffuses the next episode without diminishing the heightened atmosphere. Lucy goes indoors, snubs Niccolò who is seducing yet another girl, and makes Carlo dance with her to Nina Simone's 'My Baby Just Cares for Me'. Sparring pointedly, they jive along the portico in front of pastoral murals redolent of immortal peace. Questioned again about Lucy's birth, the war reporter says he was at the fall of Saigon before August 1975 but dodges telling what he did immediately after, in the month she was conceived. They are interrupted by the masquers bursting into the portico to perform an acrobatic dance and a parody of marching troops, as if they have tapped into Carlo's murky repressed memories. The atmosphere darkens when one of Carlo's discarded lovers drunkenly mistakes Lucy for his new woman. She squats and pisses to show Lucy his preferred sexual pleasure. Amused, Carlo dances away by himself: nothing, he implies, touches his dark soul.

A brighter magic returns and infuses the advancing hours. Almost all the company have gathered in the villa, but outside Michele hams an aria for Noemi, bewailing her deathly cruelty to him. She giggles, lets her dress fall and draws him behind a laurel hedge. In the foreground, accompanied by Stevie Wonder's 'Superstition', two masquers glide by, one strutting in slow motion, the other swimming along the grass catching and releasing the ankles of his partner. It's another Fellini moment, and the maestro's influence is carried through to the villa where revellers are literally turning each other's worlds upside down. But Lucy, still rather soberly the right way up and on the rebound from sighting Niccolò with his new conquest, hooks up with a very drunk English boy. This is Gregory (Jason Flemyng), and the two of them leave the party together.

Albeit she remains unaware of it, a deep relationship issue is propelling Lucy. The pressure she feels to find a lover is driven by the potent need to replace her mother, the lost object whose lack Lucy must fill to feel complete again. That is the role which, wholly at random, Lucy now settles on Gregory.[3] She hopes that the culmination of the evening's exhilaration will be a night of love, as it is for several couples. Diana finds Ian in his studio and they make love tenderly; Christopher and one of the masquers continue the dance in a private ritual of passion; meanwhile Richard buggers Miranda in self-adoring celebration of his power over her. But Lucy has to make do with an affectionate good night chat with Alex who from the next room has heard her come home with Gregory. The latter is too far gone in liquor for anything but sleep.

Once again, through the presentation of this night, Bertolucci's vivid aesthetics have drawn attention to their agency. The fluidity of Khondji's camera; radical shifts in pace brought about both by the actors' movements

3 I owe thanks to Joanna Dovalis for this observation.

and changes of gear between prerecorded music tracks; the linking of scenes the moral, dramatic and aesthetic qualities of which differ sharply – these devices give the sense that almost all the participants, no matter how grotesquely, are lifted out of their routine repressions for a few hours and put in touch with aspects of their selves which they do not fully command. We and they are swept up by moments of ceremonial cinema. So the presentation of the party fuses the liberating impulses of fantasy to the politics of human relations, the latter sometimes (as with Carlo and Richard) brutal, and sometimes (as with Diana's unobtrusive watching for Lucy) tender. Some scenes celebrate the bonding of lovers (Noemi and Michele, Diana and Ian, Christopher and his partner). Other relationships that have already died are ritually sundered and given formal burial (Lucy dismisses the philandering Niccolò; Carlo's former lover humiliates him). Only brutish Richard, untouched by any force other than his own solipsism, pretends lust is the same as love to conceal his indifference for Miranda. All these factors, and the mirroring of Lucy's curiosity by our own, create an engaged feeling tone that helps us perceive through the diverse mythologies the sacred and the swinish inseparably tessellated – light and dark locked together.

The party is over

The morning after the party's fine theatrics starts with banality as Lucy sees a hungover Gregory off. But Alex has suffered a relapse in the night, and his doctor insists he be hospitalised so that his pain can be controlled as he dies. Inevitably it is Diana who accompanies him in the ambulance. After taking final leave of Alex, Lucy sits alone in his room grieving for him. But then, glancing out of the window, she notices the terracotta sculpture of a mother and child made by Ian. Something – perhaps that the figures, as transitional objects, seem to return her gaze frankly; perhaps that the nearness of death has sharpened her awareness of life – causes a new realisation to dawn.

She gathers wild flowers and takes them to Ian in his studio. During the time that he has worked on her portrait, they have grown in confidence with each other. He has come under her eye just as she under his, and increased understanding brings them together. Beneath his melancholic mask she has discovered a warm human being – a figure worthy of her love. Meanwhile Ian has recognised how Lucy differs from her mother: 'You have a sort of joy in your eyes.' Now, just as she identifies him as her birth father, his life-size carving of Lucy reaches completion. The emotion of their mutual recognition at last releases her from one obsessional search.

Her animus is free to move to a lover. As if on cue, Osvaldo is waiting to talk to Lucy about visiting New York. He sits on another of Ian's mother and child statues – a lighthearted sign that the relationship between anima and animus is changing. Reinforcing the point, no sooner does Lucy leave the studio than she is stung by Ian's bees. Their stings (as if her father's emissaries were driving her in that direction) bring her closer to Osvaldo. He gently helps her apply a salve, unafraid to show his feminine, caring side. Then they walk into the countryside, Osvaldo leading her to his favourite tree on a hilltop, reminding her that he once wrote to her about it. Lucy had thought the letter in question came from his brother, and its sensitive evocation of the writer's feelings had secured her affection for Niccolò, an affection which now flows toward Osvaldo. Soon his empathy wins her heart as he recognises – the only person to do so – that she must be missing her mother. As she weeps, so does he. Their shared vulnerability and tenderness draw them together. Moved to tears by love, not daring to kiss her lest he offend, he shows a personality more responsive than his brother. He knows, without having heard M. Guillaume's moral precept, that beauty wounds the heart. As evening comes in, they make love and stay out all night sheltered by the great tree.

Return to the world

At the end of the night what has changed? They come down from their high hill together cheerfully enough, but reading their descent against a background of classical myths hints at a slightly bathetic remove from the elevated home of the gods. Lucy no longer has the bewitching aura of a muse, but behaves like a young woman relieved of anxiety, and content with her lover. So when they part to go to their homes and Osvaldo says he wants to go with her to New York, she replies without fuss, 'Then do.' They kiss and a tender smile flickers on Lucy's face as he heads down the track to the Donati villa, turning to call back, 'It was my first time too!'

As she walks away somewhat flatfooted, the camera cuts to a sequence of helicopter shots. These show her trudging along the Graysons' road, then move away to circulate over Sienna. This re-entry into the wider world is shadowed by the final music track, Roland Gift's querulous 'Say it Ain't So'.

Its lyrics could hardly be more unexpected. Instead of celebrating the joys of love or the beauty of the beloved, they concentrate on the pain of being in a relationship that has gone sour. The singer addresses his woman in terms that despair has rendered apathetic: he wishes he could believe that she won't deceive him any more. He wishes he could hate her, but he can't. Sooner or later he knows he will have to give up living the lie in which they are locked.

What are we to make of this shocking focus on the pain of betrayal? It appears to have passed unnoticed, perhaps ignored in the rush of cinemagoers to escape the end credits, or perhaps because many in the audience assume that (like marriage) sexual union in fiction guarantees the wished-for happy end. We have no information about the future lives of Lucy or Osvaldo, but the film's ending provides a jarring re-entry into the world of politicised adult domestic life where the couple have no choice but to make their way. The song reminds us that the portents, if they live out the same patterns as their elders, are not good. Almost every member of the Graysons' circle has either been unfaithful or in a broken relationship: Ian, Diana, Noemi, Alex, Carlo, Richard, Miranda, Niccolò and of course Sara. Against this tide the wish to 'Say it Ain't So' amounts to little more than a pathetic bleat.

Creativity and object-relations theory

The work of Susan Kavaler-Adler can be used to explain the psychology and actions of a number of the characters, most strikingly Sara and Miranda. The sometime near-borderline state of mind suffered by Lucy's mother also implicates the daughter to the extent that she might succumb to similar psychological pressures as they transmit down the generations.

Through a number of case studies of female artists, Kavaler-Adler describes the phenomenon of the woman who becomes trapped in the toils of her interior life. A principal symptom is her attempt to construct images that with their specific creative radiance seek to make up for the loss in the Oedipal or pre-Oedipal stage of her mother's cherishing care. The roots of this impulse lie in what Winnicott termed the 'unthinkable anxieties' caused the toddler by the mother withdrawing, often because she cannot face the child's increasing autonomy as a consequence of emotional anxieties brought on by her own abandonment fears. The toddler is not then able to form a safe, containing image of the other in the psyche (Kavaler-Adler 1996: 29). She makes up for this loss of her mother by creating internal objects, fantasy images. When early trauma of this kind has been suffered by a woman who sublimates the pain in creativity, a closed internal system may be created that perpetuates the repetition of the trauma in the theme and process of both her life and her work. Such an internal system can generate an unconscious fantasy marriage to a demon lover figure (Kavaler-Adler 1996: 3).

Kavaler-Adler (1996: 178–9) explains the genesis of this figure as follows:

> Once pre-oedipal psychic arrest takes place, as it does in the borderline, a female child's frustrated desires for empathic mothering will be transferred to the highly arousing father during the oedipal stages of development. Then, not only does the father become the object of erotic yearnings, but he also becomes the object of early oral cravings for nurturance, and a vision of the traumatically lost idealized mother is transferred to the father. Consequently, the father idealization becomes

> a defensive constellation of images used to ward off the demonic overtones of the early mother. In as far as the father inevitably disappoints the daughter in her complex of yearnings, he is turned demonic within her internal world as well, and his demonic form fuses with that of the early traumatic mother of separation.

Miranda is a clear example of a woman trapped in such a world, her contempt for the jewellery she must once have created with passion being the displaced sign in her work of her pathology. The same sickness is expressed through her having taken her demon lover Richard into her life. A generation before Miranda, Lucy's mother Sara had been just such another borderline personality type. Until stabilised by her American husband, she had flitted from one man to another, oscillating with each between initial desire and swiftly following revulsion. Now Lucy herself, offspring of an absent birth father and a mother who withdrew from her into drunken rages or the internal world of her poetry, is at risk of entrapment in a similar pathology.

Among the other older men, had Lucy adopted Alex as male muse and displaced father to substitute her lost object, he might well have moved into a place in the same psychological syndrome. As an inner object, Alex could be greedy enough to try and ensure in his narcissism that her connection with the world should only be through him. Symbolically, the fact that Alex is dying implies what introjecting him could do to her spirit. Carlo, despite his surface charm, displays many of the characteristics of the demon lover as his brief, sexually overheated relationships with Sara and the woman at the Donatis' party indicate. The same hunger to appropriate the female image shows itself in a greedy attempt at creativity in his voyeuristic tape of Lucy. Again, were she to have been tempted by him, possession by the male image might have been her fate.

As matters turn out, Lucy escapes the endless repetition of childhood trauma thanks to two transformative factors. Firstly, Ian, far from reflecting narcissistically on his own self, reflects her image back at her (both in his conversations and through his art) as different from her mother's. Secondly, Lucy herself obsesses about her missing father only before she finds him. Having recovered her lost object, she shares a sweet moment of mutual recognition with him and then projects a transformed and displaced image of her animus onto a young man of her own age and takes him as her lover. Not only does Osvaldo lack the aggressive sexual traits of his brother but, on the contrary, he exhibits a gentle, quasi-maternal aspect. That aspect is decisive in his attraction for Lucy and implies that balance has been restored to her psyche. It is in this context that the deflation of her muse-like radiance the morning after her night of love hints not only at a properly cynical view of the prospects of romantic life, but also has an optimistic aspect in returning her to the diurnal world of human interaction.

By 1996, Bertolucci had, as we have seen, often spoken publicly of his Oedipal strife with his father and its reflection in his previous films. So it is particularly interesting to consider how he has positioned himself in this film in the opposition between two types of male muse. On the one side stands the artist as psychologically vampiric narcissist: Kavaler-Adler describes Auguste Rodin's sadistic use of Camille Claudel in such terms (1996: 57–78). On the other there is the artist who does not seek to seal his female muse from the world by submersing her in the creative mystique of their shared work. Bertolucci's collaborators such the actress Eva Green (who later worked with him on *The Dreamers*) speak of him as being of the latter type (Thompson 2003). More importantly, the text of *Stealing Beauty* indicates it too.

The author, archetypes and art – politics, pleasure and desire

Turning to the archetypal structures underlying the film, we may note that in myths as in religions, the hero often has two fathers, one who belongs to this world, the other linked with the spiritual or divine. This is true of Lucy who has her well-loved nurturing and sensible father in the USA. Ian, her mysterious father, is quite other. In his studio (like Vulcan at his forge) he knows how to control earth and fire (for instance, in his terracotta work) to give his inner feelings material form. Lucy's relationship with him is quite different from that with her American father because Ian uses Lucy as his muse. Thus she has a role as the artist's anima. Conversely, Lucy experiences an epiphany and first intuits Ian as her father through the intensity of his sculpture. The manner of her recognition suggests that she has discovered her soul's father through the constellation of animus.

In Chapter 2, the classical Jungian concept of the contrasexual archetypal images was introduced. Both images are generated spontaneously from the unconscious. While the anima, experienced by men, represents the hidden feminine aspects of their personalities, the animus symbolises the concealed masculine in women. Notwithstanding the archetypal quality of anima when activated, a man usually projects it upon a particular woman who stirs his libido – for example, a mother, lover or muse (Jung 1931b: 198). Conversely a woman is likely to project her animus on father, lover or a male figure who, like an artist or priest, conveys intimations of the magical or divine. In their positive aspect, therefore, these erotic contrasexual projections can help bond a child with its parent of the opposite sex and an adult into making ties with another, loved individual. Their spiritual potential is also of high significance: 'Anima and animus lead us to religious experience, to whatever we revere or call holy. That is the function of the contrasexual archetype for our identity: to make the bridge across which we forge a link with a living Self . . .' (Ulanov and Ulanov 1994: 127). The contrasexual archetype confronts us with an otherness that is entirely apart from the ego, from what we accept as ours. It opens us to otherness itself, initially in our experiences of the body, emotions and sexual desire (Ulanov and Ulanov 1994: 128). Ultimately, when those projections are withdrawn from individual people and understood as functions of the psyche, anima and animus can relate us to whatever we find holy. This, of course, is hardly a novel idea: Dante, though he did not use the same terminology, traced this very pattern in his obsession with Beatrice. I want to argue that Bertolucci exploits this potential of the anima in providing the film with one of its perspectives.

Writing of *The Spider's Stratagem* and *The Conformist*, the films Bertolucci made a quarter of a century before *Stealing Beauty*, Noel Purdon remarks that the camera was given a wilful ability to create unreality. Some of its visions were determined by the consciousness of the protagonist; but others can clearly be coming from no consciousness but the director's (1971: 8). In comparable manner, *Stealing Beauty* replicates the intense, feeling gaze of the artist studying his muse or anima. As Ian and Alex gaze at Lucy, so the film offers its spectator a comparable desiring point of view, a fair indication that Bertolucci is willing to be seen to have adopted the same perspective.[4]

The feeling tone of the film is thus an essential key to understanding the text. Does the film desire Lucy and to a lesser degree its other characters? Yes, it does, although that is only one of its purposes. Is the film voyeuristic? Yes, but for a particular purpose, namely to politicise the anima – and hence voyeurism itself. It both presents the anima as a character and shows the effects of anima constellation on other characters. It opens an emotionally charged space in which some spectators feel the subjective experience of anima attraction while others are alienated by anima voyeurism. We see the outer and feel the inner worlds at the same time.

Desire is implicated in both the distinctive construction of point of view and the creation of a sense of the magical, close to the sacred, in scenes such as those previously analysed. Those sequences are far from unique within *Stealing Beauty* and give an indication how the film has been inflected in its function as a transitional object. Delightful, governed excess marks much of the film's imagery both visual and aural. This stylistic exhilaration is for the most part redundant to the storytelling process, but integral to development of the themes. It also, as I argued earlier, contributes markedly to an authorial presence that has developed over the years and links Bertolucci's films. In effect through stylistic excess he allows spectators to sense in *Stealing Beauty* his own involvement in anima politics.

4 Could Bertolucci have cast Donal McCann as Ian because their physical resemblance enabled the director discreetly to put his surrogate on screen?

Bertolucci has noted the intuitive nature of his aesthetics:

> For me, the cinema is an art of gestures. . . When I find myself on a set, with actors and lights, the 'solution' I find for a certain sequence, a certain situation, does not come from a pre-conceived idea, but from the musical rapport that exists between the actors, the lights, the camera, the space around them – and I move the camera as if I was gesturing with it. I feel that the cinema is always a cinema of gestures – very direct, even if there are fifty people in the crew.
>
> (Bertolucci cited by Vogel 1971: 26)

Chris Wagstaff adds that when making *The Spider's Stratagem* Bertolucci learnt the means of giving his viewers pleasure by surrendering to (rather than, as previously, resisting) the eroticism of cinema. Furthermore, he discovered he could do this while selecting images that would edify his audiences (1991: 17). Politics, pleasure, desire and the cinematic dream world combined. It is evident that *Stealing Beauty* continues in this vein.

When an artist such as Bertolucci projects the contrasexual archetype (and all the more when he does it with eroticism), the impact differs from when an individual does so in private. A fundamental tenet of post-Jungian theory crucial to screen studies holds that, just as humans in social groupings share their signifying systems and hence their discourse, so too they share the drives and unconscious energies that give rise to such highly charged images (Fredericksen 2001: 15–55; Izod 2001: 33–56). Artists, because they reinvigorate existing and innovate new forms of symbolic exchange, invoke the archetypal images such as anima and animus not only for themselves but also for those sectors of society which are reached by their work. Therefore, just as personal, private manifestations of the contrasexual archetype have the power to draw individuals into finding greater insight into their selves, so public constellations of anima and animus (as in the instance of film stars who catch the popular attention) can draw the collective imagination of large numbers of people.

Images energised with sexual power often also have a sacred quality. The converse is also true, as revealed by the history of Christian symbolism where the sacred has often been sexualised. Arguably the (albeit inchoate) desire to engage with the divine in human nature is one facet of the motivation for both Ian Grayson and Bertolucci – the artist on and the artist behind the screen – creating a representation of the anima.

Looking beyond anima and animus

So far, so positive, but two problems arise. The first is that engagement with the contrasexual archetype runs counter to the demands of social and communal life. Jung understood very well the conflict involved in people's impulse to engage with anima and animus: 'Man's instincts are not all harmoniously arranged, they are perpetually jostling each other out of the way. The ancients were optimistic enough to see this struggle not as a chaotic muddle but as aspiring to some higher order. Thus the encounter with anima and animus means conflict . . .' (Jung 1946a: 262). We have already seen that in her own right Lucy has a presence more substantial than a wraith-like anima. If she is a muse to some, she is also an adolescent struggling to establish her own point of view. While seeking her own animus she is also looking to find her place in the world, a goal that requires she work out the social structures within which she will function. Therefore she observes the micro world of the family with a gaze which is becoming politicised both by her needs and by interaction with those around her. Bertolucci shows us the Graysons' household from Lucy's point of view and with her politicised perspective. We see her deciding how to react, for example, to Ian's strangeness, Alex's flirtations or Richard's gross advances, but also to Diana's mapping her memories of Sara onto Lucy herself.

Bertolucci extends the political dimension beyond the domestic by letting the audience see the limited interest of the Graysons and their friends in what he called the 'small moments in which present day Italy enters this protected island' (1996: 23). Fighter planes pass overhead on their way to the war in Bosnia. The erection of a TV relay mast, evidence of Berlusconi's increasing control of media and national politics, portends more than the eyesore the Graysons lament. Closer to home, labourers work the vineyards and could be invisible for all the notice the incomers pay to them. The family reside in Tuscany but, as one visitor says, they have made a little world of their own so apart that it feels as though a passport will soon be needed to gain entry.

The wider spectrum of politics evoked peripherally in this way has an archetypal equivalent in the relatively wide spectrum of psychological types found at the Graysons. Just as politics outside the house are ignored by the people within it, so the archetypal energies residing in the range of character types (which have their own political potential as in Diana's Ceres caring function or Carlo's disruptive martial nature) are de-emphasised in comparison with the energy which activates the contrasexual figures. In this context, the impotence of M. Guillaume has significance because it hints at the absence of the wise old man archetype. The latter figure, were it present, would be a mana personality which might appear in the stage of development following that in which the anima and animus had exerted a semi-magical attraction. Samuels *et al.* describe a mana personality as one which 'suggests the presence of an all-pervading vital force, a primal source of growth or magical healing' (1986: 89). It appears when an individual is in a transitional stage and the ego has consciously to face the self, the personality in its entirety. Its function is to give the individual the feeling that a heightening of consciousness is possible to match the level achieved by such figures as the wise old man or woman (Samuels *et al.* 1986: 89–90). We shall have to wait until Chapter 8 to encounter such a figure. Its absence in *Stealing Beauty* seems to indicate that the protagonists have still some work to do in the way of self-discovery.

The second problem to which we must pay attention in considering the contrasexual archetype is that, as we first saw in *Eyes Wide Shut*, it by no means always has an exalted function. Some of the negative political consequences of energised anima and animus can be seen in *Stealing Beauty*. Where an intense focus on and desire for those people invested by the contrasexual archetype is found, we also see that projections of this archetype can be remarkably fickle in flitting from one person to another. Anima and animus can lead to the breaking of relationships as readily as their making. *Stealing Beauty* shows plenty of evidence for this. Anima-animus excitement can fill the consciousness, seductive as a drug, no less than the obsessiveness of new love with which, of course, it is intimately connected. In the wider world beyond this film, the politicised anima and animus are vividly evoked and endlessly exploited in advertisements. A prolonged collective excitation of this archetype (as by sexualised advertising images) can propagate a narrow cultural obsession with that which is glamorous and new.

Contrasexual projections can be so strong that they appear to consist in the qualities of the person or thing upon whom anima or animus is projected. This has the paradoxical consequence that, as a product of the inner world, the contrasexual archetype, rather than fostering greater understanding of the inner world, actually has the potential to blank off access to that world until the projection is withdrawn. One further consequence can be that desire obscures the shadow. Indeed the contrasexual archetype may itself be a manifestation of the shadow, but its voluptuous success in arousing libido disguises its dark aspect. In that case obsession with the projected contrasexual archetype inhibits the individual from recognising those aspects of his or her personality that are hidden specifically because they are negative. Miranda's desire for Richard blinds her to his shadow quality – the way his contempt mirrors her own for herself. Niccolò, read as another constellated animus figure, shadows Lucy's obsessive fear of the sex act. Many protagonists in *Stealing Beauty* fail to discern the shadow behind anima and animus, and this failing extends beyond their personal lives and loves into the social world. Lucy remarks on the beauty of rural Tuscany just as she and Osvaldo walk past a group of prostitutes soliciting motorists; and the Graysons are blind to the shadow in national politics (Bosnia, Berlusconi). It seems fair to speculate that some of those members of the audience who projected the anima onto Lucy may have been desensitised thereby to the shadow characteristics latent in an over-idealisation of sexual love. That might account for their deafness to the song, 'Say it Ain't So.'

Stealing Beauty thus offers us a world in which the individual's pursuit of anima and animus (whether ideal love or muse) cannot be dissociated from the inevitable byplay, friction and contentment of domestic (and, by implication, societal) politics. Libido and politics are shackled together, co-active. The promiscuous flitting of anima and animus from projection onto one individual to another is seen as having political consequences in shaping (and then reshaping) family structures. In return, family politics – whether spoken or barely gestural, and whether signalling approval or stricture – impact the thriving or dissolution of those same contrasexual projections.

Through *Stealing Beauty* Bertolucci shows that he knows well the anima and its effect on other men. Focusing for a moment on the director's personal psychological investment, the film's structure allows it to be read in the context of his belief in the links between his cinema and dream as well as the intuitive nature of his filmmaking. An observation he made after its release now takes on new significance. He said that making each of his films seems to bring about in him a sense of purification and rebirth (1996: 24, 38). This examination of *Stealing Beauty* suggests that his ideas of beauty and politics, contrary to his conscious assertion that they cannot be reconciled, are indeed fused at a deep level of which he appears not to be fully conscious. Certainly the aesthetic and emotional warmth of his treatment of Liv Tyler's Lucy – not unproblematic for some spectators, as we shall see – contrasts sharply with the cool facade of Kubrick's treatment of Nicole Kidman's Alice.

That the anima should fascinate a director in the later years of his life is, given the nature of the archetype, not surprising. In Bertolucci's case it can be read as a sign of his intuitive search for rebirth through the links the anima brings with the spiritual, a search that has to be navigated through political complications of the kind this film shows. However, the ineffectuality of the wise old man archetype puts this search in perspective, implying that it has not advanced to the point where the ego has confronted the self at depth and in its entirety. Perhaps it is an indication of his personal development that Bertolucci's next film *L'Assedio* (*Besieged*) (1998) opens with the song of an African *griot*, a storyteller who, gifted or cursed with knowledge of the pains that afflict his people, has the shamanic role of a mana personality.

In the public domain, Bertolucci dramatises the anima to his audiences so that, in becoming conscious of its power, they too can learn the spiritually rewarding insights it may give rise to, as well as the dangers and risks it poses. His conversion of the anima as muse into a publicly available icon is done in such a manner as to open the politics of the psyche to shared understanding. Because the film is so personal, featuring the young and nubile Liv Tyler in the lead role was a risky strategy since, as realised by this beautiful actress and Bertolucci's cinematic eye, Lucy the ingenue is the object of passionate interest which the audience is able to share too. Some spectators were troubled by what they took to be the prurient interest of a director in his late middle age in the girl. This reading of the film albeit against the thematic grain along which I have interpreted it, nevertheless provides us with an ironic indicator of Bertolucci's success in politicising anima. Thus the film allows it to be seen that the psychological projection of anima is not an illusion detached from the material world. Rather than presenting us (whether on the micro scale of the nuclear family or the macro dimension of society at large) with regimes which are governed without psychological input, *Stealing Beauty* shows how the projection and introjection of anima are integral to both interpersonal and societal politics. It not only shows spectators this, but also opens for them positions from which they may feel it. That is a mark of its achievement.

Chapter 4

Personal and national politics in Bernardo Bertolucci's *Besieged*

Introduction

Besieged (1998) reverses the pattern of *Stealing Beauty* which first drew attention to the psychology of its main character Lucy and then showed how her needs and appetites play into and are in turn modified by family politics (and marginally by Italian national politics). *Besieged* focuses first on the cultural and social differences between its two protagonists, strangers who happen to be sharing a house, as they struggle to understand each other. Only during the process of our getting to know them are the personalities of Shandurai and Kinsky gradually seen to be backed by mythological antecedents and, like Lucy's, to have qualities conforming to archetypal patterns.

The film's Italian title is *L'Assedio*. It means 'The Siege' which conveys the idea of attack, as opposed to the defensive posture implicit in the English title. We soon see how this is appropriate, though not at the very beginning when we find ourselves looking down in silence on a lake cradled in the jaws of a spent volcano. Here is a timescale distinct from the frenetic pace of daily life into which the action, handheld camera and brisk cutting will soon draw us. Lacking any obvious connection to the narrative, this mysterious opening presents us with a world which we forget during the course of the story. Yet as the Earth's other story that moves so slowly it seems timeless to humanity, it provides a backdrop, masked by the busy obsessions of daily life, of which the protagonists are never aware (see Tassi 1999: 22–3). As such it recalls the deep unconscious.

Visions and nightmares

A peripatetic musician (John C. Ojwang) links the two temporal worlds as the title sequence draws us into an unnamed East African state. The singer's theme is Africa, the raw timbre of his voice summoning a sense of the continent's suffering through the ages. As his lament unfolds, we enter the daily life of the people. Well-fed soldiers move through a township, making their bullying presence felt. Images of their leader are being posted on every available space, suggesting that a military junta has seized control, possibly in a coup. Meanwhile a young nurse works in an under-equipped centre ministering to children who have suffered terrible injuries, presumably from armed conflict. All the while, the storyteller sits chanting in the shade of a thorn tree whose limbs, busy with curious children, spread wide above him. The pain in his voice and his repeated cries of 'Africa' hint that he is both bard and shaman. He seems to be recounting the history of his people's suffering, a soothsayer gifted with mystical knowledge of their souls.

At the end of her shift, the young nurse Shandurai (Thandie Newton) is cycling home along a country road when military jeeps swoop past her. The soldiers burst into a rural schoolroom where her husband Winston (Paul Osul) is teaching his class how to understand the difference between a good leader and a cruel boss. Without a word of explanation, the soldiers bundle him into one of their vehicles and roar past Shandurai again, heading to the military jail. She collapses in the road shrieking inaudibly for her husband while the children, having learnt a lesson they will never forget, run out of the school. As they watch, silenced by the shock of what has happened to a loved schoolmaster, who but the singer should walk out of the red dust that the vehicles have kicked up. The enigma of his appearance at this moment emphasises his mystical powers as his timeless lament for Africa's grief finds its latest instance in Shandurai and Winston.

The young woman has no time to absorb the shock of her husband's arrest before the roar of a low-flying jet intensifies her terror and, in a stunning unmotivated cut, hurls us with her into a dark and strange place. The horror is revisiting her in a nightmare and, as her strangled cries go on and on, it all too slowly sucks her out of sleep. Terrifying as it was in actuality, her African trauma has now conscripted her dreams and memories. As she awakens, we slowly discover – while by degrees she recognises the place where she has found refuge – that she is in the depths of an old Roman house. A rumbling noise has woken her and she goes to a small cupboard where she finds a blank sheet of musical staves, on it nothing but a large question mark.

Facing the unknown

This question mark cues consideration of the film's dramaturgical method because it is not the only puzzle that unsettles both the character and viewers. Firstly, we cannot immediately relate the African and Roman scenes and have to wait to find out why Shandurai is so far from home. Secondly, the meaning of the question mark is nearly as heavily veiled from us as from her, though the latent homage to *A Room with a View* gives a hint. In E. M. Forster's novel, George Emerson's equally baffling interrogation mark challenges the atrophied Miss Bartlett to face the terror of the unknown – a challenge which she fails miserably. In *Besieged* the query at the first level for audience and Shandurai alike is to know what is going on; but behind that, Forster's deeper challenge is equally pertinent since Shandurai, although a much better equipped personality than Miss Bartlett, has also plunged from another world into Italy and must face the unknown in a strange language and culture.

The next puzzle is why this small cupboard rumbles. The viewer cannot readily gain the necessary factual information to resolve this query thanks to Fabio Cianchetti's camera work. He maintains the tightest of framing, explained only in part by the fact that Bertolucci was working in 'miniature' (his term, see Sklarew 1999: 17) for the television screen. This visual strategy marries with the film's dramaturgical method in that both techniques withhold information from the audience. We see the tiny cupboard on several occasions before realising with Shandurai that it is a dumb waiter (a piece of nineteenth-century machinery unknown in her previous life). As Sally Chatsworth remarks, 'Shandurai lives in a present Rome through [an African] past, an "elsewhere" both cultural and geographical' (1999: 40).

These early moments establish a pattern to the unfolding of Shandurai's new life in Rome. It is mostly shown from her point of view and the audience usually lacks sufficient information to grasp why significant events occur. For example, we must wait to find out that the interrogation mark has been sent down by the owner of the house, Jason Kinsky (David Thewlis). We have also to wait to find out that he is English, a pianist and music teacher; also that Shandurai cleans for him in exchange for lodgings and enough to live on while she studies medicine. The film's method of revealing information in tantalisingly incomplete glimpses ensures that we share the difficulty she and Mr Kinsky (as she always calls him) experience in understanding each other.

The structure of *Besieged* can be likened to that of chamber music in the interweaving of all the elements that carry its themes. The delayed release of narrative information through tight framing and the manipulation of light and dark (to enhance the sense of the protagonists' difficulties in understanding) oblige the audience to give attention to what it is permitted to make out in the music and architecture as well as the behaviour of the characters.

The contrast between the bursting energy of the African sequences and the superficial calm of Shandurai's Roman life requires the audience to experience a simulacrum of her traumatised condition. Not only is she still deeply wounded by the blow of Winston's capture, but the culture shock of her exile to Italy is amplified by the stifling oppression of her new emotional isolation. Equally Kinsky, as scion of the English upper-middle classes, has been bred to stifling repression. These factors make it hard for the two of them to get to know each other and worsen their stuttering inhibition.[1] Since they have difficulty talking to each other, their communication – initially non-communication – is signalled through the music they like and the subtle byplay of their glances, gestures and actions. She plays African pop on her music system, dancing and singing to it as she works. He seems to find it alien, while she finds his classical piano pieces cold and hostile. As Fabrizio Tassi remarks, his music is Apollonian, hers Dionysian (1999: 24).

Nevertheless each is curious to find out more about the person with whom they share the house. Early in their acquaintance, she scrutinises his rooms closely while cleaning them. Then, while she is attending classes at medical school, he examines her things equally intently, unconsciously mirroring her behaviour. Like children astonished by the strangeness of the outsider who has been thrust into their lives, they try to find out more by secretly spying on each other, touching and sniffing the other's possessions. However, Kinsky soon becomes more interested in Shandurai than she wants, watching her movements and sending down an orchid in the dumb waiter.

Mr Kinsky

What does Kinsky's musicianship tell us about his personality in the early stages of their acquaintance? We discover that, although he plays the piano with masterful accomplishment (dubbed by Stefano Arnaldi) and fills the house with delicious sound, he performs only for himself. He does almost no paid work except as a piano teacher. This makes for a tenuous link with Winston. However, whereas the latter is totally committed to shaping his pupils' moral understanding of the world in which they are to survive, Kinsky's contact with his students is cool and limited to improving their keyboard technique.

Kinsky's renditions of the masters are fluent and passionate; however, he also shows a rigidity of imagination in that he limits his repertoire exclusively to the European classical canon from Bach to Grieg. Theirs is the only language in which he is articulate. Before he utters halting words disastrously to declare his love for Shandurai, he courts her by pouring out his preferred music, in effect addressing her exclusively on his terms. More than this, prior to luring her up to the music room by sending down a ring in the dumb waiter, he rotates the grand piano through 180 degrees so as to face her when she enters the room. All unconsciously he has turned the instrument of his music into a huge phallus. Tightly framed shots of the young woman cleaning room after room convey her reaction as he hits the keys

1 This is not to deny Shandurai's linguistic skill: she learns Italian quickly and well enough to pursue medical studies.

so urgently that the penetrating noise seems to be pursuing her around the house, causing irritation rather than pleasure. So, quite contrary to Shandurai's feelings for Winston which give primacy to respect, Kinsky tries to push his despairing neediness on her without first having gained her admiration. When he confesses his love – something of which she has no inkling – her irritation turns to dismay. Kinsky asks her to marry him and urges his readiness to do anything for her to prove his love. A scream explodes from the locked abyss of her sorrow: 'Get my husband out of jail!'

In terms that set him in both a mythic and a psychoanalytical context, Kinsky is a *puer aeternus*. As with Nick Nightingale and Bill Harford, the phrase refers to the Michael Jackson type, an eternal youth locked into belated boyhood and withdrawn from the world (on Jackson see Izod 2001: 80–90). Although there is a positive aspect to the type, which Jason Kinsky will eventually reveal, the negative aspect of the *puer* usually strikes the observer first. In Kinsky's case it is signalled by his immaturity in personal relations. Here is a character who when first met shows none of the bold and practical qualities of the Greek hero whose name he bears. A man in his thirties, he lives in the spirit rather than the body (see Samuels *et al.* 1986: 125–6). It fits with this aspect of his personality that he appears to believe that his own perception of the world is universally held. So he is both pathetic and cruel when he falls in love with Shandurai. He urges his needs on her without for a moment asking himself whether the circumference of her world might not be identical with his, or whether her feelings might not coincide with his.

Mr Kinsky's palazzo

The house provides a visual metaphor for the ideology upon which rests Kinsky's ultimately complacent take on the world. He has inherited this little palazzo from his aunt. It implies a European culture whole unto itself. On the outside undistinguished, planted in what has become a commuter rat-run leading to a Metro station, indoors it is resplendent with elegant figurines, paintings, statues and tapestries. The interior contains so many beautiful antique art works that, as Dave Kehr notes, it looks like 'some kind of storehouse of Western civilisation' (1999: 8) and furnishes a visual complement to the music Kinsky plays. With his English origins and Italian connections, his Austrian, German, French and Norwegian music, the pianist is all but submerged by a European high culture ossified by its own weight. The sense of cultural decadence is complemented by the drab exterior of the house. All the foregoing characteristics associate it with the culture of the *senex*. This is the archetype of the old man which, in its negative aspect, has an authoritarian, conservative nature, tending to inhibit if not extinguish the imagination (Samuels *et al.* 1986: 137). Thus Kinsky is a *puer* locked by a *senex* culture into an endless boyhood in which he never achieves anything nor even sets himself goals.

We scrutinise the house and its neighbourhood from Shandurai's perspective. As before, Cianchetti resolutely keeps the framing tight. The resultant fragmentation of space both within and beyond the house becomes a means of representing her incomplete understanding of Rome. She sees the bits she lives in or cleans or travels through, but never the tourist vistas. This is the more remarkable in that the house stands alongside the Spanish Steps, one of the city's tourist destinations. We never see their glorious sweep because, as the truncated views of the house and the city show, Shandurai does not perceive them whole. She has no overarching frame of reference within which to amplify the sense data that her eyes relay.

Despite the stand-off between Shandurai and Kinsky, the clash of opposites that they represent will produce change. One architectural feature signals the potential. Both Bertolucci and his screenwriter Clare Peploe regarded the spiral interior staircase as an important feature in choosing the little palazzo as the film's location (Sklarew 1999: 18). Although first seen in the close-framed shots typical of *Besieged*, eventually it is shown in its entirety. At first, as might be expected, its intricate ironwork acts as a divider that separates the two lonely inhabitants of the house. But gradually its seashell coils suggest the possibility (for example, when shot from above and below while Shandurai is dusting and Kinsky is at the piano) of links between the distant pair. Then, after Kinsky makes his disastrous declaration of love for Shandurai, leaving her nervous of addressing him, renewed contact occurs as if by accident when, while observing him leave the house from a vantage point high on the stairwell, she happens to let her duster fall. It drifts down and settles on his head intriguingly like a novice's veil. She runs down the several flights of winding stair that separate them to recover it and they exchange a few tentative words. Thus the staircase is simultaneously both rigid (we frequently find ourselves looking through the elegant wrought-iron banisters which Shandurai cleans and which separate her from Kinsky) and fluid in its spiralling form which leads the characters toward each other.

The meaning of the spiral has deeper ramifications still. Amplified in the context of ancient symbols, it gives us clues as to how the psychological deadlock between the characters might be broken. This interpretative tactic, justified by the emphasis on antiquity in Kinsky's palace, encourages us to take note of the stairway's geometry: for the spiral combines the idea of a circle with forward movement. The circle has an obvious association with the cycle of time, for example in the turning of the seasons through both calendar and ritual years. It also has powerful associations with the unconscious (*vis-à-vis* the square which has equally familiar connections with the concepts of rationality and the conscious). The person who follows a spiral track, however, does more than circle, since he or she also advances. Hence the spiral is an eloquent indicator of the potential for personal progress made through circling around the unconscious ('circumambulation' was the term used by Jung) so as to tease into light some of its troubling contents. It is, in short, a symbol of the possibility of further development through the integration of unconscious contents (Von Franz 1964: 248–60; Chetwynd 1993: 320). As presented in *Besieged*, the spiral is not an inert figure but the structural basis for the characters' lived expression of their gradual rapprochement. Since Shandurai and Kinsky are by no means fully aware of what is happening to them, it is all the more apt as a symbol of their potential for development – development which will only occur when each character deciphers what the other holds of her and his unconscious. This is not an intellectual exercise, but one which, led by their emotions, they have no choice but to go through.

Irruption of emotion

The first signs of this in Kinsky lie in the aggressive-pathetic way he declares his love for Shandurai. Emotion begins to rupture his fixed persona. Equally strong affects govern her response – fear of him as her employer (there is a decidedly unequal power balance in the household) and anger at his intrusion into her privacy. In turn, the release of these emotions opens her to the far worse pain of Winston's loss, which now overwhelms her. Yet as soon as the constrained emotions of both characters have surfaced, things begin to change – just as Jung's analysis of the nature of emotion anticipates (see Introduction). Shandurai, distressed to the point of physical sickness, starts by looking for a room elsewhere. However, the incident with the falling duster seems to give her pause – perhaps because Kinsky is startled and shows a wry self-deprecation of his frailty, gentle and unthreatening in comparison with his earlier behaviour.

Soon after, Kinsky attends worship at an African church, looking, we will eventually realise, for a contact with Shandurai's homeland. There he hears the joyous passion of the choir and the conviction of the priest (Cyril Nri) in recalling Christ's words that anyone who tries to preserve his life shall lose it and anyone who loses it shall be kept safe. The new experience of attending to the passions of other people – Shandurai, the congregation and their priest – will change Kinsky's life. The first symptoms quickly surface when he plays a disc by John Coltrane. Shandurai, cleaning the risers, is astonished by the sound of jazz in that house. She works her way down the spiral and sees him sprawled across a sofa relaxing. Finding him a less frightening being than she had thought, she offers to make him coffee.

Messengers of change

The underlying change, which as usual both Shandurai and the audience have to wait to discover, is that Kinsky has decided to sacrifice everything he holds dear in order to give her the help for which, from the agony of her soul, she cried out. She discovers that precious artefacts are disappearing from the house when she goes to clean them. But initially neither she nor we can tell what this means. Nor does Shandurai consciously notice the implications when she finds a discarded envelope addressed to Kinsky from her own country. But she has registered something unconsciously and when she falls into a slumber her world turns upside down in a dream which prepares her for knowledge that will come later. It takes her back to her township and the peripatetic singer. This time she sees herself tearing down the posters of the military ruler. The singer, dressed in smart western clothes instead of the rags he wore before, directs his song to her rather than the world at large. While she listens, she sees one last poster, but on this one the ruler's face has become Kinsky's. She tears it down too, as if refusing to be governed by such a male figure. Is this a political or a personal dream? For the moment it remains a mystery.

At this, the film's mid-point, Shandurai leaves the house on an errand and passes an antique shop. The clatter of something hard falling in the road (an ingenious aural metaphor for understanding falling into place) triggers her sense that she has half glimpsed something significant out of the corner of her eye. She goes back to the window and recognises one of the figurines she has been cleaning – Mercury. The presence of the little statue in the shop window brings her closer to realising what is going on, and the messenger god is an appropriate figure to provide this help. In myth he linked the world of the gods to that of mortals. Here he is the counterpart of the African shaman who has been stirring Shandurai's dreams. In psychoanalytic terms, both Mercury and the shaman function as psychopompi. As such they mediate not so much between the gods and humanity as between the *dramatis personae* of the psyche, drawing energies from the unconscious and introducing them as images which the conscious mind can grasp and convert into ideas. Mercury and the shaman will help bring self-knowledge and mutual understanding to each protagonist. This they do by making connections between African and European culture. At the personal level this shift is essential because the two cultures are strongly embodied in the inner worlds of each of the two protagonists – and each finds the other incomprehensible.

More than in the spheres of these two individuals alone, each culture occupies the unconscious of the other. It is certainly open to question whether Kinsky's first approach to Shandurai, given his lack of thought about her feelings, was tainted by an element of racism in the unthinking assumption that he might command her love. This is a man who knows so little about the woman who lives in his house as a servant and is the object of his desire, that he has no idea she is married. The personal relations of these two have obvious parallels in the realm of sociopolitical relations. Shandurai visits a Roman market run by friendly African traders. These are represented as vigorous and responsible citizens, yet are pushed so far to the margins as never to be seen in the company of white Italians. At the turn of the millennium in the world outside the cinema, the ignorance of Europeans about Africans is all too apparent in the hysterical fear of refugees and asylum seekers. Specifically, the idea that they were under siege concerned many Italians who feared their nation would be overwhelmed by the numbers of migrants pressing to enter the country from, among other places, the African territories bordering the Mediterranean.

As our two characters adjust to each other after their emotional clash, the influence of the messenger psychopompi makes itself felt. Back at her cleaning duties in what had once been a heavily adorned music room, Shandurai finds Kinsky composing hesitantly at the piano. For the first time the windows have been opened onto the garden, abundant in greenery and voluptuous wisteria. Kinsky, rather than shut himself away as he once did, invites Shandurai to hoover the carpet rather than interrupt her work for his sake. While she runs the machine back and forward over the expanse of what is almost the only furnishing left in the room, a variety of stimuli blend in his head and issue through the keyboard. Minimalist classical progressions mix with the repetitive riffs characteristic of African music and jazz. They take on a pulse prompted by his glances at the young woman working – the curve of an arm, the thrust of the vacuum cleaner, the snarling crescendos of its motor. Shandurai in turn begins to move to the music's rhythm as it evolves, so the piece develops into a celebration of shared work in progress. Although not fully aware of it, both have a part in shaping the new composition. Pianist and cleaner smile shyly at each other, pleased at feeling connected for the first time.

Some days later Shandurai receives a letter which brings news of her husband's transfer from military jail to a civil prison. However, the envelope has been mailed locally, not in Africa, and the realisation dawns in her that Kinsky is responsible for it. The swirl of emotions that this unleashes is communicated by radical jump cutting as thoughts of Winston's improved fortune beat against her perception that it is owed to Kinsky. She hears the piano swell with romantic fervour and runs to the music room; but Kinsky, far from sitting at the Steinway, is not even in the house. Shandurai strikes the keys and stills the performance: but his music has invaded her mind as a living presence, just as the man is doing.

This moment signals the renewed energising of Shandurai's animus. She has, of course, an established animus in Winston, but the longer she is in Kinsky's house, the more her husband comes to seem like a respected mentor and father figure than a lover. Although she resists, the psychopompi are leading her to new animus projection. The implications run deep because understanding the contrasexual archetype will lead her to integrate her inner and outer life, ultimately enabling a fuller knowledge of the self.

Despite her desire to celebrate for Winston and quell any feelings other than friendliness toward Kinsky, Shandurai's acute awareness of the latter is evident when next he plays. This time the current of musical influence flows from him to her. Upstairs he plays Beethoven while, way down the seashell spiral of the main stairway, she washes the marble floor of the entrance. A lovely connection is subtly established as she mops to the piano's rhythms while the printed dots of Beethoven's score shimmer in counterpoint to the sparkle of the floor's mosaic.

Shandurai

Where Kinsky began as a *puer*, uncomfortably close to Narcissus in self-regard, Shandurai too has a mythological predecessor, and Mercury connects us to her. The messenger of the gods was charged with entering the underworld to fetch Proserpina (Persephone in the Greek version) and restore her to the world above (Bolen 1985: 198). Although there is no Ceres in *Besieged* since no mother features in the film, a variant of the archetypal daughter figure (known as the Kore) underpins Shandurai's personality. In being forced out of Africa, she has been thrown into a completely unknown milieu that is to her an underworld. So the African messenger acts toward her comparably to Mercury in the myth of the Kore.

Shandurai differs from Proserpina in being a married woman, but she behaves with a maiden's demureness, nor does she wear her wedding ring. Although confident in her professional studies, she is wary in dealing with Kinsky. This is not surprising since there is a serious imbalance of power in their connection such that, whether aware of it or not, he occupies the role of Hades in their domestic set up. That imbalance is evident in several ways. He always uses Shandurai's first name and she always calls him Mr Kinsky, even later when writing him a love letter. Her room is at the bottom of the house (and on the servants' stairwell) while he occupies the upper part of the palazzo. Thus her work as Kinsky's cleaner recalls the labour of African housekeepers throughout the continent for their European employers.

Having said this, Shandurai arrives at Kinsky's house the more mature of the two. Where he has locked himself in stale boyhood, her commitment to dealing with the effects of corrupt political power has exiled her before time from her own youth. The dream she has of the peripatetic singer addressing her directly signals the kind of change her psychopomp is preparing her for by renewing her inner strength. When Kinsky's face replaces that of the African military leader on the township posters and she tears down his image too, she begins to take control. In doing so she adopts another of Proserpina's characteristics – self-empowerment. Through her suffering, the goddess, first victimised in being abducted from her mother, eventually grew strong and became Queen of the Underworld (Bolen 1985: 197–9). In comparable manner, Shandurai, exiled from mother Africa, was parachuted into Rome with no wish to remain in that alien place longer than she could help. Yet her comings and goings into the city from the house, like

Proserpina's seasonal movement from the underworld to the Earth's surface, provide the link that connects Kinsky to life (Tassi 1999: 24). By the time Winston arrives she has become an empowered woman able to determine her own future on equal terms with both him and Kinsky. Her animus has shifted from a projection which acknowledged Winston's quasi-parental authority over her to one that reflects a newly-made relationship of relative equality with Kinsky.

Sacrifice, pain and play

An equally fundamental alteration occurs in Kinsky's personality, triggered by the presence of Shandurai. When he falls in love with her, she becomes his anima and draws the projection of the hitherto stultified feminine in him, making it available for him to know. Experiencing the anima for the first time is invariably emotional because (whether understood as such or not) it is (like a woman's meeting with her animus) an encounter with an aspect of one's largely unknown inner life. In Kinsky's case the shock is healthy and triggers his evolution from *puer* to rounded adulthood even though he discovers that the woman he loves is not available to him. His love is so complete that he sublimates it to the attempt to achieve what she most wants. Unable to tell Shandurai what he is doing lest he seem to be manipulating her, he acts silently with a deep, unselfish sense of love and sacrifices everything, including nothing less than his music and any hope for the woman's love (Sklarew 1999: 17; Tassi 1999: 24).

Kinsky's psychological development is not merely personal but has social and political dimensions too. When he makes the dreadful sacrifice of selling his Steinway to raise the last tranche of funds needed to buy Winston's freedom, he decides to give a concert to his pupils before the instrument goes. It will be his only chance to play his new composition before an audience. Things do not go as planned, however, and the concert ends up in disarray – a further sign of old moulds breaking. The occasion is interrupted by a telegram from Winston for Shandurai announcing his arrival two days hence. She runs off confusedly, bewilderment and sorrow battling with her joy. Back in the music room, the children's attention wanders. A football bounces into the garden, distracting them, and they creep away to search the shrubbery for it.

Bowing without rancour to the inevitable, Kinsky abandons his performance and joins the youngsters. While one of his pupils plays a Chopin waltz, Kinsky entertains the others in the garden by juggling fruit and clowning. Shandurai returns to the party in time to share the children's delight at the surprising playfulness of this hitherto solemn man, which makes a clear contrast with the static emotions and still objects that used to dominate the house. That Kinsky does not regret the first performance of his only composition turning into a sort of playtime for his pupils is a signal moment in his personal and social maturing – yet another sacrifice. It seems he learns from his pupils to become like a child again. The *puer* – the false child – rediscovers the direct honesty of the true child, a sign that his rebirth is underway. In his acceptance of sacrifice, Kinsky comes to embody the positive side of the *puer*, the innocence of whose vision opens the way for others to perceive what Hillman describes as 'our own first natures, our primordial golden shadow . . . our angelic essence as messenger of the divine' (cited in Samuels *et al.* 1986: 126). It follows, Hillman argues, that people can derive their sense of destiny and meaning from the *puer*. This is indeed the gift that Kinsky brings Shandurai in the process, which she has initiated, of revealing more about himself.

Irresistible emotions

Their need for self-discovery is too profound to be achieved in a single moment and soon they are again weltered in emotion. The confusion of the concert precedes a night of drunkenness for both Kinsky and Shandurai. Although they spend the evening apart, both are dismayed by the prospect of Winston's arrival next morning. Neither is accustomed to alcohol, so it soon allows their repressed emotions to surface. Kinsky joins the priest at a bar to celebrate the success of their joint campaign. He drinks to dull the pain of losing Shandurai; but the wine enables him at last to admit that he is not a good enough pianist to perform in public. This is a confession made on the spur of the moment, but no less effective for that, marking a step toward a shared acceptance of who he is – simultaneously achieving a measure of self-recognition and his return to the world.

Shandurai meanwhile, alone in her room, tries to write to him expressing her gratitude. The words will not come out right, so she opens the champagne intended to celebrate Winston's arrival and drains the bottle as the hours pass. In opening her heart, the wine washes away a self-deception. Previously, trying to explain her feelings for Winston, she had spoken of his bravery and her respect for him. Now her feelings reveal to her that respect is no substitute for love. What started as a letter of thanks becomes after many drafts a simple note: 'I love you Mr Kinsky'.

Shandurai's self-confession and the effect of the champagne release her into a lustful half sleep from which Kinsky's crashing return awakens her. Going silently to his room to remove the sleeping man's boots, she stays and ends the night in his bed.

The lives of both Kinsky and Shandurai have veered away from the goals they once willed – his in music, hers in marriage. Although their actions are voluntary, neither would have altered as radically had not the affect aroused by the other's presence laid siege to their prior state of mind. As indicated in the Introduction, Jung recognised that emotions are irresistible, allowing drives of which we are wholly or partly unconscious to take over and alter our attitudes (Jung 1939: 278–9; 1956a: 442). They are 'instinctive, involuntary reactions which upset the rational order of consciousness by their elemental outbursts' (1956a: 278). And their import for human affairs is great because they are the chief originating source of consciousness (1954c: 96).

As a metaphor, the film's title expresses through the idea of a blockade the deadlock that occurs when, as with our protagonists, emotions are fiercely resisted for fear of their impact. John Donne's Holy Sonnet XVI invokes a siege of the emotions, the voice of a terrified but passionate suitor crying out . . .

> Batter my heart, three person'd God; for, you
> As yet but knocke, breathe, shine, and seeke to mend;
> That I may rise, and stand, o'erthrow mee, and bend
> Your force, to breake, blowe, burn and make me new . . .

It concludes:

> Take mee to you, imprison mee, for I
> Except you enthrall mee, never shall be free,
> Nor ever chast, except you ravish mee.

Donne links the idea of sacrifice to the breaking of a metaphorical virginity – the suitor's reluctance to bind himself like a bride to his creator. God is the lover simultaneously to be welcomed and feared as an aggressor who will break in after laying siege but, having done so, will renew in glory all that he has wrecked.

The Holy Sonnet is relevant in reading *Besieged* because sacred and secular love have often been expressed through similar imagery. There are at least two reasons for this. Each can function as a powerful simile for the other. And secondly, the intensity of love, whether secular or religious, causes a transforming psychological upheaval in those who experience it. If Donne's God is imagined as a human lover, the sonnet declares emotions close to those that rule Shandurai and Kinsky. Their nascent feelings are confused by the need for, and terror of sacrifice. Furthermore their discovery of love forces them to face the divine in themselves – but at a heavy cost.

As an archetypal figure imposing itself on consciousness, sacrifice often prepares people for a painful realisation. In order that personal development can occur, their familiar and trusted values have to die to make way for the formation of a new symbolic order in the psyche. This is the venture upon which Kinsky, having given away everything that once shaped his being, has embarked. His new playfulness shows that he is coming through his ordeal with the reserves intact that will enable him to find a new life.

Meanwhile Shandurai is besieged by the conflict between her desires and the dictates of her conscience (Sklarew 1999: 17). By the time Winston reaches Rome, she has tasted for the first time nakedly erotic love. As the Hades of her Roman world, Kinsky has caused her to face and conquer her shadow – her fear of Eros. Her newly-budded passion, however, will only be free to take root if she gives up her marriage.

The film ends with Shandurai having to consider a second, unseen question mark: which relationship and which mode of being to sacrifice? She has not yet made her choice when she rises from Kinsky's bed to answer the door to Winston's ringing. Bertolucci cuts the film before we can find out how she greets her husband.

Sacrifice, psyche and society

The painful personal sacrifice necessary to make way for the psychological changes that Kinsky and Shandurai are undergoing does more than open up the inner world of each independently. For his part, Kinsky made his sacrifices to achieve a political as well as a personal goal. Conversely, Shandurai's introjection of a new animus image has allowed her to discover and make use of certain facets of personality which in her previous cultural milieu would have been deemed inappropriate to a woman. Specifically, these manifest in her assertiveness with Kinsky and her readiness to alter her life to fit her intuitions. So what has already passed between Shandurai and Kinsky has altered radically the previous power imbalance between them. Although we cannot tell how the quandary with Winston will be resolved, their readiness for sacrifice has already had an impact on the politics of their relationship.

In many great narratives, sacrifice does indeed clear the way for rebirth of not only the individual but also the community. The motif surfaces in the myths and religions of many places and times, remaining, for example, a concept of high significance for Christians and fundamental Islamists. In *Besieged*, Bertolucci does not show what if any impact the principal characters' personal sacrifices may have in their societies beyond the sphere of domestic politics. However, the personal and the political are already deeply implicated. Winston was arrested simply because he acted out of concern for his pupils, wanting them to recognise the difference between tyranny and leadership. The ruling African cabal judged him an enemy of the state because, in the paranoid logic of dictatorship, any teaching which might encourage people to question the authority of dictators has to be seditious politics. It follows that where social paranoia drives a dominant power to repress opposition to its policies, there the cultural unconscious and politics are linked.

As for the future, Shandurai's embarking on medical training must have been intended to enable her to return to and tend her people. Her crisis of conscience will therefore have consequences not only of a personal nature but also for her people. *Besieged* ends without showing whether her potential as a member of society or that of the two men is fulfilled – what life Kinsky will make for himself and whether Winston might follow the direction implied in his teaching and join a new generation of leaders in exile waiting for the junta at home to fall.

Told from Shandurai's perspective, *Besieged* offers its spectators a position from which to engage with her in a double hermeneutic as she makes sense of Rome and her new acquaintances, and we make sense of her. The sweet nature of the young woman cannot but entice some viewers to empathise with her through both an involuntary affective mimicry (in response to Thandie Newton's finely tuned performance) and the voluntary emotional simulation which the character's predicament invites. The film's power lies in dramatising her and Kinsky's relationship, and for many spectators that will be read within (to use another of the concepts of Murray Smith described in the Introduction) a structure of sympathy. However, after the opening sequences, the politics of Africa are held in the background, something for the spectator to feel more than experience as a source of high emotion. Thus it seems unlikely that audiences of *Besieged* found their own imagined worlds turned upside down by it.

Bertolucci's next film *The Dreamers* completes the links between psyche and society, dramatising the mutual connections between desire, culture, and both personal and political responsibility. It seeks to draw the audience not only as in *Besieged* into the personal conflicts of its characters, but to go unambiguously beyond the sphere of feelings, however deep, aroused in personal relations. *The Dreamers* was to attempt to inseminate in spectators more than a recognition of the need for political change in distant nations, a passionate appetite for change at home.

Chapter 5

The politics of youth remembered: Bernardo Bertolucci's *The Dreamers*

Introduction

As indicated in Chapter 3, Bertolucci's experience of psychoanalysis left him fascinated by dreams and their resemblance to cinematic sequences. He had long harboured the desire to make a film dealing with the Events of Paris in 1968 and finally realised this ambition with *The Dreamers*, Gilbert Adair's adaptation of his own novel *The Holy Innocents*. Here at last was the Bertolucci film that wove together in a rich tapestry sex, psychoanalysis, memory, dreaming, history and culture, revolution and filmic style.

A city made strange

Bertolucci has always been concerned to make cinema new and strange to eye, ear and mind. Starting with *Il Conformista*, he sought to make his films innovatory to the degree that they should attract close attention from his audiences yet not so inaccessible as to discourage their interest. *The Dreamers* (2003), no exception to this principle, opens tightly framed on steel girders through which we are descending, restricted to a travelling close shot of the structural components themselves. The structure – punctuated by the main titles razoring in and out of the spars – is not easily identified until the duration of the descent and our knowledge of Parisian iconography assure us that this must be the Eiffel Tower. We get a perspective on it quite other than that which tourists ascend to enjoy when they gaze out at the view across the city. Bertolucci's director of cinematography is once again Cianchetti; but any expectation that he might, as in *Besieged*, be working exclusively in miniature is banished by Jimi Hendrix's roaring music (both spatially and emotionally huge) that accompanies the descent. In fact, diverse visual styles attach to different sequences and vary both the mood and its implications.

Twenty-year-old Matthew (Michael Pitt), a visiting Californian student, is exploring the city. He leaves the Tower to attend a screening at the Cinémathèque Française and crosses the Pont d'Iena over the Seine with

Steadicam shots following him to reveal a wide panorama over the river toward his destination in the Palais de Chaillot. However, the joyful sense of liberty that this elegant vista elicits in the viewer is made strange by the camera momentarily gliding to one side to pick up police vans howling past. Matthew soon finds that his way into the cinema is obstructed by demonstrators, many of them students whom he recognises as, like him, regular members of the audience. They are protesting against the dismissal by André Malraux (President de Gaulle's Minister of Culture) of the Cinémathèque's founder Henri Langlois.

Bertolucci has placed Matthew in February 1968 at a nodal point of political fermentation – right at the start of what the young man refers to as 'our very own cultural revolution'. For the French youngsters around Matthew, the sacking of Langlois was symptomatic of their government's autocratic ways. The generation in power was out of touch with young people. The latter, not having lived through the occupation, lacked their parents' reverence for de Gaulle's wartime leadership against the Nazis. Nor was the issue at the Cinémathèque the only ground for their disaffection. They were also angered by the antiquated conditions in the overcrowded universities, their outdated curricula, remote professorate and inflexible bureaucracy. Added to this, social relations had not changed at the same pace as in the USA and Britain where rigid hierarchy and deference were rapidly being eroded (Forbes 1992: 15).

Cinema and culture on and off the screen

However, none of these factors explains why the government's intervention at the Cinémathèque had such an inflammatory effect. Malraux had sacked Langlois on the justified grounds that the latter was an inefficient archivist (Forbes 1992: 17); but the minister failed to understand that Langlois was less interested in cataloguing and preserving the prints he collected than in screening them. In doing so he performed a key function in invigorating film culture for Parisian cinéphiles at large and, more particularly, for the young filmmakers who had by 1968 emerged as the French New Wave. Among the film buffs demonstrating outside the Cinémathèque were a number of cinéastes of whom we get glimpses in *The Dreamers*, including Godard and Truffaut. That pair went on some weeks later to close down the 1968 Cannes Film Festival, by which time social unrest had intensified (French 2004a). Langlois had by that time been reinstated, but the issues at stake had widened to embrace much larger sectors of society, and in particular significant parts of the country's labour force (Forbes 1992: 17–18; Hayward 1993: 237–8).

Programmes at the Cinémathèque were notable for the way they recovered for Parisian audiences films which had gone out of circulation or had never (often because of World War II) reached French screens. They were also known for their apparently random sequencing: Hollywood classics jostled with New Wave recent releases, with French classics, German expressionists, Italian neo-realist films and American pot-boilers (Insdorf 1978: 20). All enthused the Cinémathèque audiences. Whether deliberately or not, Langlois's educational programme intensified and perhaps reflected the cultural stew that excited this new generation. Its significance was all the greater in a 'pre-video, pre-DVD culture when movies did not exist outside the temple of the cinema' (Bradshaw 2004). One ingredient was admiration for the *cinéma d'auteurs* of American directors – those such as Ford, Fuller, Hawks and Ray whom French cinéphiles discovered to have distinctive and sometimes personal themes and styles. Those directors had worked all but anonymously in so far as US audiences were concerned, but the French were now absorbing and celebrating their artistry. Passionate interest in charismatic American film stars added to the ferment. Other significant ingredients to the mix included love for the old masters of French cinema; contempt for 1940s and 50s translations of novels to the French screen (the heritage fashion dubbed by Truffaut *la tradition de la qualité*); and, incidentally, indifference toward almost all British cinema. Above all, the 1960s were in France no less than in the Anglo-Saxon world the decade of the (commercially backed) emergence of a pervasive new youth culture. This was marked by the seizing of heady new sexual freedoms; gaudy, exuberant and affordable fashions for young men and women alike; the rapid erosion of the old forms of deference; fierce debates on political and philosophical topics; and exhilarated enjoyment of rock 'n' roll and jazz – all to the dismay of the parental generation. In the rich ambience of this cultural explosion, the old cinema of France was scornfully dubbed *le cinéma de papa*. Meanwhile films of *le Nouveau Vague*, the New Wave, with their deliberately eye-catching editing, handheld camera work and direct sound that produced a rough-cut aesthetic counter to seamless mainstream American products were easily (if not entirely accurately) associated with the younger generation and became known as *cinéma jeune* (Hayward 1993: 234–5, 238).

Enthusiasm for youthful American culture coexisted with resentment against that nation. In part this was directed at US economic dominance, the market cause of the very cultural invasion French young people were enjoying. But their anger was sharpened by American involvement in Vietnam. This anger together with their desire to see old and entrenched power structures overthrown found outlet in passionate approval of the Latin American revolutionaries Fidel Castro and Che Guevara, as well as a largely ill-informed endorsement of Chairman Mao's Cultural Revolution. This is not only the territory that Bertolucci makes the common ground for his young French characters, but also the cultural milieu that provided a major stimulus for the aesthetic and political concerns of his own early films.

Revolution and cinephilia

The crowd through which Matthew is making his way is being roused by passionate speeches in defence of Langlois, the Cinémathèque and Liberty delivered by Jean-Pierre Kalfon and Jean-Pierre Léaud. Bertolucci cuts between documentary footage of these seminal New Wave figures giving their speeches in 1968 and shots of them delivering the self-same words to his characters. His editorial method dovetails today's fiction to past actuality and underlines both the historic significance of the *événements* and the debt *The Dreamers* owes to them.

Matthew pushes through the crowd to the gates of the museum. There, chained to the railings like a suffragette, he finds a strikingly handsome young woman whom he has noticed in the Cinémathèque audience. Isabelle (Eva Green) asks Matthew to take the cigarette from her lips because she cannot reach it, and they begin to chat. But when he asks why she is chained, she throws off the shackles with a twist of elegant wrists. While she may be amusing herself by dramatising the situation, the CRS (France's feared riot police) are not playing: they charge, clubbing anyone slow to move, and break up the peaceful demonstration with needless brutality. This is the first occurrence of a contrast that *The Dreamers* sets up recurrently. Matthew and his new friends, like all the rebellious students, will dream altered futures and begin to act out subtle flowerings of change; but the politicians and their factors do not dream at all but take leaden steps to preserve things just as they are.

Isabelle and her twin brother Théo (Louis Garrel) lead Matthew away from the mêlée and walk with him along the banks of the Seine. Friendship quickly blossoms. As A. O. Scott (2004) observes, the ensuing triangle is like an updating of Henry James. They are the same age and share eagerness for life, contempt for the tired old ways of their parents and above all a passion for cinema. Matthew asks Isabelle when she was born and she answers, 'I entered this world on the Champs Elysées in 1959, and my very first words were, "*New York Herald Tribune*!"' On cue, Bertolucci cuts to the scene in Godard's 1959 film *A Bout de Souffle* (*Breathless*) in which Jean Seberg is selling the newspaper on that very boulevard. Isabelle claims that the New Wave, rather than her parents, gave her life.

The reference to *A Bout de Souffle* is not, however, exhausted by such a first-level reading. *The Dreamers* is richly embellished with clips from, citations of and oblique references to films and music. This early example serves vividly to illustrate not merely an aesthetic approach but also a number of themes that run through Bertolucci's film. *A Bout de Souffle* revealed the era's deep fascination with the collision of French and American values which echoes throughout *The Dreamers* when the three young cinéphiles debate the superiority of Chaplin over Keaton; of Clapton over Hendrix; and the relative demerits of Mao dragooning the Chinese people into uniformity of thought versus America's attempt through war to impose its ideology on Vietnam. We are being shown cinema as it records cultural change, *A Bout de Souffle* marking a key turning point in generational culture. However, there is yet more to it than this. We have already seen in the case of *Stealing Beauty* the way in which for Bertolucci the arts magically free the imagination to discover new ways of being. His use of archival clips, as Scott remarks, makes gloriously literal the idea that living in and through the movies is a mode of communion (2004). There is no question that the director's love for cinema dreaming is at one with the passion of his principal characters in *The Dreamers*. With this film's focus on revolution, the question that needs attention will be whether it propagates cultural change in its own right.

Taking the revolution home

Another question *The Dreamers* poses as intimately as any of Bertolucci's films is in what way sexual discovery will change the protagonists' personalities. As in many of his films, the sex drive moves his characters into discovering new ways of being – whether that drive expresses love, hatred or self-loathing. Although in some cases (as in *Last Tango in Paris* with Paul's intense death drive) it may do no more than deepen an urge that was already active, in other instances (Lucy in *Stealing Beauty* being a case in point) sexual discovery no less than the arts magically frees the imagination. In *The Dreamers* movie games will lead to sex games and the film will draw close links between the arts, sexuality and revolution.

Before this happens, Matthew is invited home by the twins and experiences dinner *en famille*. A conflagration between the generations, a miniature of the quasi-revolutionary dispute in society at large, flares between Théo and his father. Georges (Robin Renucci) complacently accuses his offspring of believing naively that demonstrations can change the world. Angrily, Théo charges his father with failing to take a stand against American intervention in Vietnam and abandoning the political fervour for which his poetry had once been famous. The meal ends with Théo muttering that he would hate to be like his father, and his fury leaves the older man hiding his hurt behind ineffectual pomposity. There is more than an echo here, of course, of Bertolucci's repeated need to 'kill the father' in order to emerge as his own man. The difference here is that Georges is an ineffectual figure finding refuge in his library and seldom emerging other than under the tutelage of his wife. In the family he represents the *ancien régime*, already teetering on the edge of ideological extinction.

Meanwhile Matthew, given his gauche manner, surprises both the dinner party and us by coping deftly with a no less inflammatory challenge.

Georges accuses him of fiddling with Isabelle's lighter (flame again) instead of paying attention to his disquisition on the way inspiration comes when it chooses. Delicious irony: Matthew has at that exact moment been struck by inspiration. He shows how the lighter's dimensions marry with all the lines of the tablecloth's box patterns and also with the dimensions of his fascinated listeners' bodies. And, he argues, it doesn't stop there because every part of the world fits in a cosmic harmony of shapes and sizes with all the others. 'I was wondering why,' he says. 'I know that it is.' Matthew appears to be experiencing that magical once-in-a-lifetime moment which comes to some young people when they find all too briefly that they seem to understand everything – a revelation of perfect order in the universe during which all its mysteries lie open. The incandescence of Matthew's illumination contrasts with Georges's humdrum assertion that for him the universe is chaos.

Incandescence, the pervasive metaphor in the dinner-table scene, weaves together diverse experiences including rage, illumination and, before the evening ends, the beginnings of love. All these inner experiences will lead to change, though it is not always immediately seen. Almost the final instance of conflagration that evening occurs when Isabelle bends over the table to kiss Matthew good night and her hair catches in the flame of a candle. Matthew, calm and practical, claps hands on the flames and puts them out instantly – a rare moment in the friends' early acquaintance in which he knows exactly what he is doing.

Matthew usually looks the naive American trying to keep up with European sophistication. However, lest we be deceived into fixing too simple a label on the young visitor, it is already apparent (as Georges, to his credit, perceives) that he has a personality more interesting than his friends at first know and in significant ways more fully developed than theirs. Another instance of his entwined immaturity and imagination is his cod philosophical explanation that true movie buffs like Théo, Isabelle and himself sit in the front row so they can be first to receive the images coming off the screen. As Scott (2004) points out, logically this is a silly notion, not least because the Cinémathèque was devoted to showing old movies. It is, however, also beguiling – less a wilful delusion than a consciously impossible metaphor expressing Matthew's romantic passion for the seventh art as well as his intuition that the cinema has the capability to change the world's order.

Movie games and sex play

After the parents have left for a long holiday at the seaside, Matthew accepts the others' invitation to move in with them and we focus principally on the three young dreamers. With the passing of the days they leave the apartment seldom and become increasingly preoccupied with themselves.[1] As they play out roles borrowed from the screen and quiz each other's knowledge of favourite moments, Bertolucci treats their seriousness with tender solicitude, as Scott (2004: 000) notes.

> [He] revels in their unselfconscious intensity, gazing affectionately at these children who speak solemnly of 'cinema,' who quote André Bazin with reverence and for whom the movies, far from being an escape from the world, are a means of entry into it.
>
> This idea that living in and through movies is not a solitary neurosis but a mode of communion is made gloriously literal by Mr. Bertolucci's use of archival clips . . .

A clip which makes the point comes from *Bande à part* (1964). Isabelle and Théo challenge Matthew to help them break the record time for running through the Louvre established in that film by Anna Karina, Sami Frey and Claude Brasseur. Bertolucci cuts between Godard's film and his own characters as they race down the galleries, the earlier film acting like a memory prompt that urges his young heroes on. The challenge is an early test of Matthew, but it is also the trio's entry into a world reshaped through cinema. Unconsciously too, it functions as a kind of foreplay. Having beaten the record, the twins chant 'We accept you, one of us!' Matthew joins in the victory celebrations, and Bertolucci cuts to Tod Browning's *Freaks* whose deformed characters they are imitating. The exultant friends mean that they are cinema fanatics; but, as in a dream, the quote seems to have been triggered by an idea of which none of them is yet conscious. The idea will take on a different resonance when Matthew tries to break the psychosexual triangle that is about to form by challenging the twins to grow out of their freakishly frozen childhood.

Isabelle and Théo bear matching birthmarks on their shoulders. Bertolucci does not confirm whether they were physically conjoined because, as Théo says, they are Siamese twins in their minds. During Matthew's first night in their apartment he spies on them sleeping together naked; his voyeuristic peek at this quasi-primal scene upends his neatly ordered world. But what he does not know until later is that, appearances notwithstanding, they are not lovers. In psychoanalytical terms, the twins are in an uroboric state. Natural

1 Writing for *The New York Times*, Scott (2004) remarks that, 'The ensuing triangle is like a soft-core updating of Henry James, with Matthew representing an open-minded, skeptical sensibility exposed to the dark shadows and gothic mysteries of Old Europe.' Except that the contrast is slightly overdrawn (from a European perspective, Matthew's untried puritanical streak is hard to miss), the comparison with James is illuminating.

in childhood, it becomes 'freakish' in later life because the uroboros needs to be outgrown if the individual is to achieve complete adulthood.

The uroboros is an ancient Egyptian symbol, a snake which lives by devouring its own tail. In post-Jungian psychology it invokes the self before ego consciousness has emerged from the unconscious. As Neumann says, it is a highly charged image because the snake constantly slays, weds and impregnates itself. In one aspect it is an image of perpetuity and hence of eternity; but in its circularity it also signifies the germ cell of creativity. The round, self-contained uroboros is 'the symbolic self-representation of the dawn state, showing the infancy both of mankind and of the child'. It signifies 'the unconscious state . . . the original, basic, psychic situation that is everywhere the rule' (Neumann 1954: 11, 271). Ego consciousness normally develops only later as the infant grows. The uroboros with its completeness unto itself and its closure from the outer world is, therefore, a symbol that does not convey the idea of a mature self, but rather of origins. The thrust to achieve maturity is dependent upon the evolution to the fullest capacity of consciousness, the distinguishing mark and *sine qua non* of the human species. However, the urge toward growth has to fight against the psychologically fatal attraction of continued submersion in the unconscious. That attraction is great because it holds out the illusion of a safe return to an earlier, known state, and escape from the fears which come with the enforced adventure into the developing world of consciousness (see Neumann 1954: 39–101). This is in effect what Matthew will eventually realise, telling the twins that they will never escape the impulse to remain locked in belated childhood unless they give each other freedom to find their independent lives.

Where as here images occur that imply uroboric incest, they point to a regression – the surrender of ego consciousness in whole or in part to the womb-like unconscious which reabsorbs it. Neumann (1954: 17) points out that such symbolism is always accompanied by the insignia of death to signify the abandonment and dissolution of consciousness before it has flourished completely. Sure enough, by the end of the film Isabelle will attempt to include the boys in her suicide; and although they survive, the black images of the CRS police charging the rioters and bearing down on herself and Théo have a deathly quality.

Matthew does not achieve his full understanding of the twins until both their *ménage-à-trois* and the *événements* on the streets are moving toward crisis. In the meantime, Théo and Isabelle draw him into their 'humidly close' relationship (Bradshaw 2004). At first he finds his puritanical values repeatedly discomfited by their flagrant and insouciant dishabille. When their games shift from movies to sex play via the forfeits levied on failure to guess a charade, the twins' psychological sadism makes him distinctly uneasy (Scott 2004). Isabelle obliges him as a reluctant voyeur to watch Théo masturbate over a photograph of Marlene Dietrich (a poster which redoubles emphasis on the sadomasochism of the moment). Then a few days later Théo exacts revenge when the other two fail to recognise his performance of Edward G. Robinson's demise on the shadow of a cross in *Scarface*. He ups the stakes, insisting that Isabelle and Matthew make love while he watches.

It is – or should be – a crucial turning point in all their relationships. Isabelle accepts the challenge and puts Charles Trenet's rendition of 'La Mer' on the turntable. She strips and helps her brother capture Matthew who, mortified by the violation of both his sense of propriety and his feelings for Isabelle, is hiding in a kitchen cupboard. As they rip off his clothes they discover that he has filched a photo of Isabelle and tucked it under his penis. Matthew realises that further resistance would fly in the face of his obvious desire and goes to Isabelle. His motivation for assenting to the sexual forfeit is clear, but Isabelle's and Théo's are less apparent, perhaps even to themselves.

As the others go to it on the kitchen floor, Théo mimics Belmondo's tough-guy demeanour. A cigarette hanging from his lip, he fries up an absurd number of eggs, from time to time glancing as if indifferently at the couple. The breaking of shells counterpoints the lovemaking: Matthew is causing Isabelle pain but, a virgin himself, he has little idea of it. When they climax, noises from the street below draw Théo to the window. Pursued by the *flics*, demonstrators are racing past flaunting communist flags. The juxtaposition of the mould-breaking activities inside the apartment and on the street cannot be missed.

When Matthew and Isabelle move apart, Théo goes to his sister tenderly, touches her thighs and with satisfaction observes blood on his fingers. Astonished to discover that he rather than Théo is Isabelle's first lover, Matthew is overwhelmed by joy and love for her. He appears not in the immediacy of the moment to appreciate the politics of his situation; but consciously or not, the twins have put him in the position of a go-between, consummating the instinctual unity that they cannot quite bring themselves to express in the flesh.

Incest, anger and revolution

Andrew Samuels has considered the potential uses of the incest motif (carefully insisting that he is concerned with the fantasy and not the actuality) (2001: 67–8). It was not in 2003 a new theme for Bertolucci; in *La Luna* (1979) the incestuous relationship bonded mother (Jill Clayburgh) and son Joe (Matthew Barry). Caterina masturbates Joe to help the unhappy boy break out of the uroboric state. In Samuels's terms, she provides Joe with 'erotic playback', communicating admiration and love of her son (albeit through riskily intimate physicality) to enable his development toward sexual and psychological maturity (pp. 85–6). However, the meanings of such a parent-child incest fantasy are in significant respects distinct from those raised by the twins in *The Dreamers*. In considering the topic of sibling incest, Samuels takes as his starting point an observation by Jung that it could be defined 'as "kinship libido," a kind of instinct which, like a sheep-dog, keeps the family group intact' (Jung 1946a: 224). In some societies, like the early Christian communities, endogamous marriage (i.e. within the family) was recognised. Kinship libido had a function in organising those communities which has completely disappeared in the West (1946a: 233). Samuels argues that because exogamous marriage (i.e. outside the family) is the cultural norm in our time, incest fantasy has taken on a transgressive nature 'that makes it a useful metaphor in developing transgressive politics' (2001: 68). The idea marries with Bertolucci's themes in *The Dreamers* where the trio seem revolutionary in refashioning sexual mores in their private microcosm and as such are juxtaposed with the political *événements* unfolding in the city.

At first, new love and vigorous physical appetite focus Isabelle on Matthew to the exclusion of Théo. However, it is not long before the twins' psychological sadism resumes. Théo initiates it by slipping back into her bed when Matthew goes in search of something to eat. When the latter returns, he has to lie on the floor and Théo warns him not to get in the way of love between himself and his sister, conjoined as they are in the psyche. Since Isabelle does not demur, the most powerful current of libido swings away from the axis between Matthew and Isabelle and returns to its former alignment between Théo and Isabelle. Although it will take him some while to mount a challenge, Matthew cannot miss seeing that he has a rival.

In the meantime, other needs and appetites make themselves felt. Pushed into cooking by Théo, Isabelle serves up a couple of appalling casseroles of burnt goo. Perhaps this 20-year-old daughter of the Parisian bourgeoisie truly has no idea how to prepare food, but it's a seductive thought that, as the woman at the fulcrum of a *ménage-à-trois*, Isabelle is mocking the forms of patriarchal marriage. Then, with the increasingly messy apartment empty of food, Théo mocks the hunter-gatherer's role by collecting the neighbours' garbage and serving it up for lunch. As their domestic scene undergoes disruption of the patriarchal politics and economics to which the twins' parents conform, it resembles life in the city where (although offscreen) food shortages were experienced during the disturbances as nervous housewives hoarded supplies. In the apartment shortages occur, however, because the cheques left by the parents have all been spent – probably (since Théo only breaks into his father's cellar after the money has run out) on wine and dope.

Despite the fact that, to the annoyance of his student friends, Théo is no longer helping organise demonstrations at the university, politics also enter the apartment in dope-fuelled arguments with Matthew. When Théo proclaims that Mao is no tyrant but resembles a great filmmaker in directing his people to march together, Matthew 'makes an equally passionate case against this incestuous utopia of shared minds' (Feeney 2004). He says that, since Mao's foot soldiers are all required to devote themselves to the same single text, it leads to the death of the imagination. The boys also argue fiercely about Vietnam. Théo is angered both by the American armed intervention, and contradictorily that Matthew has avoided being drafted by enrolling at university. Hurt by this, Matthew insists that there is no escaping the draft by claiming to be a pacifist.[2] Besides, if Théo's radical politics matter so much, why does he not take part in what is stirring on the street? The debate about music is integral to this argument. Matthew tells Théo that he is mistaken to think that American GIs listen to Clapton. Hendrix is the man, his greatness that he plays fucked up music for a fucked up time, and that is what the soldiers in Vietnam respond to.

Jealousy disturbs the boys, as the track behind their argument, Hendrix's 'Hey Joe', emphasises. It is the song of a lover preparing to shoot his woman for taking another man. So politics, film aesthetics and psychology have come together again and remain interlocked when Matthew complains that the twins don't love him as much as he does them. Isabelle responds by challenging him to prove his love and he accepts eagerly, not caring that she is demanding the reverse of what he had wanted. But when he realises that they intend to test him by shaving his pubic hair, he is outraged: 'You're trying to turn me into a freak. "One of us, one of us, one of us."' Because it quotes a much-loved film, the charge dwells in Isabelle's memory and will unsettle her. Meanwhile Matthew tries to make the twins understand that they must let go of each other if they are to grow into adulthood. He challenges Isabelle to prove her love by going out with him without Théo.

Battling the uroboros

Isabelle accepts. She and Matthew enjoy a date at the Cinémathèque. They see *The Girl Can't Help It* and for a short, sweet moment join the entranced audience in swaying to the Ink Spots' crooning. The evening is a success and back in the apartment Matthew overcomes Isabelle's reluctance to let him into her room. No one, not even Théo, is allowed to see it and when Matthew does charm his way in, we can see why. It is a girl's room, revealing a personality by no means as fully formed in adult configuration as the sophisticated mask that she favours makes her intimates think. The decor is indeterminate, a pastiche of sentimental Regency probably to her parents' taste, its furnishings a curious mix. Remembrances of childhood (a twinned pair of teddies) sit alongside materials for the study of anatomy.

2 Note the hint in Matthew's letters home of alienation from his father, implying that the latter may be a war veteran who has pressed his son to follow his footsteps.

Nothing in the room would give her mother cause for anxiety, so it could hardly be more different from Théo's, whose posters and icons declare his generation's rebellion.

Isabelle's admitting her lover looks like a promising move toward adulthood. She comes to him as the Venus de Milo in long black gloves which cut her arms from view – a living image of the almost perfect goddess of love. When Matthew correctly identifies the statue (a loving gift as a quiz question), she rewards him sexily. But Théo, in the next room with a girl whose giggles reveal that they too are sexually excited, puts 'La Mer' on the record player with something quite other than loving on his mind. This is his revenge for being excluded from the date with Matthew. For the twins, 'La Mer' has never been an instrument of seduction but the love song that binds them and celebrates their uroboric unity. It symbolises this well. First of all, compared with the rock that they usually prefer (Janis Joplin, Hendrix and The Doors), it is *musique de papa*. Then the ocean ('La Mer') is a figure which has for centuries been associated with the deeps of the unconscious: life forms there; images within it can only be seen, when at all, fleetingly metamorphosing; and it drowns those who become lost in it. By playing it while fucking another girl, Théo cold-bloodedly violates the bond between himself and Isabelle. Like a person drowning, distraught beyond control as the music sucks her directly back into the uroboric unity which her brother is destroying, Isabelle ejects Matthew as if he were a stranger. All the while she beats helplessly on the connecting door to her brother's room with hands which (one further, ironic indicator of the risks of dwelling in the uroboros) are still clad in the deathly black gloves that belong to the other girl.

A deep need to save the uroboros now dominates Isabelle. Sometime later, she finds the boys in Théo's room drunkenly arguing over politics once again. Although there are, not for the first time, hints in their intimacy of a developing homosexual erotic interest which might restabilise the *ménage-à-trois*, she brushes aside Théo's invitation to join them, leading the way instead to a tent she has built in the salon. Made with bed linen and cushions, it is immediately recognisable to Théo as the luminous, candle-lit recreation of a childhood fantasy palace. Delighted, the boys rush into it, but the wine soon induces sleep. When certain that Matthew cannot overhear, Isabelle prods her inebriated brother into half wakefulness, asking urgently for reassurance that he will love her forever. But Théo is too far gone to mutter much more than 'I love you too' – which hurts because she recognises the mirroring of their coolness to Matthew. Desperate, not least because Matthew has called them freaks, she is left struggling for breath, on the brink of trauma.

In the morning, the twins' parents return from holiday to the filthy apartment and discover the three sleepers entwined naked in the tent. It is a voluptuous and erotic scene, the young bodies casually exposed as in a romantic painting of exotic nudes by Ingres. During the night they have shed their clothes and their limbs weave around each other. It seems as if the dark must have brought them love, all three, whether awake or not, and whether in the flesh or in the spirit alone. Georges, shocked beyond speech by a vista for which nothing in his experience has prepared him, cannot decide what to do. His wife has wit enough to see that waking them would be calamitous and capably manages her husband back to their car after depositing yet another of his cheques near the trio. Although she acts pragmatically rather than in distress, their departure can be read as a political defeat within the family wherein the young usurp the domestic *ancien régime* exclusively by cultural shock tactics and without a struggle. It is an inexact miniature of what is transpiring on the streets of Paris.

Isabelle awakens before the boys and, with no less shock than her parents had felt, finds the cheque placed where they could not have avoided seeing into the tent. She has always been deeply disquieted by the thought of her parents discovering her feelings for her brother. Now she rushes round the apartment making sure that they are no longer there, and her eye falls on the gas supply. Fixing a hose to the stand pipe, she pulls it through to the tent, lies down between the sleeping boys clutching its hissing mouth to her bosom somewhat like Cleopatra's asp and – not checked by the thought that she will take Théo and Matthew with her – prepares to die. Even though there is something self-dramatising in her preparations, as if she were hoping for a *deus ex machina* to save her, her actions vindicate Neumann's observation that incest symbolism is usually accompanied by the insignia of death to signify the abandonment of consciousness before it has flourished completely (1954: 17).

After a long hissing silence, but before the gas can have its fatal effect, a gathering brouhaha heralds the passage of demonstrators below the apartment. A cobblestone smashes through the window and rousts the young people from the tent's womb. *Deus ex machina* indeed. Noise and air flood the apartment as, in the ensuing chaos, Isabelle throws windows open and conceals the hose. When the others ask what has happened, she says, 'The street came flying into the room!' This curious formulation does more than merely reinforce Isabelle's penchant for dramatising situations. It also draws attention to its metaphoric undertow. Those on the street are in effect calling on the trio of friends to affirm their solidarity, and with it the life of consciousness, by rejoining their peers and the would-be revolutionaries.

The psychology of revolution

The friends dress and race downstairs, thrilled by the unexpected summons. For the first time none of them takes the lift which (shot always claustrophobically from within and accompanied by the disorienting roar of Hendrix) recalls the title sequence at the Eiffel Tower. Both representations make machinery monstrous and hint at the repressive effects of the old structures. Now on the street, far from experiencing a tightly constrained, vertical descent, the youngsters are swept into an enormous crowd, far bigger than any previous march, and move forward, taking up the chant that calls others to turn out and join in solidarity.

Matthew has been aware of the gathering impact of the *événements*, having observed on his date with Isabelle the immense piles of uncollected garbage in the streets and having seen televised news coverage of demonstrations. By May 1968, as Jill Forbes notes, the popular base of the *événements* had widened well beyond the cinéphiles and students who had started them to embrace large numbers of workers (including, for example, many from both the service industries and factories). These men and women were aggrieved by poor wages which had failed to improve in line with France's postwar rising prosperity but also by antiquated industrial management and authoritarian labour relations (1992: 15).

Some reviewers, perhaps with the scale of the historical *événements* in mind, have claimed that the film's ending is glib (Vincendeau 2004: 42), unsatisfactory (French 2004a) or forced, striking a false note (Bradshaw 2004). These objections appear not to recognise that the macro and micro political events are entwined to the very end. The break-up of the trio (the domestic *événement*) is brought about by another of Théo's stratagems. He resolves to join a group throwing Molotov cocktails at the CRS and challenges the others to go forward with him. He may be responding to Matthew's charge that he fails to act on his radical ideals. However, he has a more immediately self-interested motivation. Théo knows full well that the pacifist Matthew would never follow him into violent rioting whereas his sister cannot resist an opportunity for dramatising herself. His challenge is thus a device to reclaim Isabelle and sever her from Matthew, and it succeeds. Defying Matthew's attempts to persuade him that the proper methods of resistance use reason and love, Théo grabs his sister's arm, runs forward with her and takes shelter behind an improvised barricade before lighting and tossing his bottle. Matthew has time only to turn and make his way back through the mass of demonstrators before the black forms of the heavily armed CRS silhouetted against the flames charge forward in slow motion, overwhelming the camera and the crowd.

At this, the film's conclusion, our three young protagonists are lost among the marchers, themselves also dreamers conjuring in their minds the death of the old and birth of a new social order in France.

After the storm

What was the impact of the *événements* on France? Roger Ebert, a tourist in Paris that spring, had vivid memories of being caught between the barricades and the CRS. Reviewing *The Dreamers*, he recalled the excitement felt by young people such as himself on both sides of the Atlantic. Fifty years later, however, his analysis of that period was coloured both by nostalgia and what glum middle-aged men like to term 'realism': 'It is clear now that Godard and sexual liberation were never going to change the world. It only seemed that way, for a time. The people who really run things do not go much to the movies, or perhaps think much about sex. They are driven by money and power' (Ebert 2004).

Whatever the motivation of politicians, Ebert dismisses the impact of 1968 too sweepingly. Other commentators put a more positive cast on the issue, observing that agreements and laws were put in place which provided for across-the-board pay increases, greater recognition of trade union rights, participatory management and reforms of the higher education system. In the broader perspective, although the political consequences of May 1968 were not seen immediately and were produced by a wider set of circumstances, the death of Gaullism and the rebirth of the left can indirectly be attributed to the *événements*: 'Above all, the Events of May 1968 led to a questioning of the exercise of power in society. They revealed the possibility that power structures could change and that political activity could alter human relations . . .' (Forbes 1992: 16). That, of course, is what excited Bertolucci about that year – and that the fever for change had an international dimension since 1968 was also a year of protest in America. There massive anti-war marches occurred in Washington and the Democratic Convention in Chicago was disrupted when demonstrators clashed with police for several days. Although it was to be seven long years before the USA finally withdrew humiliated from Vietnam, the pressure of the American peace movement was in part responsible for bringing that infamous war to an end.

Heroes and siblings

Matthew's rejection by the twins brings his personal journey to a turning point. It can be mapped onto the archetypal mythic and psychological quest of the hero. As we saw in Chapter 2, the classic quest of the hero, if it succeeds, entails some or all of the following phases. The adventure starts with separation from the individual's familiar milieu and a journey across borders. For Matthew, quitting San Diego to go to Paris, the move is geographical, cultural and spiritual. The aspirant undergoes one or a number of tests or trials and is exposed to conflict at the risk of injury or even death. The events in the apartment conform to this pattern no less significantly for their having occurred between intimates. Should the individual succeed, he or she will have undergone transformation at a deep level. Although Matthew has not gained the visible trophy which often signifies the achievement of this goal, there can be no doubting the transformation of his personality.

Formerly his mother's son, a clever, innocent and somewhat puritanical boy, he has been changed through the joy and suffering of his love for Isabelle and Théo into a well-rounded man with his own strong moral convictions that are now based on lived experience. Although his refusal to hurl firebombs does not conform to the behaviour of mainstream action movie heroes, his confident assertion of what he knows to be right reveals the inner metamorphosis that has taken place and truly qualifies him as such. Eventually, like the archetypal hero, Matthew will return home, taking with him the self-knowledge gained from his journey.

The case of the twins is other. They are still living in their family milieu. Although the parents' departure on holiday does alter their circumstances so that they are free to explore their sexuality in ways that would not have otherwise been possible, separation from their prior circumstances is only partial. They devise all the tests, except only for Matthew's challenging invitation to Isabelle; and the underlying dynamic of all these tests strengthens the *status quo*, the twins' psychologically incestuous union. They are in command, as opposed to Matthew's experience of undergoing trials enforced upon him. Only after Matthew has become Isabelle's lover and challenges the twins to divide do they face conflict: Isabelle a conflict of desires, Théo a fight for control. In the outturn, as we saw, they refuse the separation that would break them out of the uroboric state. If Isabelle and Théo change psychologically at all, it is only that they end up being more intensely what they always were.

In terms of their individual psyches, therefore, the twins do not take the heroic journey. Yet, pulling Isabelle along with him, Théo makes the film's only grand gesture like an action movie hero, a risky all-or-nothing dash forward to the barricades. Given that he is toting a Molotov cocktail and the CRS are armed with riot guns, it is a quasi-suicidal act. It can be interpreted, when read as a personal statement, as the twins' assertion of refusal to change no matter what destructive consequences may befall. To limit our reading to the personal, however, would leave out of account the political dimension of their actions. By joining the rioting on the streets, the twins contribute to the movement that was to bring down the old authoritarian regime.

It is possible, thanks to Samuels's discussion of siblings, to see their activism as symbolising a redistribution of power. He argues that siblings provide an image that stands in the family microcosm for a certain kind of politics in society at large. In this, horizontal relationships (of the kind nurtured between siblings when in opposition to parents they develop radical new ideas cooperatively) challenge vertical relationships with authority (the child's struggle against parental power): 'In their ineluctable resistance to parental and societal authority, siblings speak for a decentralized style of leadership that eschews the erection of authority figures . . .' (Samuels 2001: 98).

This is the structure underpinning the dynamics of the societal struggle represented in *The Dreamers*. It has the potential to undercut, or at least reduce emphasis on the 'heroic leadership' of a lionised patriarch. Such a structure can, in Samuels's judgement, lead to a politics of temporary alliance in which the partners educate each other and a beneficial fluidity of policy-making results. In practice, however, such leadership usually fails in political terms because the siblings grow up and become the parents, losing their radical edge (2001: 99). The history of French government since the 1970s attests to the acuity of this insight and confirms the accuracy with which Adair and Bertolucci positioned Théo and Isabelle precisely in the psychological nexus between the personal (sexual) and the public (political).

Politics, audience and author

Bertolucci had a political objective in making *The Dreamers*. He wanted it to offer 'a message of hope to the youth of today. There's a big difference between then and now. In 1968 there was a perception of the future, an assumption that the world could get better and that you'd be a part of that. Today that's not the case' (Bertolucci cited by Brooks 2004). To achieve his political goal, *The Dreamers* would at least have had to dramatise the *événements* more fully, giving today's young audiences opportunities to feel the urgent motivation driving those who took to the streets. As it is, the film offers only glimpses of the manifestations – too little for those who do not know the history of 1968 to understand its significance. Therefore *The Dreamers* communicated more effectively with the generation represented on screen (audience members in their fifties and sixties) because in 1968 the dreams and voices of the young made themselves felt on campuses across Europe and the USA in ways not previously known and which touched many young people deeply at the time.

Bertolucci seems not to have been aware that the young in the early twenty-first century – certainly in the UK and USA – pay scant attention to the political history of their parents' and grandparents' eras. They know little of 1960s cinema and nothing of the European New Wave that Bertolucci celebrates so lovingly. Although they are better acquainted with the rock and pop of that decade, their knowledge is owed to the music industry which finds it easier and more profitable than the film industry to recirculate its products. It might have helped the young audience engage with his political themes had he found a way of referring to demonstrations against the second war in Iraq – a burning issue which for months before and after the release of *The Dreamers* aroused the anger around much of the globe not only of the young but their parents too. Then the film might have pointed a clear direction for its time. That it did not was particularly sad in a period of history when governments claiming to be the moral leaders of the western world had, on the most favourable assessment, been guilty of appalling judgement in invading Iraq. And in the all too probable worst case, they had lied, deceived and misled their peoples. The moral force of what was achieved in 1968 could indeed have offered a message of renewal in 2003–4.

Bertolucci, taking command of the material and revising Adair's novel to fulfil his vision for the screen, is the first and last dreamer here (Brooks 2004). In this film he finally resolved the conundrum he had cogitated on more than 30 years earlier: 'For me it's very difficult to succeed in mixing together the idea of beauty that I have as a moral fact and a reduction of reality in political terms, exactly because I think they are two irreconcilable things' (Bertolucci cited by Purdon 1971: 7). *The Dreamers* is indeed the Bertolucci film which weaves together sex, psychoanalysis, dreaming, politics (albeit primarily a personal politics) and cinema. I argued when discussing *Stealing Beauty* that he allowed spectators to sense his own involvement in anima politics through that film's stylistic excess. In *The Dreamers* too, aesthetic control guides the weave, but to a different end than in the earlier film since on this occasion anima politics is not his concern.

For reasons touched on in Chapter 3, it has been a long time since Bertolucci employed a rough-cut aesthetic comparable to the 1960s French New Wave. In this film he deploys wherever possible a gliding Steadicam to produce a mysterious way of moving as if on wings (Bertolucci in Thompson 2003). Steadicam shots tend to show objects in the world around the characters sliding into and slipping out of the frame. In the apartment, for instance, the gliding camera makes the relationship between characters and place organic, as Bertolucci intended, turning the place into a sort of character. In this context, the visual device links actuality and dream. *Mise-en-scène* develops the political aspect of both: the contrast between Théo's room with its posters tacked up over torn wallpaper and the genteel decor of the rest of the place projects the conflict between the generations into the narrative after the parents have decamped. And the increasing seediness of the apartment signals the shift in power as between old and young. The camera draws the audience in, seeking to make them part of what it witnesses. For a scene inside the Cinémathèque, Bertolucci asked Cianchetti to have his camera as nearly as possible invade the cinema screen when Sam Fuller's *Shock Corridor* is playing. He wanted to show fusion between the screen and the Cinémathèque audience. The Steadicam's gliding movement throughout much of the film seems to express the desire to extend that attempt at fusion to produce the same effect for audiences watching his own movie.

The clips intercut throughout *The Dreamers* play into Bertolucci's narrative in complex ways, affecting the mood and anticipating or echoing plot developments. Some have a playful function, like the citation of *Bande à part* and *Queen Christina*. Some are elegiac (*A Bout de Souffle* and Françoise Hardy's 'Tous les garçons et les filles' have this quality), others sombre (suicide in Robert Bresson's *Mouchette*). Several have an undertow which in the context Bertolucci places them in is menacing (*Shock Corridor*, Jimi Hendrix's 'Third Stone from the Sun' and *Freaks*). And Marlene Dietrich revealing herself, by stripping off the paws and head of a great ape costume that conceal her, combines the eroticism and sadism for which she was renowned.

These various factors, added to Bertolucci's long-standing wish to direct a film about 1968 and the wit and passion of *The Dreamers*, all make it impossible to doubt that there is an authorial energy behind it. The ambivalent values of the clips enhance rather than detract from this presence. Their conflicting registers enrich a characteristic that pervades the film. Its ambivalence produces the sense that Bertolucci has (to adapt Jung's term) circumambulated his material, perusing it from a variety of psychological perspectives. For example, in the personal drama we see that the three young people are mature and childish, gorgeous and slovenly, intelligent and naive. We are perfectly positioned to view them both tenderly and with amusement. In the political domain, replaying the fiery speeches of '68 switches us back to that year and gives us a lived sense of history through documentary footage. But the device also functions to the contrary end by showing us the comfortable bourgeois figures that Jean-Pierre Kalfon and Jean-Pierre Léaud have since become.

Bertolucci's overarching vision offers perspectives on the characters and *événements* from a variety of points of view, holding opposites in tension. Notwithstanding the substantial contributions of Adair, cast and crew, it bears (appropriately for a film that celebrates the New Wave) the stamp of a passionate, thinking authorial personality. That personality seems to me to have the qualities of a wise old man. An archetypal figure which Jung found surfacing when guidance is needed, the wise old person points to the future by bringing meaning out of bewildering confusion (1948: 217–20). The thought that this figure is energised is particularly interesting given that Bertolucci had lost his own father three years before the release of *The Dreamers*: '. . . having a father who is 90 means that you are still in the position of being the son. Then he dies and you grow up, and already you are an old man. So I feel as though I have gone straight from adolescence to old age without ever being an adult' (Bertolucci cited in Brooks 2004).

In *The Dreamers* the wise old man has overseen a therapeutic process of anamnesis (recovery into memory) of material that had once been conscious and later lapsed (Jung 1946b: 95–6). If the film is now read as representing the psychological self-exploration of the *auteur* as wise old man, anamnesis of 1968 suggests that the parents' departure complements the reframing (albeit regretful) of incest fantasies. They are now set in a wider context where uroboric attachments, however seductive their invitation to resist the world into which the young adult must move, can be recognised as, even for an artist, a potentially injurious entrapment. Thus recognition of the demerits of the twins' uroboric interdependency *vis-à-vis* Matthew's new, albeit painful, self-sufficiency hints at a clear step toward self-discovery or individuation. It vindicates the sense that, although the film may not have had the kind of impact on its audiences for which Bertolucci hoped, he succeeded as *auteur* in summoning his wise old man in fashioning his text.

Chapter 6

Anima and the political dynamics of cultural stasis: the case of *S1møne*[1]

Introduction: the provenance

S1møne (USA, 2002) is a reworking of the Pygmalion story set in present-day Hollywood. Only one character recognises the likeness to the older story of the events which have caught up the lead protagonists. But Lainey (Evan Rachel Wood) is a teenager, and all the adults in this satire on Hollywood's paranoid potentates (her parents among them), *know* that nobody understands stories other than themselves. As if never off camera, these loud empty vessels act larger than life to reassure themselves that they matter to the industry and the movie-going public. Their arrogance fails to conceal ignorant vulgarity; it also lets them ignore the child's perceptive ideas.

Lainey, who has read the original story, is the only character in a position to appreciate that a strong current of misogyny and an even stronger current of self-delusion run through the several generations of the Pygmalion tale. In Ovid's *Metamorphoses*, Pygmalion, King of Cyprus, had for many years lived a bachelor existence because he was 'revolted by the many faults which nature has implanted in the female sex' (1955: 231). Eventually he carved for himself an ivory statue of a woman which he found to be lovelier than any living female, and fell in love with his own creation:

> Often he ran his hands over the work, feeling it to see whether it was flesh or ivory, and would not yet admit that ivory was all it was. He kissed the statue, and imagined that it kissed him back, spoke to it and embraced it, and thought he felt his fingers sink into the limbs he touched, so that he was afraid lest a bruise appear where he had pressed the flesh.

1 I owe grateful thanks to Joanna Dovalis for her guidance on the psychoanalytical reading of the film.

In response to his prayers, Venus gave the statue life and presided over Pygmalion's marriage to the newly-created woman. Nine months later a child was born to the happy couple.

In George Bernard Shaw's play *Pygmalion* (1912) (as well as *My Fair Lady*, the Broadway musical spin-off of 1956, and the 1964 film of the same name) the story centres on the transformation of Eliza Doolittle, a Cockney flower girl, at the hands of Henry Higgins. Shaw too made his male protagonist a bachelor in his middle years, but his was a comic figure, a cantankerous, self-opinionated snob who cannot see himself as others do. His brutal manner with the young woman is so crude it speaks of both his insulation as a cocooned upper-middle class Londoner, and his complete lack of self-knowledge. Yet his physical and social clumsiness endow him with a ghastly innocence which, together with his enthusiastic energy, becomes a source of amusement for the audience and one of his redeeming features (Morgan 1980: 51–2). So strong are his self-centred delusions that Higgins believes he is Eliza's teacher. As a researcher of phonetics and teacher of elocution, he attempts to turn the flower girl into a fine lady by giving her lessons in received pronunciation, not caring whether the forced translation from poverty to the social insulation of upper-middle class mores will benefit or ruin her. In truth, however, Higgins is really Eliza's clueless student, and the play focuses on his education into the ranks of humanity.

S1møne draws on both these predecessors but reworks them. Andrew Niccol, who previously scripted *The Truman Show* (1998), wrote and directed this film, turning his satirical eye away from megalomania in the TV industry toward the same condition in the movie studios. His Pygmalion is Lainey's father, Hollywood film director Viktor Taransky (Al Pacino). Niccol drops Shaw's silent allusions to *Cinderella*, but plays with his idea of mutual education between a powerful man and a young woman. The film preserves elements of Shaw's comedic but serious register and darkens it with satire. It also draws from both its predecessors the theme of a man bringing his ideal to life by art.[2] Shaw politicised the impact of this folly by focusing on the class inequalities between Higgins and Eliza; and the film version *My Fair Lady* was faithful to Shaw in this respect. Since *S1møne* mocks the stereotypes both of the creative genius and of Hollywood as a political minefield, it too follows Shaw's play. In Hollywood, art and industry politics go hand in glove, so it is no surprise to find that Viktor's creation of his ideal woman cannot long remain untouched by industry and public expectations. She too becomes politicised.

2 Although Higgins is too blind to himself to know it, the same desire to bring to life his ideal that drove Ovid's Pygmalion motivates his meddling in Eliza Doolittle's life.

Trading in goddesses

Where Ovid linked his story with the supernatural, Shaw dropped this aspect altogether. Nonetheless, Ovid's verses resonate intriguingly with *S1møne* in that, like Pygmalion's statue, Simone (Rachel Roberts) is a virtual, not a real woman. As such she takes on characteristics of the anima. Far from being real, she comprises elements of the women of overweening significance to Viktor, film stars, since he draws upon the traits of many of them in composing Simone. So in the first instance she is his projection, but her genealogy makes her a distillation of the screen goddess stereotype. She soon begins to awaken a passionate fan base. Then both indirectly through their appetite to see more of her, and directly through her personality, she commences to exert influence over Viktor's life.

Viktor was in deep trouble before Simone came into his life. Despite his panic-driven best efforts, he had failed adequately to groom his then leading lady with the absurd flattery she demanded as a bankable star and would-be goddess. He had not managed (though only by an inch) to provide tyrannical Nicola (Wynona Ryder) with the biggest trailer on the studio lot. But that was insult enough: ranting at the imagined humiliation from the depths of her empty being, she stages a preplanned walk off the movie. Her pathological sense of entitlement is fed by a need to be seen, acknowledged and validated as if she were truly known by the whole world. In her narcissism she suffers from the morbid lack which lies behind the craven appetite for popularity endemic in Hollywood. It soon becomes apparent that Viktor is possessed by the same sick state of mind.

Rescued by the trickster

With his production *Sunrise Sunset* half in the can, Viktor finds himself in desperate need of a new leading lady. It makes matters no easier that his studio head is Lainey's mother, his ex-wife Elaine (Catherine Keener), who has lost faith in his capacity to deliver a saleable product. Facing professional meltdown, he is unexpectedly rescued by a computer genius. Hank Aleno (Elias Koteas) bequeaths Viktor a software package, Simulation One, which enables its user electronically to generate a virtual actor so perfect that her performances pass as those of a live player. Viktor deploys the software secretly to insert Simone (her name an abridgement of the package that gives her existence) into the role that Nicola has abandoned. The studio executives, including Elaine, are taken in. Thrilled with Simone's performance and under the illusion that they have a new flesh and blood star on the lot, they release Viktor's film. Simone receives overwhelming media attention and soon becomes the object of rising public acclaim.

A number of reviewers have remarked that *S1møne* touches on Hollywood's fear of digital visual effects. For example, Kate Stables writes:

'Viktor surely represents a consoling fantasy for Old Hollywood that Art, in the person of the director, can win out over ever-encroaching Science, as film becomes increasingly a digital domain' (2002: 56). This is what Viktor believes about himself; but as an argument concerning the film's themes it is mistaken. It might be convincing if firstly, Viktor had control of the figure he has created and secondly, the movies he directs with Simone were artistic triumphs. In fact his lead actress wins the plaudits while reviewers knock the films themselves as inferior product. The clips that we see confirm their scepticism. However, audiences are so caught up in the adulation of Simone that they do not notice the quality of the films. Instead they clamour to see the star in the flesh (or failing that on TV). Greedily amplified by the media, this demand is a main factor ensuring that Viktor cannot fully control his invention.

It was objected that the film does not sufficiently acknowledge 'the real-life mixture of graft and infatuation involved in the painstaking creation of vactors [*sic*]'. This overlooks the catastrophe that destroys Hank. He dies from an inoperable tumour of the eye contracted through overexposure to the screen during countless hours spent crazily creating his phantom mate: 'I licked skin, I licked hair, I licked every part of her.' Karten (2002) notes the likeness between Viktor's story and Mary Shelley's *Frankenstein* (1818), the mad scientist who, seeking fame, creates a monster that kills its human creator. However, it is Hank who plays *S1møne's* Frankenstein and hands the role to Viktor as his legacy. The terminal damage Hank has suffered to his eye suggests blindness inflicted by obsession which, metaphorically speaking, Viktor contracts through his own fixation.

Viktor's success with Simone is based on a fraud which Hank tempts him to carry out. Seen from the perspective of Jungian psychology, the very manner of Hank's furtive, late-night appearance at Viktor's side as the latter prepares to leave the studio for the last time reveals Hank's shadowy nature. He represents Viktor's liability to suffer a Frankensteinian calamity should he not reach some understanding of his inner desires, at present so seriously out of kilter with his outer life. But Hank, who bequeaths Viktor the software only because he thinks that the director will bring his dream woman before the public eye, is that special instance of the shadow, the trickster. As we saw with Kubrick's Milich, the trickster can be thief, prankster or cheat, but at the same time has the power to bring revelation and with it the reconciliation of the opposing elements of a personality. By endowing Viktor with Simone, who turns into a dangerous anima, Hank (because of rather than despite his sinister qualities) faces Viktor with the darkness implicit in his own personality and thereby offers him the most valuable gift conceivable. Viktor has looked at the screen (and at life off the screen too) with only his conscious mind, and not his inner eye. He has long suffered a form of blindness himself, but through Hank's gift he will eventually gain a measure (albeit quite limited) of painfully hard-won insight. As John Beebe has shown in relation to Hitchcock's *Notorious* and Spielberg's *Schindler's List*, the trickster plays a pivotal role in integrating the anima into the personality so that the individual can increase his or her self-knowledge (1990: 33; 1996: 584–6). Viktor's sanity and life will be imperilled by the anima as she deploys with increasing potency her monstrous aspect; but in the outturn, she will fail to destroy him because he reaches an accommodation with her.

Ego's adventures with anima

Simone has been described as Viktor's (or any director's) dream; an actor under his complete artistic control who will do anything he wants and never complain (Haro 2002). Of course no human being, whether actor or not, can in reality be totally subservient without injuring the personality. But images that rise from the unconscious and semi-conscious realms of the mind may for a time (though not indefinitely) appear to obey the wants and desires of the individual. Simone, viewed through the analytical psychologist's lens, can be read as a projection by Viktor of such an anima figure, the supple, bewitching and endlessly transforming wraith which tends, exactly here, to play a major role in the life of a man when he is going through a period of psychological change. In such a case it can help open an individual's inner life (Jung 1935: 188–211). At the same time, as the object (more accurately the creation) of emotionally driven but ill-focused desire, the anima is a dangerous seducer because she can take over a man's soul and trammel him in a thousand painful knots. This also is true of Simone. But, equally typical of the anima, the pain Simone causes will eventually lead Viktor to a measure of self-knowledge and help him rebalance his life. Ultimately, as that process moves on, she herself will change with Viktor's changing take on the world.

As I mentioned when discussing *Eyes Wide Shut*, Jung believed that the anima stands in compensatory relationship to the persona, the mask that an individual shows to the world (1935: 192–5). It follows that where, as with Simone's vapid blandness, the anima is restricted in its range, the persona must be equally limited. This is true of Viktor, 'so monomaniacally focused on his career' (Grady 2002) that his specious persona as a supposedly gifted film director has locked onto him to the point of almost excluding other personality traits. Every imagined threat to his position in the film industry seems in his paranoia to condemn him to oblivion. Moulded by fear, the mask with which Viktor faces the closed hothouse of his professional world seldom deviates from the media man's false bonhomie. It's a fair guess that his emotional rigidity has contributed to his failure as a husband; and, although he says he loves Lainey, as her father he gives her little of his time.

As we have already had ample occasion to notice, every archetypal image, including the anima and persona, expresses more than the psychological particularities of the individual in whose mind it first arises. Just as humans in social groupings share their signifying systems and hence their discourse, so too in post-Jungian theory they share the drives and unconscious energies that give rise to such highly charged images (Fredericksen 2001: 15–55; Izod 2001: 33–56). To follow this line of thought in connection with *S1mone* is to find that the much remarked vacuity of the film's virtual screen goddess should be read to reveal not just Viktor's personal delusions but those harboured by the film's other characters, since she is adopted as an anima figure by them all. They include the director's industry peers, the media and Simone's on-screen audiences. The supposed universality of Simone's allure cannot be missed when Viktor blends into her face, voice and mannerisms the traces of many stars whose mass appeal is beyond question – Jane Fonda, Audrey Hepburn, Grace Kelly, Meryl Streep and Lauren Bacall.

The attraction that fans feel for stars, tending as it may to encompass a sense of identification and even empathy, has its source in affect. Devotees respond to stars with what can be intense emotions. Their enthusiasm elevates stars to the status of icons – and strips them of glory when the popular passion wanes. From the psychoanalytical standpoint, stars have much in common with religious icons. They express the archetypal drives of those people (in films, the key creative members of the teams around them) who shape them as representations. Complementing this, they stimulate the constellation (the arousal and focusing) of similar energies in those spectators who respond to them (Beebe 2001: 209–11; Hockley 2001: 116; Izod 2001: 79–104). Simone as anima not only expresses something of Viktor's need for soul-making, she chimes with and amplifies the like needs in her fans. Her image exemplifies the manner in which popular culture, when it coalesces around star icons, amounts to more than the negotiated exchange of the signs that construct human discourse (though it depends upon that process too). It engages ineluctably with the symbolic and the archetypal – and in Simone's case, the expressing and popularising (politicising) of a particular inflection of the anima.

The popular response to Simone's first screen role is so great that Viktor has to deal with it. With no woman to reveal in the flesh to studio executives, not to mention the press and her clamouring public, he has no choice but to embark on an unending series of deceptions. What makes the hoax psychoanalytically all the more telling is that, although Simone has her own synthesised voice, her words can only mimic Viktor. When the press interviews her by remote link, he speaks her response into a microphone. A nanosecond later the simulation package utters his words through Simone's mouth as inevitably as Echo followed Narcissus. Indeed, Pacino plays these scenes like just such a lonely, self-obsessed man as Narcissus, with a persuasive blend of vaingloriousness (Simone endlessly praising his work) and pathos (at those times when she becomes his sole confidante).

The psychological dynamic of the relationship between these two was described by Susan Kavaler-Adler writing about the Pygmalion type before this film was made. As here, typically, both parties are narcissistic; but whilst in that respect they mirror each other, there is an imbalance of power. Although they are each other's muse, Pygmalion always tries to dominate as a father figure. In due course the intensity of the relationship between them may form a quasi-incestuous passion, whether actual or in the imagination, in which (as we saw when describing the psychology of several women in *Stealing Beauty*) the male's possessiveness can be felt as the demon lover's sadistic lust (Kavaler-Adler 1996: 89). Yet the male muse also confers an incandescent, god-like aura on 'his' female artist. Male muses who confer this mystique enact the same psychic function as narcissistic parents because they mirror her as a special figure, while neglecting her emotional needs. Those needs form a vacuum which nurtures an addiction in the female artist to a grandiose self-image. Kavaler-Adler shows that the female artist's cravings for control can combine with her lust for the sadistic aspect of him to the extent that she becomes possessed. And although Simone is a virtual rather than an actual being, in sense she does become possessed in that Viktor's and her quasi-incestuous love will in due time give birth to a creature which threatens to become a monster (1996: 56, 89).

Anima plays with ego

Many of the words Viktor puts in Simone's mouth are those which the press and her public require of her. The perfect actor over whom he had total control, now, through her popular dimension as a cultural phenomenon, proves anything but biddable, however demure her on-screen presence. Simone as the anima, an activated archetypal image, is beginning to take over his life. Given the nature of their electronic and psychological relationships, it is not surprising that occasionally they let fall words which tell us more about him than her. Explaining why she will not be present on the set for her second film *Eternity Forever*, Simone tells her co-stars, 'I relate better to people when they're not actually there.' ('Of course. Of course!' they gabble enthusiastically.) As a revelation of intimate titbits, this is public relations gobbledygook uttered by Simone for the tabloid press. But before they became hers, these were Viktor's words, and they speak his Narcissus nature.

After faking public appearances for Simone, electronically keying her into a TV chat show and even arranging a concert before 100,000 adoring fans, Viktor finds he has succeeded only in amplifying the clamour of press and fans alike for more contact. The turning point comes when Simone wins Oscars for best actress in both her films! In her acceptance speech (supposedly live by satellite from a shanty town she is visiting on her Third World tour) she thanks all her collaborators but omits to name Viktor. This is crucial because as always he both wrote and recorded her script but, in an untypical Freudian slip, left out her usual warm acknowledgement of him. The omission signals a crisis. As a figure generated in Viktor's unconscious, Simone has been gathering strength for some while. We have previously seen her interrupt him disconcertingly with thoughts he would rather not have uttered, but which just, as it were, slip out, such as 'You're going to get in an awful lot of trouble, Mr Taransky!' Now, however, as a voice from his unconscious, she has actually succeeded in obstructing the expression of Viktor's conscious will.

Slighting the goddess

This incident jolts Viktor and he decides to free himself from Simone by desecrating her image, in effect attempting to quell the anima. However, as we saw when discussing *Eyes Wide Shut*, Jung identified the ability of archetypal images to take on a degree of autonomy through the ungovernable energy with which they constellate. It gives them what appears to be an independent existence of their own. In extreme cases, 'If there is already a predisposition to psychosis, it may even happen that the archetypal figures, which are endowed with a certain autonomy anyway on account of their natural numinosity, will escape from conscious control altogether and become completely independent, thus producing the phenomena of possession' (1954a: 39). When an individual tormented by an archetypal image tries to repress it, Jung's observations suggest that it can become charged with even greater dynamic energy to rebound into consciousness in a darker or more monstrous form (1954a: 63).

In Viktor's first doomed attempt to destroy the goddess, he gives her the starring role in *I Am Pig*. The only clip from it that we see ends his film with Simone on her knees in a wedding dress covered with muck and grubbing for food among penned swine. The filth of her wedding dress signals the state of her and Viktor's relationship and the silent pun Pig/Pyg[malion] reminds us that, since Simone is his anima, he too is made pig by his treatment of her. Viktor has assumed wrongly that he can manipulate the image of the female as he wishes without suffering any personal damage. The injury to his mental health will become all too clear when he tries to kill off his star.

The psychology of tabloid culture

In the meantime *I Am Pig* delights Simone's public. This is particularly interesting given the activities of the film's populist press. As Steve Rhodes (2002) says, the tabloids have been on a feeding frenzy since the release of *Sunrise Sunset*: 'They desperately need answers to some important questions about the never seen-in-person actress. The first of these crucial questions is, "Who is Simone dating?" The tabloids go wild trying to get the dirt on her, using everything from spy satellites to bribery'.

This is our cue to detour and link cultural theory with post-Jungian concepts of anima and animus by examining the brutalising pattern of the British and North American tabloid press in conferring stardom on individuals who are in the public eye. Each is made a cynosure, lauded for looks, personality or talent which the press, working in conjunction with the celebrity's agents, augments (or invents). However, these gifts are only loans and the papers' editorial teams call them in ruthlessly at any moment they choose. Having first fed, the tabloids next disgorge, smearing the star with all the muck they can rake and spew (*I Am Pig*!). Thus they pursue an endless cycle of raising, then fouling the anima and (since famous men also fall victim of the same process) its converse, the animus. Whilst this vicious circle does not destroy the career of every celebrity the tabloids manhandle (since stars' survival requires an addictive dependency on publicity), it must do psychological damage. For the stars themselves it augments the tendency to unhealthy narcissism. And the cumulative impact of an endless succession of king-making and regicide injures audiences by diminishing their sensibility while slighting ancient rituals of growth and decay.

The economic interests of the press are plain. Lionising the famous only to demean them through tittle-tattle and calumny is their policy because it has sold newspapers for more than a century. No denying then that in this theme the popular press stimulates and holds the interest of large sectors of the North American and British publics. But what psychological processes are at work here? The cycle is so insistent as to declare that the unconscious or semi-conscious needs of large numbers of people must be excited by this form of trough-feeding. For two reasons, however, we cannot assume we are dealing with a universal phenomenon; and as a consequence we cannot refer it directly to the collective unconscious – which Jung's observations taught him all humanity shares at a deep level. First, every fan offers devotion to a particular star but may well dismiss other luminaries in the same firmament; and second, there are many people who are not touched by the star phenomenon at all. It is therefore preferable to infer an excitation of unconscious or semi-conscious appetites in self-selecting segments of the population.

The concept of the *cultural unconscious* enables this differentiation. It extends post-Jungian theories of the psyche, positing a less deeply buried level of unconsciousness based on the recognition that social and cultural pressures conjoin their considerable influence with many other factors in forming all but those images generated by the most profoundly hermetic psychological forces. Jung himself said that conscious and unconscious 'have no clear demarcations, the one beginning where the other leaves off. It is rather the case that the psyche is a conscious-unconscious whole' (1954d: 200). Richard M. Gray developed this thought, remarking that 'the closer to consciousness the archetypal influence is led, the more easily its external form is determined by environmental factors' (1996: 72). This is the realm that has become known as the cultural unconscious.

Rushing and Frentz describe the cultural unconscious as the site of a collision of psychic energies from two separate origins – archetypal images having their source in the collective unconscious, and repressed contradictions from oppressive social formations (1991: 391). Their formulation is unnecessarily constrictive. Repression is indeed often a key contributor to the building up of psychic energies that show when the cultural unconscious gives up its secrets in such projections as those upon popular stars. However, the joyful enthusiasm of fans for the stars with whom they say they 'identify' provides evidence that many people introject images that are desired. Such images may well possess an archetypal quality felt in the deep emotions that they arouse. Rather than only permitting a recovery of repressed complexes, they may equally well represent a blossoming in the individual's psyche – healthy new growth embedded in the shared excitement of a star's fan group.

There is, then, much at stake here. Andrew Samuels suggests that the cultural unconscious may be thought of in two ways. Firstly it may be conceived as a repository of cultural experience. Alternatively it could be understood as the means, already existing as a potential, by which the human psyche gives birth to cultural difference and then reinforces it. In fact, for analysts of popular culture attempting to account for the production and consumption of symbols, there is much to recommend Samuels's guess that it has both functions (1993: 328). Such a perspective endows the cultural unconscious with a sphere of influence far wider than that described by Rushing and Frentz. The way that film stars are propagated by the studios and received by the public helps demonstrate the point and shows how culturally available images can be seized upon as markers of difference which arise, seeming to be almost (but not quite, since collective consciousness also has a function in perpetuating these images) ready-formed, from the cultural repository to which Samuels refers.

What then is the meaning, considered in terms that might complement our understanding of the cultural unconscious, of the ceaseless cycle of creating and destroying stars in tabloid journalism? A good place to start is with Jung's concept of *enantiodromia*. He argued from observation of his patients that every archetype, every psychological extreme, contains the seed of a conversion into its opposite. In time it will show a tendency to run toward that opposite (1954b: 266, 271–2). So good turns to evil and dark eventually returns to light. The creation and subsequent destruction of heroic or godlike figures can be comprehended within this cyclical pattern. It is not a new phenomenon in human culture, as the fate of the year kings of old, tied to the changing of the seasons, testifies. In our own epoch, the elevation of sporting stars and their subsequent early sacrifice to time as the years despoil their prowess has much the same quality (see Izod 2001: 124–42). But nowhere in our culture is *enantiodromia* shown more clearly than in the accelerated cycle of elevation and desecration of celebrities in the tabloids. Here we witness the conjunction of archetypes with the cultural. Archetypal images – such as the gods and goddesses imbricated in the formal religions – change slowly and over long periods of time. By contrast, cultural images – such as those of screen gods and goddesses – alter according to a rhythm dictated by the interlinked changes in discourse and culture which themselves are connected to the historical movements of the societies that generate and receive these images. The pace of cultural change in western societies, it hardly needs noting, accelerated through the twentieth century.

The tabloids urge onward a cyclical process already deeply embedded in the cultural and economic structures of capitalist societies – the elevation to the highest good of the rights, needs and expressions of the individual. If the great corporations are to survive, they must constantly increase the felt needs of the people who constitute their markets. This they achieve by marketing their products to satisfy the wants of the individual as paramount. In doing so, advertisers, marketing departments and the media combine to propagate the values of individualism. They have done much to establish a value system which ties wants and desires in an endless cycle to the certainty of built-in obsolescence. What you want so badly today, you obtain not without cost tomorrow, only to find that it soon becomes tiresome when advertisers proffer new objects of desire to supplant the old.

Stars, because they are each identifiable by their unique appearance, are icons *par excellence* of individualism. But they are also little deities who express simultaneously our need for gods and our revulsion from them. The need is as old as human kind and expresses the projection of the human self into the universe. However, the values of individualism are at odds with most formal religions because the latter encourage the devout to subsume their personal sense of selfhood to a belief in the commonality of all those within the Church. While religion tends to de-emphasise the individual's sense of uniqueness, the requirements of advanced capitalism pull in the contrary direction. Mass revulsion from the gods is a modern phenomenon arising from our refusal (as the autonomous, self-defining individuals we believe ourselves to be) submissively to accept being shackled to images of unchanging deities. An unalterable godhead commands an unchallengeable authority which in turn diminishes our significance as individuals. The tabloid processing of stars therefore coincides with, augments and expresses a deep cultural *enantiodromia* surrounding western societies' need for and fear of gods. That fear easily transposes into contempt and envy. It is this which drives the besmirching of star images. Sometimes the loss of reputation amounts to destruction of the particular star. Sometimes the star will recover public favour. Either way the tabloid media orchestrate what amounts to a trivial and corrupting form of sacrifice and rebirth. It is trivial because so little is implicated in the rise and fall of these paragons of individualism. And it is unhealthy both for that reason and because the ordering of these petty but nasty sacrifices and the concomitant manipulation of both stars and audiences occurs only to satisfy the most cynical of commercial considerations.

How does all this connect with the activities of the media in *S1møne*? In the person of tabloid hack Max Sayer (Pruitt Taylor Vince), the press is indeed simultaneously orchestrating devotion to the star and doing all it can to dish the dirt on her. However, the irony is that Viktor has inadvertently timed the release of *I Am Pig*, the production through which he intended to destroy his own media star, so that it anticipates the downswing in press favour. It catches the rhythm of popular expectation and, by desecrating the goddess before the media can do so, elevates her even further. The cycle develops when Simone appears on a morning TV chat show and gives vent to a barrage of counter-orthodox soundbites: 'I just think all elementary schools should have a firing range . . .' 'Immigration: God, isn't it crowded enough?' All this and more is a wild success with her audience. Do they hear what she says or is it just the fact that she has the courage to be controversial and present herself as a drunken, chain-smoking slut that appeals to them? *Time* names her Person of the Year, and the increasingly desperate Viktor remains trapped by his creature.

Style and the perception of meaning

From the point of view of the individual receiving the symbol (the spectator watching the screen), the specifics of a text's rhetorical address are of formative significance. To a significant degree it is the style or manner in which a text addresses recipients which touches the emotions and the deeper layers of the psyche. When spectators experience a culturally-specific symbol that works for them, they feel an excitement which is not aroused by other images, despite the fact that those other images may appeal deeply to many different people. The stardom of Simone illustrates this phenomenon well. Her address to the film's internal audience is integral to their reactions. The ungovernable frenzy of not only her fans but the Hollywood crowd at an A-list party suggests that her image is intuitively perceived as bearing meaning. Meaning is conveyed not only in the words and deeds of the characters she plays, but also through every stylistic facet of her performances – that is, through the rhetorical address embodied by her total screen presence. The strength of feeling of her fans arises from the excitation of cultural unconscious in its role as a repository of differentiated and value-laden experience.

Jung wrote of archetypal behaviour patterns that they 'are the ever-present and biologically necessary regulators of the instinctual sphere, whose range of action covers the whole psyche . . . We may say that the image represents the *meaning* of the instinct' (1954d: 201). He was referring to the collective or transpersonal unconscious. *Mutatis mutandis*, something rather similar can be said of the cultural unconscious where the image, anchored to drives which do not run as deep into the archaic nature of humanity, represents the meaning, usually unrecognised by both those who produce and those others who receive it, of the ideological mesh in which they are caught up.

In *The Armies of the Night* (1968) Norman Mailer expressed the significance of this cultural conjunction with a clarity the prescient acumen of which has not diminished in the intervening years. Mailer, arrested during the October 1967 peace march on the Pentagon, records the experience of being taken to jail with other demonstrators. They are driven on a military bus through the suburban shopping streets of Washington, and Mailer (observing both himself – in the third person – and the scene outside the bus) gazes at the high-school adolescents on the sidewalks . . .

> . . . the kids looking surprisingly like high school kids in Hollywood and TV, the long pants, sweaters, sneakers; the girls in variations on middie blouses and mini-skirts, saddle shoes. A part of him had always tried to believe that the America he saw in family television dramas did not exist, had no power – as of course he knew it did – to direct the styles and the manners and therefore the ideas of America (for in a country where everyone lived so close to their senses, then style, precisely, and manner, precisely, carved ideas into the senses), ideas like conformity, cleanliness, America-is-always-right.
>
> (Mailer 1968: 167)

Mailer's observation, taken in conjunction with post-Jungian hypotheses concerning the cultural and psychological efficacy of archetypal images, supports the idea that, when constellated, anima can (as it were secretly) contribute through the shaping of fashion to the shaping of ideas. As I have said, the fashion that an anima figure might embody reaches to more than clothes, make-up and hair. This is true for Viktor's exact attention to every detail of Simone's appearance, gestures, movements, vocal patterns and soundbites so that her overall style fits with the propagation of an ideology which she embodies implicitly. Thus we move from the anima as manifestation of personal malaise to its politicisation across a culture, all the more potent in that Viktor is one of the elite who have the power to activate the great dream machine of the western world.

Lest the idea of anima embodying political passion seem improbable, we may cite the evocation in late eighteenth-century France of *Liberté* as the figurehead of the revolutionary movement, and contemplate the evolution of that figure. A hundred years later, the French gave the American people a monument to celebrate the centenary of the United States gaining independence. The Statue of Liberty nicely illustrates the *enantiodromian* reversibility of the anima, whether public or private. Once the universally admired celebration of a triumphant revolution against the British, the statue now to half the world signifies quite the opposite – brutal American oppression.

What then does Simone's style mean? It is clearly the product of careful control, evident in the perfection (except only on those occasions when Viktor tries to destroy her image) of her immaculate looks and mannequin gestures. In the domain of the personal, her style and mannerisms convey a solipsism so pure, so monomaniac that she shows no sign of self-awareness. This level of solipsism is the consequence of the intense and unhealthy self-regarding narcissism remarked earlier. It imbues the film's Hollywood personnel in general and both Viktor and Elaine in particular. They esteem other people solely according to the professional advantages that will flow from knowing them. So Simone represents a distillation of the Hollywood 'Me, me, me' ethos. Not surprising, then, that her image intervenes in the dynamics of power relations, as revealed by reactions of the other characters. She also has a striking impact on family politics. This is unmistakable in her effect on Viktor, despite the fact that he is notionally her creator. But it goes further. Thanks to Simone, Viktor recovers professional kudos, which reawakens Elaine's interest in him. Her reaction mixes a new-found sexual jealousy with an attraction to the power he once again commands.

Simone's stardom signifies that the ideology she embodies extends beyond the domain of family politics to infiltrate the mores of substantial sectors of the American people. She is an immaculate icon for beliefs strikingly similar to those of Mailer's middle America revisited 35 years on. The constellation of her meaning across the wider realm of her audiences amplifies narrowly-focused ideological values. Like the kids Mailer gazed at sorrowfully, Simone embodies ideas that complement the solipsism that blinkers her personal vision, 'ideas like conformity, cleanliness, America-is-always-right'. On the national scene the appeal for her on-screen public of those Teflon values is plain enough. For the actual audience, there is an echo here of the bullying political narcissism that characterised the Bush administration's conduct of international relations after the trauma of September 11, 2001.

To take this further, because Simone is an anima figure, her meaning, as with all archetypal images, must have both positive and negative qualities. Both aspects are inherent in her golden-girl beauty. The negative aspect is indicated when Viktor adjusts Simone's appearance. The girl's exquisite image is achieved through an electronic equivalent of the cosmetic surgery that perfects so many Hollywood beauties. The cumulative effect amounts to a sterile passivity which shows in her inability to initiate vigorous action.

It fits with claims made on her behalf that she suffers from the immobilising anxiety disorder agoraphobia. Yet although her pathology is discussed by Viktor, the glamorous syndrome of the golden girl in the golden southern Californian clime is so potent that it veils Simone's sickness from her public.

Simone has her own on-screen animus who complements her negative characteristics. Her co-star Hal Sinclair (Jay Mohr) amplifies her fatuous statement about relating to people better when they are not actually there. A figure no less vacuous than Viktor's original female lead Nicola, Hal boasts to the media about his closeness to her – even though they have never met (Grady 2002). His craven need to claim relationship with her clearly expresses his unhealthy narcissism. Conversely, however, we can read him in inverse mode to show how his need to attach himself to her hints at a potential *enantiodromia* – a way in which Simone's negative associations could (although this never occurs) be transmuted into positive ones.

Her potentially positive qualities, like the negative ones, centre on her looks. Here a concept which analytical psychology adapted to model one form of psychological growth is relevant. It is the idea that beauty has the power to draw the mind toward enlightenment. This thought can be traced back through numerous literary sources – for example, poems by Keats, Spenser's *Faerie Queene*, Dante's love for Beatrice – to Ovid's Pygmalion. Beauty is perceived as having power to transform the beholder. It can bring inner peace and harmony after turmoil, leading the conscious mind to a connection with the Self and drawing the person who observes it toward the realm of religious experience. In order for beauty to lead the mind in that direction, however, the devotee requires an awareness that something numinous lies beyond the image attracting his or her devotion. Simone's beauty is not used in a sacramental way by any of the film's characters because her fans, like their goddess, lack any self-awareness that might reach deeper than the ego.

Revenge of the trickster

Having failed to extinguish Simone's stardom by denigrating her, Viktor tries virtual murder – and fails once again. He destroys the Simulation One programme by attacking it with a virus, then locks the software in a trunk and dumps it at sea. What stronger metaphor could there be, given that the ocean has for hundreds of years been associated with the unconscious, for Viktor's forcible repression of an unwelcome complex? As it happens he is witnessed loading the heavy trunk onto his yacht by the tabloid hack Max Sayer, who has been tailing Viktor in the hope of finding Simone. Possessed by the same frenzied need to touch the hem of the goddess with which he infects his readers, and fearing the trunk contains Simone's corpse (metaphorically not so far from the truth), Max plays a familiarly disruptive role.

As a journalist he is the messenger type. In myths this archetypal figure can attain high dignity through its labours when, functioning as a psychopomp, it links sweetly the conscious and unconscious spheres of the psyche. We saw it playing this part in *Besieged.* But as befits a tabloid scavenger dedicated to digging up the dirt, Max fills the variant of this role as both trickster and another instance of irrepressible archetypal energy. Entering Viktor's life not long after the death of Hank Aleno, Max inherits the latter's psychological function.

As we saw in the case of Kubrick's Milich, the trickster is no less a psychopomp than any other messenger with the power to link the conscious and unconscious spheres. But tricksters do so in ways that annoy, disrupt or even endanger the subject. When Viktor announces Simone's sudden death and arranges a fashionable studio funeral, Max tips off the cops. They interrupt the ceremony and open the coffin – which contains only a life-size cardboard cutout of the star. The trickster has delivered Viktor to the lowest point in his fortunes as he is arraigned for her murder and faces the death penalty. Yet the calamity Max has engineered will ultimately initiate processes that lead to Viktor's restoration to a renewed, though different, form of life.

In attempting to kill off an anima image that has excited a mass audience, Viktor has sundered himself from the cultural unconscious. Because the collective image of Simone has grown so strong, he imperils himself by denying it. Seen from the media-led perspective of Simone's public, he is both mad and (since the tabloids swiftly find him guilty without the need for trial) culpable. Psychologically speaking, he is out of balance. By trying to kill off his feminine side (Eros), he has delivered himself to the masculine Logos: the Law has him caged. To save himself from the executioner's needle, Viktor is obliged to confess to the simulation-deception. But he is not believed, not least because the software (Simone's 'body') has disappeared from the sunken trunk. Once again an autonomous complex has taken on a life of its own; and Jungian theory leads us to expect that it will constellate again somewhere else or in some other form.

An all-American family

In fact it is Lainey who recovers her father's anima when she manages to reactivate his software, drive out the virus and thereby save him from a murder rap. A common role of the child in religion and mythology, hence also in analytical psychology, is to offer to the adults with whom it interacts opportunities for rebirth into renewed self-understanding and even spiritual life (Jung 1951: 162–4). We had an earlier glimpse of such a figure with Helena in *Eyes Wide Shut*. Child images in cinema that have this potential include Christine Baxter in *Don't Look Now* (Nicolas Roeg, 1973) and Flora in *The Piano* (Jane Campion, 1993) (see Izod 1992: 77–80; 2001: 77–

8). But Lainey is not an infant Christ-child but an adolescent and, as shown earlier, savvy with it. As a child-woman she blends the unconscious directness of the child with an early sense of the passions that move adults. Lainey's saving of her father permits his reunion with his anima, but will be a strange rebirth.

In its earliest telling the Pygmalion tale featured marriage and childbirth, but Viktor's and Elaine's divorce adds a new twist. Further variations now follow. Thanks in part to Lainey's rescuing her father from the Law and restoring him to Eros, Elaine asks Viktor to move back in with her. But she also asks him to bring Simone along too. Elaine plainly has not only her relationship in mind but also film-industry economics and politics. The virtual actress has far too firm a grip on her public to be allowed to slip away. She brings to both the studio and the Taranskys immense financial rewards and concomitant power in the industry.

Elaine as studio boss evidently has in mind breeding a whole cast of virtual actors. Some months later, Simone makes a television appearance alongside Viktor to introduce her public to their new baby, Chip. The implications for Viktor and Elaine's marriage are, to say the least, interesting. We are left to ponder how well founded their reunion might be or whether it is merely a political alliance calculated to enhance their professional positions in Hollywood. The resuscitated marriage must be secret, a fact which leads to the suspicion that this new public deception must be playing politics with the souls of the actual family members concealed from public view. And questions must arise about the extent to which Viktor's damaged anima has been healed, given this split between its public and private manifestations.

In the same television interview Simone also lets the world know she intends a career change: she has decided to go into politics. This confirms what has all along been latent – that anima is a political force active in the overlapping spheres of the individual, the family and society at large. And what politics will this cynosure endorse? Her public can read anything it wishes into her final utterance: 'Viktor and I are both very concerned about what kind of world our new son Chip is going to grow up in.' Nobody, whether Republican, Democrat or Independent, could argue with these catchall words. They give rise to the suspicion that Simone will become a politician with the main aim of wielding power – perhaps presidential power – in an America which, if her influence prevails, will continue always to be right. Is this the monstrous gestation resulting from the union of Viktor and Simone as quasi-incestuous muses to each other's narcissism?

S1møne's audiences

In the light of all this, it is worth speculating on the way the film played to North American audiences. Released by the independent distributor New

Line, *S1m⌀ne* opened late August 2002 and received mixed reviews in the American press covering the spectrum from delight to outright hostility. It secured ninth place in the North American box-office returns for its first week (*Screen International* 2002a), but over the next two weeks declined to thirteenth and nineteenth places respectively before falling out of the top 20 (*Screen International* 2002b, c). During that three-week period its reported takings amounted to slightly less than $10m (2002c). By way of rule-of-thumb comparison, there were at the date of its release nine films listed, each with cumulative North American takings exceeding $100m; and the market leader was *Star Wars: Episode II* with receipts in excess of $300m (2002a).

The box-office returns make it pretty clear that ironically, as opposed to her reception by the audiences on screen, Simone was not embraced as an anima figure by the mass American audiences of 2002. A number of factors may help explain this.

Firstly, the demography of the North American movie-going audience would have reduced the likelihood of mass anima projective identification with either Simone or Rachel Roberts. Approximately three quarters of those who go regularly to movies are no older than 25. Simone herself resembles a mature woman in her physical prime at about 30 years of age. For most of the audience, therefore, she would not be an obvious recipient of anima projections as either mother, lover or alter ego.

Secondly, we need to consider *S1m⌀ne's* subtle deployment of register. The film opens with a blue tinted vista down a breakwater to the sea. Samuel Barber's *Adagio for Strings* backs this shot in the version reworked for a choir. It sets up an elegiac, timeless opening frame. There follows a shot of the empty studio lanes with parked trailers looking like a surreal scene from a science fiction movie, as cold and desolate as an Edward Hopper painting. The weird, electronic wind effect underlaying this shot also universalises time and reinforces the sense that we are in dreamland – an ideal location for the anima to appear. With the third shot (an extreme close-up of Nicola's candy being sorted by Viktor), we move from the macro to the micro – the action commences with music producing a perky pseudo-Gamelan effect, the recurring aural motif that perfectly underscores the empty busyness of Hollywood. A repeat viewing reveals, however, that we have been deceived: the opening shot is actually a clip from Viktor's *Sunrise Sunset*. Meanwhile careful attention to the rewriting of Barber's *Adagio* establishes that the choir is singing 'Agnus Dei' – words that belong to a requiem. Our first viewing invites us to share the elegiac setting for a loved anima. A second viewing shows that we have been taken in by Viktor's typically overheated melodrama (anima seduction being, of course, the theme of all his movies). But the point is that in the first instance we actually were drawn into that elegiac dream register, and the surreal look of the parked trailers (which are not in Viktor's film) confirms it.

This leads us directly to a third factor inhibiting the anima impact of Simone. Dark comic satire is the register which characterises most of the film – not one of the genres that usually draws large numbers of young people. At odds with the warm feelings generated by the opening, satire inevitably has a distancing effect as it undermines not only the human characters but also the magic of Viktor's dream creature. So the film functions in two registers: the one seductive (as when Viktor communes in his studio with his muse) and the other (for example, when they go into the wider world) satirical. The tensioned balance between the two modes enhances the text's wit, but it diminishes the raw impact of anima precisely because the business of the satire is to make the machinations of this archetypal image known – to repoliticise it, so to speak.

Before Mailer's bus journey ended, he drew a distinction between those young Americans who allowed themselves to be groomed for conformity and the bright kids whose active intellects made them resist social cloning (1968: 168). Simone, as we have seen, possesses specific anima characteristics: she is an archetypal projection of a damaged man, a semi-functional family and a society ignorant of its own motivations. But an elegiac and bland figure whose particular languor promises inaction and continuation of the status quo is more apt to appeal as satirical object rather than as anima to that brighter section of the populace where a film as intelligent and lively as *S1møne* was likely to have found its audience. That the lead female did not become an image cherished by the passionate devotion of her actual audience may be taken as a marker – albeit ironic – of the satire's success in politicising the anima.

Chapter 7

Myths in British documentaries of the 1980s and 1990s

Introduction

Documentary, with its roots in observable fact, is a sub-genre that might not be expected to reveal much in the way of mythological foundations. Yet Don Fredericksen demonstrated the contrary with his work on *The Song of Ceylon* (1935). Jungian methods can enhance the reading of documentary films no less effectively than feature films (Fredericksen 1980, 2001). This chapter analyses certain trends in British documentaries of the past 20 years to discover whether they succeed better than the features we have so far looked at in communicating with the audience with archetypal force.

Once more with feeling: the British docu-soap

As Richard Kilborn (2000) has shown, docu-soaps are similar to reality programming in their tabloid deployment of short episodes from the lives of those they observe. Usually they feature easily-digested dramatic incidents embodying readily-identified themes. They also resemble soap operas not only in weaving together short segments of storylines, but also in filming people, social actors, who have distinctive personalities. Programmes made in this mode concentrate on what happens to these 'characters'. Typically they focus on what these people's work or domestic circumstances require of them; or what they themselves identify as the central dramas of their lives. Alternatively the production crew may manoeuvre them into unexpected predicaments and film their reactions.

In practice what results has often had unexpected historical antecedents which are probably accidental rather than designed. The connection I have in mind links them to the 1930s films of the British Documentary Movement. It is well known among students of the Movement that in Britain these filmmakers were acting as pioneers when they represented working people as the heroes of labour. Reminiscing in George Stoney's critical assessment of Flaherty's work *How the Myth Was Made* (1978), Harry

Watt, one of the Movement's more vocal members, remarked that workers of the 1930s had previously seldom been shown on screen other than in comic roles. The documentarists, as a matter of policy stemming from deep conviction, set about rebutting such demeaning images. Heroic images of people at work formed the dominant tenor of their imagery.

Dai Vaughan, however, detects a minor, covert theme which he infers runs counter to the dominant tenor. He starts by observing that in these films the workers' heroism rests upon their dedication to production. In performing useful work they form a mutually interdependent group whose labour gives them dignity. So far so good, but the other part of the binary couple that comes to mind when one thinks of production is consumption. Vaughan believes the films of the Documentary Movement imply that people who are not heroes of labour will be too poor to consume more than the basics needed for survival. In their poverty they lack the dignity of those in productive employment and will be 'victims of circumstance'. Whilst the films themselves seldom show the disadvantaged in their imagery, this binary pairing of heroes of labour with victims of circumstance forms what Vaughan regards as one of the governing ideas behind British documentaries of that decade (1983: 41–2). His analysis invites our attention because docu-soaps of the 1990s often feature a similarly split master set.

Many docu-soaps take as their subject matter the functioning of a complex organisation with which the viewing public regularly comes into contact without knowing how it works. For example, *Airport* (BBC, 1996–), a programme that has run through numerous series, featured the operations that keep Heathrow functioning. Another, shorter-lived series focused on people working in an out-of-town shopping mall (*Lakesiders*, BBC, 1998). So, just as in the 1930s documentaries, British workers are represented as fulfilling a vitally important role: it is they who keep the country's essential services running. Many docu-soaps make it plain that the British are looked after every hour of the night and day by a labour force whose heroism these programmes resolutely sing. Implicit here is a representation of aspects of national identity which clearly relates the 'political' to the personal.

It would be this straightforward were it not that, in order to maximise audience ratings, docu-soaps tend to offer viewers more than one perspective on their subject matter. In fact they sometimes provide us with the chance to adopt what logically should be mutually exclusive points of view on their real-life characters. Even when these programmes celebrate loyal and dependable workers, some of the very individuals who in that perspective are viewed as heroes may also be regarded by the audience with a sly sense of superiority because they are simultaneously shown as victims. But they are not victims of circumstance suffering under an adverse social or economic system as would have been the case in the 1930s. Now they are more likely to be the dupes of their own delusions of self-importance.

Victims of delusion

Presented against the backdrop of their labour-in-service, the occasional self-delusion of a few of these heroes commutes to something close to forgivable comic screen eccentricity (a long-established minor vice much celebrated in British popular culture). What in the 1930s and 1940s documentaries had been a purposely inspiring record of working people based on John Grierson's democratising principles returns in the 1990s docu-soap as farce. In effect the viewer is given the opportunity to collude with the filmmakers in victimising the characters.

Of the many possible examples, it will suffice to mention two here. Maureen Rees in *Driving School* (BBC, 1997) was heroically determined to get her licence, but was clearly shown to be deluded in thinking she would ever be able to pass the test. Her ludicrous ineptitude made her the principal attraction of the series and for a short time something of a television star in her own right – that and the fact that, like a true British hero, she persevered unabashed and eventually did pass her driving test. Equally, Jane McDonald, the chanteuse on board the holiday liner in *The Cruise* (BBC, 1998), showed relentless courage in her determination to break into show business; but anyone with half an ear could not miss that her brassy vocal performances seldom surpassed mediocrity.

Occasionally docu-soap makers go for the jugular and screen an individual afflicted with a self-delusion so nearly pathological that it drives the form to burlesque. In such instances, like much other entertainment-driven television worldwide since the late 1980s, these programmes do not always rise above allowing their victims to humiliate themselves. Jane McDonald's grotesquely distorted echo Aisha was to be heard (thankfully only in one episode) in *Airline* (ITV, 1998). This was the teenager with a voice so off-key that she tormented all who came within earshot of her endless warbling. Aisha's barely credible mania, unfettered by sense or sensibility (there was a kind of heroism in so energetic and innocent a self-assurance), was the belief that she could break into the entertainment world by singing at a holiday resort in Ibiza. As we never doubt for a moment, she fails. However, this humiliation was not sufficient for the programme makers. Exiting the airport terminal on her return home, Aisha tripped and fell in front of the camera – for the director an irresistible metaphor which remains in the final cut.

Avoiding anxiety

The celebration of heroes and incitement to deride the self-deluded do not exhaust the recurrent themes of these programmes. There is something else that generates an unverbalised subtext. Beneath the surface of several docu-soaps (*Airport*, *Airline*, *Lakesiders*, *Paddington Green* (BBC, 1998–2001) and *Jailbirds* (BBC, 1999) for instance), it is possible to sense a deep anxiety. It shows in the relentless pressure inherent in the organisations under the lens to get work done efficiently and according to plan. Despite the hectic efforts of the heroic protagonists, they often miss their goal. Planes and trains do not leave on time. Machines break down at critical moments. In *Paddington Green* the material fabric of the environment is all too obviously crumbling – like the lives of some of the local residents. The recurrent subtext of such programmes makes it almost impossible not to infer that the whole social system is on the verge of spilling out of control. Here is a theme which has familiar psychological roots in an affliction that has endured through countless epochs. Felt by both individuals and societies and manifesting in a variety of forms, it finds its core in the fear that things fall apart. It is an anxiety that undoes us both in personal dreams and collective waking nightmares, the terror that, where control is slipping away in some manner difficult to pin down, calamity will surely follow. At root personal level, this is likely to be caused by fear of the dissolution of body and mind that will come with death – an archetypal nightmare indeed. In the social arena, the nightmare embodies an awareness that is hard to accept into collective consciousness, namely that all cultural achievements are temporary and prone to more or less sudden change. Given that it has such a strong archetypal basis, there is a theme of substance here that is well worth exploring.

Rather than acknowledge this theme explicitly and look at it square on, however, the docu-soap swerves away from the political back to the personal. This ideological shift occurs so commonly in screen fiction that it is in effect the norm. By comparison, it was rare in documentary where the norm prior to the later 1980s held that programmes should centre on seriousness of purpose. Viewers expected that social problems would be dealt with as such and without thematic displacement. So when a documentary focused on a single individual, more often than not that person typified a group or social sector.

It is not that docu-soaps show no interest in the individual's professional role; but as they build the elements of their principal subject's character, their prime concern appears to lie in identifying the unique marks of the individual as an object of scrutiny wholly absorbing in his or her own right. Nonetheless, it should be added that the viewer's reading process does cause these social actors to surrender some of their individuality: not so much in favour of a seriousness of purpose as to draw them toward stereotypes. This occurs because the docu-soap sets its 'characters' in cultural contexts designed to make them easily recognisable. Thus in their treatment of the people in front of the lens, the key difference between traditional documentaries and docu-soaps is that the former seek to discover the social type through the individual; the latter use familiar social and cultural norms to persuade us that behind the stereotypical exterior of a 'character' lies an authentic and psychologically unique individual.

Sexuality in the docu-soap

When docu-soaps swerve from the political to the personal they often displace the current of social anxiety that they might otherwise have explored in its own right onto sexual attitudes and relationships. It's a diversion which confirms the sub-genre's links with soap-opera. Sex tends to be treated in one of three popular cultural modes – the sentimental romance, the camp and the bawdy. All are inflected in peculiarly British ways.

Sentimental romance

The first mode is sentimental romance, an illustration of which is furnished by *The Cruise* (BBC1, 1998, dir. Christopher Terrill). The series followed the fortunes of staff on board a luxury liner as they served the wealthy holiday-makers who are their clients. Those staff whom we get to know are, despite their disparate personalities and ambitions, bonded together by their sense of having a distinctive group identity *vis-à-vis* the passengers. I have already said that one of the attractions of these programmes is the way docu-soaps celebrate the men and women who keep services running, and *The Cruise* is a good example. Typically the crew on the liner have to work hard at routine tasks, the boredom of which is alleviated by their contact with other human beings – contact which the docu-soap cherishes, of course, in its search to focus on characters.

Another factor that bonds members of the crew featured in the series is their struggle to achieve success on terms that they themselves respect. Jane McDonald makes great play (over more than one episode) with her determination to be a star of the entertainment world. As we get to know her character, she spouts the full litany which every novice seems to need to learn by heart if she is to succeed as a professional performer: the necessity for a high degree of motivation; the way the performer suffers from exposure and lives on her nerves; and the greatness of those professionals who have made it.

We are left in no doubt about Jane's ambition. As a plucky fighter she has the potential for heroism. But when she first takes the stage in the ship's so-called Celebrity Theatre, her opening number is noticeably off-key, and the performance lacks lustre. It is a bad night, with many patrons walking out while she is working. As Jane says shrewdly enough, the punters are used to getting entertainment whenever they want it from television, but the round-the-clock eating offered on-board is something not found everywhere. However, although her audience have gone to shove more food into their bursting guts, she also realises that she has not sung well. So at this point we witness the awakening of the victim of self-delusion – a self-discovery that is a significant way marker on Jane's road to heroism.

Sure enough, Jane's story ends well. The final episode showed an altogether more successful performance that she gave after being tutored in some new tricks by a more experienced singer. When adversity conquered leads to triumph, there results a reliably heart-warming story formula. The audience can be expected to forgive earlier failures. And in Jane McDonald's case, far from merely forgiving, the audience became markedly enthusiastic. Television executives are paid to notice these things, and before long she was presenting the midweek lottery draw on TV and had recorded her first album (which reached no. 1 in the UK album charts in 1998). Thereafter she became host of her own prime-time show.

This much success for an unremarkable singer would ordinarily exceed anyone's expectations, even when the *chanteuse* had shown the fortitude of Ms McDonald. But there was another element which added to the television audience's affection for the performer – sentiment. While working with the director of *The Cruise* (with whom she had struck up a good professional rapport), Jane did not conceal her longing for marriage, a desire as intense as that for success. Just before transmission of the series ended, the BBC was able to announce that she would wed her boyfriend some months later. Once again Christopher Terrill was commissioned to cover the event and the BBC broadcast a special show featuring the wedding in the Caribbean. As if this were not enough, her wedding photo occupied the cover of the UK's principal listings weekly the *Radio Times* accompanied by a three-page spread (Ogle 1998). The nation's sentimental and middle-aged at heart gladly reached for their hankies.

Notwithstanding Jane's popular reception, it appears to have been in Jung's terms an expression of the audience's feelings rather than emotions, a topic to which we shall return.

Making camp

The second popular cultural mode in which the docu-soap exploits sexual interest is camp. In this mode, the sexuality of the social actors is framed so as to arouse the voyeuristic curiosity of viewers. This usually occurs when the sexual orientation and behaviour of the social actors are foregrounded as differing from the heterosexual paradigm. Two instances of such subjects are Jackie (formerly Jason) McAuliffe, the transsexual prostitute in *Paddington Green*, and Toni, the energetic lesbian in *Jailbirds* who, once recovered from drug addiction, cut something of a swathe through the other women inmates with her frank sexuality. Their respective filmmakers portrayed both women not without sympathy. Each had plenty of opportunity to speak about herself, her desires and fears. Each became something of a minor celebrity, though only Jackie showed a willingness to exploit her new-found fame.

All the same, there was always a risk that they might be perceived by audiences as part of a freak show. Images of people transmitted through any medium inevitably take their place in a cultural setting that is already formed. This symbolic context affects not only the way that programme makers represent their subjects, but also how viewers understand them since the latter select what seems to them the appropriate cultural register through which to make sense of what they are shown.

The camp mode in docu-soaps has the power through its representations and style to elicit deeply embedded cultural attitudes in the audience. It is capable of doing so even when the sexuality of the subject is peripheral to the programme's ostensible topic. A case in point is Jeremy Spake who was featured as the Aeroflot traffic supervisor at Heathrow in numerous episodes of *Airport*. The episodes that involved him focused on the endless tribulations in his professional life as he battles to get passengers on board planes so that they can leave on time. Although he is relentlessly camp in manner, his sexuality does not become a theme that the programme explores openly. However, a robust, if silent, subtext is firmly in place here.

When docu-soaps play to a British audience and signal camp (as Jeremy Spake did through his speech mannerisms and body language), they engage a popular cultural form of address that dates back to music hall variety acts of the late nineteenth century. Stand-up comedians kept the tradition alive throughout the intervening period, and since the middle of the twentieth century the work of a significant number of television comedians and game-show hosts has ensured that mass audiences are familiar with it. In addition, there has existed in parallel since the 1930s a popular genre of cheerfully vulgar comic postcards.

The comic seaside postcard that found its apogee in the garish work of Donald McGill was described by George Orwell as 'something as traditional as Greek tragedy, a sort of sub-world of smacked bottoms and scrawny mothers-in-law which is a part of Western European consciousness' (1941: 100–1). Observing that well over half these postcards depended upon jokes about sex, Orwell found that (with women's bodies obscenely exaggerated in breasts and buttocks and often featuring gags about male sexual inadequacy) the pictures lifted the lid off a widespread repression (1941: 101–4). However, the repression he had in mind was different from the attempted suppression of either the erotic or pornographic. The comic postcards represented, he argued, 'a sort of saturnalia, a harmless rebellion against virtue' (1941: 110). They expressed the anti-heroic self, 'the voice of the belly protesting against the soul', depicting the part of oneself that is 'a little fat man who sees very clearly the advantages of staying alive with a whole skin' (1941: 108). This was an aspect of the human condition that Orwell found most literature and painting of his day preferred to ignore.

The cinematic heirs to the vulgar postcard were the *Carry On* films, as Marion Jordan has demonstrated persuasively. Although they met with no critical recognition in their day, they formed an institution in British popular culture, no fewer than 28 being made between 1958 and 1980 (1983: 312). Their stylistic consistency can be partly explained by their box office success and partly by the recurrent presence of the same people in their talent line-up. They were all produced by Peter Rodgers and directed by Gerald Thomas who used the same two scriptwriters on 21 of them. A small group of actors played leading roles again and again, so that what resulted was nothing less than a self-contained genre (Jordan 1983: 314). A further factor added to their consistency – the deliberate presentation of the principal roles as highly stereotyped caricatures the main features of which (no matter what the narrative context) were repeated in film after film. As Jordan points out, certain situations and character types which recurred in the postcards moved readily into the *Carry On* films. Plots were calculated and locations (such as hospitals) chosen to ensure that characters would be discovered in a state of undress. Women are seen by men as either fantastically desirable or shudderingly repulsive. Men for their part are either sexually deficient or grotesquely well endowed. As for couples, they are either young and amorous or locked in grim-visaged and desexed middle age. The extremes are the more marked in that there are no mid positions, no sign of transition between the seeming opposites. The division between the polar extremes is further emphasised by the repeated casting in successive films of the same actors to play roles with the same sexual characteristics (Jordan 1983: 317–19).

The postcards make no reference to homosexuality (Orwell 1941: 102). The *Carry On* films, not least because Kenneth Williams was repeatedly cast in them, do, though allusions to homosexuality come more through verbal byplay than dramatic action (Jordan 1983: 320–1). Typically the films make much of the comic situations that arise when large institutions such as the army, hospitals and schools try to impose their disciplines on people but fail to take account of their animal needs and desires (Jordan 1983: 316). Jordan sees as cheering – despite their being dominated by the male point of view – the cheeky resilience of the films in celebrating the liveliness of a sexual interest that exists without having to be tied to high romantic ideals or passions (1983: 322). This is close to Orwell's harmless saturnalian rebellion of the ordinary man or woman and permits the hypothesis that the response of the films' audiences may have been much like that of those who enjoyed McGill's postcards.

Thus there exists in British popular culture a well-established practice of encouraging a camp view of sex. Towards the end of the last century, when heterosexual behaviour had become an almost universally accepted topic for detailed and open discussion, that camp view focused particularly on transgressive sex. A number of high-profile chat show hosts and guests took advantage of – and exaggerated into grotesque stereotypes – the masquerade of scene gays and transvestites. In the first category Julian Cleary and

Graham Norton played at being shocking, while Lily Savage refurbished a theatrical tradition that had been brought to television by cross-dressing performers like Dame Edna Everage and Danny Le Roux.

I have shown how docu-soaps position the viewer to expect the exploitation of stereotypes through character-centred real-life drama, and camp does nothing if not deal in stereotypes. It is for this reason and because producers know that audiences enjoy it, that docu-soaps sometimes foster camp. Once again the sub-genre can be perceived as opening up opposed viewing positions from which to gaze at certain people who become subsumed to stereotypes. We can see them as heroic representatives of sexual minorities, beneficiaries of the gender revolution unabashedly claiming their right to public acceptance. Conversely, however, at least two of these 'characters' can be viewed as updated versions of the figures in salacious postcards, *Carry On* films and popular television showcases. In the case of the jailbird Toni, the possibility of spillover from camp stereotypes is there because she is an unashamed transgressive sexual hunter. The reading of her image splits in the way described above, the positive side being that, although by definition not a hero of labour, she appeared to have become a gender icon – still featured on a lesbian and gay website two years after the programmes' transmission (SpiceUpYourLife 2001). Jeremy Spake's credentials as a hero of labour have already been mentioned. The viewer of *Airport* is, however, also offered a raft of cultural signs – for example in Spake's mannerisms, speech patterns and delight in innuendo – that invite a reading of him as a camp queen. When in this way docu-soap characters are perceived to be members of a sexual minority, innuendo and *double entendre* are seldom far away. Interestingly, Jackie from *Paddington Green* was not shown as a camp figure because her serious purpose in attempting to make a new life for herself and the extent of her suffering rendered her immune. The representation of suffering has to be incompatible with camp because it would wreck that mode's sardonic stance.

Boozy, bawdy breaks

We come now to the final mode, bawdy sexuality. Its base register is the gross sexual appetite of its participants: 'Fuck me! Look at the arse on that!' Series on the holiday industry such as *Holiday Reps* (BBC 1997–8) and *Ibiza Uncovered* (Sky One and ITV 1997–2000) make much of their characters' urgent, booze-fuelled sex drives. Predictably this register is more evident in docu-soaps directed at the young. A television listings website announcing a new series for 2000 of *Ibiza Uncovered* sets the tone:

> Ibiza is the holiday location for many young people due to it's [*sic*] incredible dance scene and hedonistic offerings. The island offers you sun, sea, sex and much more. In this fly on the wall docu-soap meet Jay

> and Dee as they try and become 'Club 18–30' reps, watch them survive the gruelling training and qualifying for their official 'shag-tag' – the reps badge.
>
> (TV Library 2000)

The holiday docu-soaps are demotic and celebrate sexual frenzy enjoyed by all (provided 'all' means all who are young). They encourage the ravers to speak out in their own right. It turns out to be a simple device by which to gain access for the cameras to record the exuberant debauchery of ordinary young people of differing class and economic background – the girls no less than the lads. As Andrew Billen wrote in 1997 in response to the first series of *Ibiza Uncovered*:

> Its producer, Natalka Znak, had the inspired idea of going out to Ibiza at the beginning of the summer and following a dozen Englishmen and women over eight weeks. Each weekend the video tape is flown back and edited for transmission the next Sunday night. Out in Ibiza's bars the stars . . . watch reruns of their own worst behaviour – unrepentantly.

In the way of these things, their boasting often outpaces achievement. It is not uncommon that some of the young would-be heroes of their own sexual Olympics – both male and female – fail to win a bout. Their deluded expectations of instant conquest culminate, after long nights addled by drink and drugs, in bathetic attempts to pull. Sometimes the objects of their lust rebuff them scornfully. Other hopeful predators are so far off their heads that they pass out as soon as they lie down. But however their fellow vacationers may mock them for their far from heroic performance, the filmmakers are more circumspect. As Billen comments, the producers are clever enough to have made programmes that make a show of sharing rather than ridiculing their subjects' sensibilities. Far from lampooning their subjects, televised docu-soaps convey complicity with these people in their desire to become stars. Indeed a number do so, and the prospect of stardom appears to provide a key mode of identification for young people with these shows, as the ongoing attraction of *Big Brother* for would-be contestants no less than viewers suggests.[1]

Docu-soap heroes: stereotypes or archetypes?

Where popular stereotypes are found, there the scholar interested in cultural formations looks for the bedrock of contemporary myth. Jungian academics take a further step and seek archetypal images that reveal

1 I owe this idea to Philip Schlesinger.

through today's myths the psychological tendencies of the age. It is therefore interesting that some hero-victims of docu-soaps have exploited their celebrity and become stars and presenters on British television. After early successes with her album, Jane McDonald presented her own show *Star for a Night* (BBC 2000) and followed up with *Junior Star for a Night* (BBC 2001). Jeremy Spake fronted *The Toughest Job in Britain* (BBC 2000–1). Meanwhile Jackie McAuliffe released an album of her piano playing which reached no. 14 in the charts, and then set about writing her autobiography (McAuliffe 2001). Likewise some of each year's survivors of *Big Brother* have secured work in front of the camera.

Despite being minor celebrities, the 'stars' of docu-soaps cannot be said to have archetypal influence. Firstly, it is rare for any individual to attain major starring status in the crowded universe of television without constant exposure of the kind that these newcomers have not yet enjoyed. Having said that, two of them do bear some of the marks of their mythological antecedents. Although Jackie McAuliffe's painful physical treatment was in the hands of surgeons, she set her own objectives for psychological as well as physical healing. Her drive toward self-realisation was striking and made her heir to the wounded healer Asklepios who practised medicine with a view to healing the injuries of both body and mind (Hillman 1988: 121–2). Finding personal illumination despite the injuries she had suffered was the heroic task which Jackie set herself.

Toni, perhaps the most intriguing of our four characters, soon disappeared from public view. Her invisibility tantalises because there are points of contact between her life on-screen and the tribulations of Psyche. That classical beauty was forced by a jealous Aphrodite into the Underworld to fetch a flask of the water of youth. But Psyche did what she had been forbidden and opened it. As a consequence she fell into a deep sleep and was only saved when Eros's arrow struck her (Grimal 1991: 379). The order of events is different in the case of Toni, 'so fetching in her white singlet, and so droll once she recovers from addiction' (Bennett 1999). As a heroin addict, she had opened her forbidden flask before being jailed and entering her Underworld, but while in prison Toni too was awakened by Love's dart. Before the *Jailbirds* series ended she made clear her intention to form a lasting union with her new partner, so her disappearance suggests that like Psyche she too found wings to fly.

Nonetheless, checking the reactions of viewers – family, friends, colleagues, press columnists, and one's own responses – it seems certain that these docu-soap 'characters' engage viewers in a potential structure of sympathy but do not stir their emotions deeply. They would have to were they to become vehicles for an energy sufficient to entice their audience to mythologise them. In part, as already indicated, this is a consequence of insufficient continuing media exposure; but the instances of Jeremy Spake and Jane McDonald clearly illustrate another factor. Although they could be perceived as heroes in their own lives, they were not epic figures capable of providing viewers with role models that might either deepen or shake the roots of their own beings. Rather, their perceived images were suborned to stereotypes by existing British cultural values. So Jeremy and Jane actually had a minor function in reinforcing a cozy sense that those values are sufficient. They helped defend their British viewers, since the familiar that they embodied was so enjoyable and safe, from the need to encounter the disturbing or unknown. They were, therefore, far from being the kind of heroes who renew and utterly rearrange our sense of reality, and who (to quote Jung in an altered context) 'rend from top to bottom the curtain upon which is painted the picture of an ordered world, and allow a glimpse into the unfathomable abyss of the unborn and of things yet to be' (1950a: 90). On the contrary, Jeremy and Jane helped keep the curtain in place. As servitors to our comfort, they bore witness to some of the less epic desires and fears exercising the British cultural unconscious. In short, they engaged viewers' feelings, not their emotions.

I now analyse two televised documentaries which I first wrote about with my colleague Richard Kilborn in *An Introduction to Television Documentary* (Kilborn and Izod 1997). In what follows I advance a post-Jungian approach that I thought inappropriate to develop in the earlier work.

Lido, poetic documentary and semi-conscious awakenings

Documentarists who want to catch their viewers' attention can opt to deploy a number of striking devices (see Kilborn and Izod 1997: 84–5). Among these, they may focus on challenging or fresh subject matter; they may adopt a controversial point of view in their coverage; or they may present the material in a vigorous, eye-catching style. Examples are legion, from *Coalface* (1935) and *Night Mail* (1936) through *Chronique d'un été* (1961), *The Thin Blue Line* (1987) on to *Fahrenheit 9/11* (2004). In its era each expounded a polemic in a distinctive manner which drew attention to the force of its representations. However, films properly described as poetic documentaries are distinctive in paying less attention to the referent in the historical world (the people and events passing in front of the camera and microphone) than to the anticipated effect on the viewer of the text's expressive elements – its aesthetics, structure and themes. Poetic films do not always commit to the original principle of documentary work that they should construct an argument about something. Rather they tend to replace argument and telling with showing and implication. They can construct a strong sense for the viewer of being present. When they do this, however, it is more usually designed to encourage emotional experience than to offer conceptual explanations of what is seen and heard (Nichols 1994: 100).

Thus in the poetic mode the expressive elements dominate and take on the function of organising the film such that the viewer, at least as much as the world portrayed, becomes a primary referent. Films like Basil Wright's *The Song of Ceylon* (1935) and Lucy Blakstad's *Lido* (BBC, 1996) have a dreamlike surface which encourages viewers to free their emotions and enjoy the sense that at some not fully conscious level they are sharing a moving experience with other members of the audience. In his study of the earlier film, Fredericksen demonstrated that the organisation of its imagery sprang, without Basil Wright being consciously aware of it, from archetypal roots. That gave the film a dimension additional to its ostensible purposes firstly as a documentary evocation of past and present ways of life in Sri Lanka and secondly as a public relations exercise for the Ceylon Tea Marketing Board. Fredericksen identified as an additional, arcane dimension to the film celebration of the eternal mystical cycle between darkness and light. While this took its form from Sri Lankan religious ceremonies, Fredericksen argued that its originating energy sprang from the unconscious of its director as a compensation for the dominance of conscious control in the rigorously programmed work of the 1930s British Documentary Movement under Grierson (Fredericksen 2001: 17–55).

Like *The Song of Ceylon*, *Lido* reveals a characteristic typical of poetic documentaries in offering itself as a deeply-felt, personal view of the subject.[2] Poetic films often give the viewer the sense that they are authored and convey the point of view of a single originating personality. Not least because its way of looking at its subject (both visually and thematically) is so distinctive, *Lido* is experienced by viewers as if it were personally addressed to them by a gentle and talented individual having a generous capacity for wry observation. That makes for an intimacy which marries sweetly with the film's lyricism, relaxing viewers and readying them for a release of emotion.

On the surface, the subject matter of *Lido* is simple. It features the open-air public swimming pool that gives the film its title and the Londoners who frequented it during the hot summer of 1995. Apart from an introductory helicopter shot that shows the location near a housing estate, the entire film was shot within the pool's perimeter. A strong sense of place is established from the start. All the footage was taken outdoors and, with the exception only of the night-time party which rounds off the film, in broad sunlight. Here is an immediate gratification for British viewers stuck in a cool, sun-starved climate, which reaffirms of one of the great dreams of the past half century. It hovers beneath the eyelids of all those who ache to escape from work or the tight confines of city dwelling. In the case of *Lido*, the dream of summer Paradise is shared by bathers and viewers alike. Clear light and

2 An earlier version of this section appeared in Kilborn and Izod (1997: 84–5, 109–12).

aquamarine water are thus the principal visible elements contributing to the film's strong poetic aura. But something else glimmers deeper and finer in the water's sheen.

The film is carefully structured, and although it does not draw attention to its formal properties, they add to the viewer's pleasure. The first of these devices is handled discreetly. It is an implied chronology, in effect a double movement through time. The baths are at first empty except for a few early morning swimmers. They gradually fill as people on their lunch break and after them families, couples, singles hoping to find lovers, the elderly and the very young all join the afternoon rush. But mapped over this cycle of a day in the life of the lido is a longer timescale. The film ends with its only night sequence as a party of friends celebrate a ceremony of commitment between a lesbian couple who have featured in a number of earlier sequences. So when the wedding vows have been exchanged and several guests celebrate by leaping into the pool, this symbolic consummation of a joyous public union brings with it the closing of the day, the summer season and the film itself. This structuring component achieves a sense of completeness. It typifies the poetic mode in arousing feelings in the spectator, feelings of pleasure at a fitting culmination. And it also invites simultaneous contemplation of the two scales – the diurnal and the seasonal, micro and macro, the personal and the collective – a doubling which the entire film sustains.

A second formal device consists in an alternation between three kinds of sequence. The first comprises interviews with the bathers and the second observation of their antics. Both types of sequence are recorded with the camera out of the water. The remaining kind is assembled from shots taken by an underwater camera. Each format serves a function distinct from the others; and each encourages the viewer to take a different perspective on reality. The three are interlaced.

Lucy Blakstad conducts the interviews herself from beside the camera. She is never seen, but some of her questions can be heard off-screen and almost off-mike. Occasionally respondents address her by name, which adds to the feeling of intimacy as if they have got to know and like her during the shoot. All this adds to the sense that *Lido* is an authored text. Around the pool Blakstad finds people from all walks of life – the powerful (senior civil servants) and the powerless (unemployed women and men); the well-to-do and the poor; gays, straights, unmarried parents; and folk of many races – and she talks to a representative selection. Typically her questioning starts with an enquiry about what attracts each individual to the lido. From that starting point she encourages her respondents to open up about their lives, needs and desires. She also asks what they know of the other people who use the baths. By degrees this line of enquiry uncovers a polyglot community, all wanting different things from their lives but residing together – at least in this space – in easy-going and contented tolerance. The interviews harmonise the diverse worlds of the people around the lido. The benign image of a utopian social collective that results creates enjoyment for the viewer because it fulfils the dream of peaceful coexistence, a powerful aspect of many people's idea of Paradise on earth, and all the more potent in that it is so difficult to realise.

From the pool's margins the camera observes the visitors as they change their clothes or swim (some lazily, others for exercise, a few as if to break personal records) or spread towels and sunbathe on the warm flagstones. In these scenes, the camera is quiet, often static; and in many shots it takes up an unusually low angle which mimics the point of view of the sun-worshippers. Ambient sound is handled distinctively in these sequences. Sometimes it complements what is on screen by providing a naturalistic aural perspective to the view; but it is not constantly motivated by what the images show. For example, there are occasions when the lido is packed with people and the sound level of the summer revels will suddenly be lowered or cut to a silence which may then be leavened by a soft, luscious music. Such moments have the quality of Shakespeare's interludes in *A Midsummer Night's Dream* or *The Tempest* in communicating a sense of magical delight. And a recurring motif augments the mood: a boy juggles a few balls, always in slow motion. Never identified (the framing excludes his face) and sometimes only seen in a ballet of shadows on the flagstones, his harlequin role is authenticated by the return of the same delicious music. This second mode, observation with no spoken commentary, unifies the other two worlds by introducing the magical.

The remaining sequences were shot underwater. They augment the element of fantasy to which the harlequin's presence has already alerted viewers. Streams of bubbles and blue light embellish the swimmers as they fishtail past the camera in slow motion – a pregnant woman, a skinny old man, young men and women flaunting their bodies, kids having a rumbustious good time. A disembodied pair of spectacles swings downward as if suspended from an invisible pendulum. Someone drifts to the bottom locked into the lotus posture. Individuals find the peaceful isolation they seek. Meanwhile, silky music accompanies the weightless bodies and the camera too swims free, tilting and swaying in the shifting waters of this miniature ocean.

Some of the people we see in these underwater sequences are known to us from earlier poolside encounters (lotus man, for example, is HIV positive and had earlier reflected on the way the baths allowed him to rejoin the human race as an equal rather than being stigmatised by discriminatory labels such as 'gay' or 'HIV'). The element of fantasy seamlessly dovetails with the sunlit life above; and the wonderful light that falls on everything above and below the waterline dissolves the boundaries between illusion and actuality. The grace and beauty of everything seen and heard beneath the surface make for a feeling of infectious delight that colours our perception of the world within the lido. So the fluid underwater visions of the people become as integral a part of them as their earthiness. By fusing the fantastic with the factual, the film offers the viewer a metaphor for wholeness of the individual in the union of mental and physical impressions. But it also presents an image of collective wholeness through the harmonious union of diverse people relishing their differences yet coexisting amicably in a thriving community. It fits nicely with the theme of union in diversity that the film ends by celebrating a lesbian wedding.

Lido is not merely poetic in its aesthetics and structure. It invites reflection on a number of themes. These include the nature of the community and changing patterns of personal interaction in contemporary British society – examples being openly homosexual relationships and unabashed single parenting. Because Blakstad's subjects respond well to her empathetic enquiries, they talk about themselves without restraint in a manner which gives the lie to many worn social stereotypes. Two single mothers, for instance, while not concealing the relentless demands of bringing up young children on low incomes, express the pleasure of friendship and the loving pride which they derive from parenting. All these concerns give the film ethnographic overtones. However, the poetic element dominates through not merely the complexity of the themes but also the feeling tone. That made watching *Lido* an emotional experience at the time of its first and second transmission, and continues to do so for many of my students to this day. The affect stirs the imagination to a sense of possibility – for collective integration both social and spiritual and for reconciling within the self the diverse currents of our individual personalities.

The film features a happy confluence of sun and water. The light of the sun is commonly associated with consciousness. Water, by the same token, carries long-standing associations with the unconscious. In *Lido* we are not peering into the deeps, however, but exploring not far beneath the surface where the familiar is agreeably altered. Meanwhile, bathing has to do with both inner and outer purification. Nothing drowned in painful obscurity is signalled here, but rather the sweet and creative renewal stimulated by dipping into realms of fantasy which hitherto lay on the periphery of awareness, only semi-consciously glimpsed. The people, the weather and the water make for the delight found in the lido. Take any one of those away and the magic is gone. Remove from the finished film Blakstad's poetic interpolation of all three components into the minds of her viewers and *Lido* would fail to engage their imagination with a vivid idea of a richer way of being that lies within the grasp of ordinary people. Fredericksen found that *The Song of Ceylon* compensated for the dominance of conscious control in the work of the British Documentary Movement through its mystical perspective. *Lido* allows the viewer vicariously to enjoy a sensual and social pleasure that introduces a sense of well-being embracing physical, social, emotional and spiritual facets of life.

My Demons: The Legacy – archetypal images and the first-person documentary[3]

The origins of this sub-genre lie in the individual's desire to record his or her own thoughts and experiences. Where once they would have been recorded on paper, now they can be registered on tape or disc. This mode of documentary depends on the belief (which must be shared by broadcasters as well as electronic autobiographers) that such recordings of personal experience will be of interest to a general audience. Before the late 1980s technical difficulties made it hard to produce from the home a well edited, polished movie with broadcast quality synchronised sound. Therefore few first-person screen documentaries were made on 8mm, the cheapest film stock for domestic use. However, home movies, finished to the less demanding standards of the domestic audience, did make extensive use of 8mm technology. The great wave of first-person documentary was made possible by two factors. One was the recognition by broadcasters in the 1980s and 1990s that they could find an audience for such material. The other was relatively inexpensive high-quality camcorder technology, with its ease of use, not to mention the narcissistically satisfying attraction that it permits immediate playback.

The undeniable overlap between the home movie and the first-person documentary makes it tempting to say that the latter has existed ever since families with portable cameras began making home movies. Certainly the aesthetics of the one have left their marks on the other. Camera angles differ from those that polished professional work has made familiar in that images are not composed with the same eye for a balanced 'speaking picture'. Filming is rarely planned with a view to editing in cutaways and inserts. As a consequence there is a great deal of inaccurately hand-held camera, and scenes tend rather to be built within the camera than in the edit suite.

Among significant differences, the home movie has a domestic audience to which its proud maker shows footage of people and places which that audience usually know well because they are socially connected with them in some way. The documentary, on the other hand, always has an audience outside the domestic circle (although first-person programmes are often made with an awareness of the filmmaker's milieu). Indeed a key difference from the home movie is that the documentary will aim to show or tell its audience things that it does not already know. In addition, the first-person film always has a theme and some sort of shape. Neither is essential to the home movie, as family and friends (but seldom the filmmakers themselves) are all too often horribly aware.

3 An earlier working of the following analysis is found in Kilborn and Izod (1997: 81–3, 104–9).

Self-evidently, first-person films license subjectivity. Indeed there is almost an obligation to feature one individual's idiosyncratic observations. We want to know how the filmmaker's view of the world relates to our own, and this is one of the strengths of such work. Furthermore, imagination often supersedes observation. Thus such films have the potential to reverse one of the founding dictates of the Documentary Movement, that it should respect the objectivity of the outside world, if necessary at the expense of subjectivity. This is not to deny that there must be something that is faithful to actuality in front of the lens. An autobiographical film will usually put on screen the images of the filmmaker's life in family, community and beyond. That may indeed be the limits of its ambition. But it can do other things – its business may be with the documentarist's fantasy life.

A young man obsessed with the idea of a monster abandons a good safe career, buys a battered old library bus with the proceeds of his pension fund and quits South East England for the chilly shores of Loch Ness. There he sits for a whole year watching through the changing seasons, gathering lore from local people, reading up his topic and shooting footage of the whole venture. He does not achieve a sighting. This is Steve Feltham's *Video Diary, Desperately Seeking Nessie* (BBC 1992) and it is riveting in large measure because it reveals his personality simultaneously from the inside (via interior monologue) and the outside (through the opinions – some of them pungently dismissive – of people whom he meets). It grabs the attention also because he discovers in the process of recording and reviewing his thoughts that it was the quest itself more than achieving the desired goal that mattered to him. Making the film has fed a process of self-discovery. Indeed, the evolution of the filmmaker's personality is one of the recurring features of first-person documentary. Feltham's imagined monster, although it has a lively existence in his fantasies, was no demon, but a friendly psychopomp – an image sprung like a dark messenger from the unconscious that led him on his geographical and spiritual journey. Had it been hostile, however, the journey might have become something more than a personal biography.

This is what happens in Willa Woolston's film, *My Demons: The Legacy*, also made for *Video Diaries* in 1992. It extends the first-person format beyond the confessional form which it quite often takes to the point where it has a therapeutic function. Her film records a journey from London across North America. It takes her through Los Angeles (her daughter's home), on to Detroit (where her son resides with his wife and their infants) and culminates in Philadelphia, the city where she grew up and the rest of her family still live. Her purpose was to visit her family with the specific aim of finding out more about herself by recovering memories of her childhood. The record of her travel across the States becomes the trail of an inner journey in which she goes back into the past to get to the psychological roots of the physical and mental torture she and her sisters suffered at the hands of her stepmother. That mistreatment has left her a lifelong slave to savage apprehension and relentless traumas. Frequently in crisis, she has been pushed to excessive drinking and suicide attempts. All her intimate relationships, not only with men but also with her children, have been damaged.

Willa Woolston acts as her own narrator, and so the voiceover, far from being a dominating Voice-of-God address in the manner of many expository documentaries, quietly utters the painful truths that have shaped her life for decades. At the core of the film are very long takes during which the camera rests, more or less static, on individual members of her family while she talks to them from behind the lens. The camera is always in Willa's hands (except when very occasionally one of her sisters turns it on her), and from time to time members of her family, either mildly embarrassed or when agonising memories thrust back into their conscious minds, request her to switch off. She seldom obliges – and the effect is to build our respect for a group of singularly courageous people. Other moments of equal weight occur when she puts herself in front of the lens and resists cutting until she has managed to utter all the horrors that are flooding her memory. Taken together, these shots – which form entire sequences – record the moments when Willa probes her sisters' and her children's memories, and they quiz her about hers, slowly moving together towards a fuller understanding of the woman who tortured them.

Together those of the older generation bring back the traumatised memories of childhood as uncomprehending victims of their tormentor. They recall being hanged by the thumbs from pipes in the basement and left there for the entire day. One sister was once tied to a chair and abandoned in the summer sun until her skin blistered. And they remember other terrible abuses and assaults. Worst of all, they come to realise with dreadful horror that their father, whom they loved dearly, must have known all this was going on and yet did nothing for fear of losing the vivacious woman who had rescued him from widowhood.

As I have said, most of these memories are recovered in long, close-up takes. They are therefore also harrowing for the viewer to witness. Into these prolonged takes the editor (Alice Forward) has inserted home movie footage taken by their father. In these shots, the sisters and their stepmother are always serenely happy. Cutting deeper than irony this racks up the pain and gives authority to the eldest sister's words when she says that, try though she might, she could never get the neighbours to intervene and help them in any way. Because the family looked as comfortable together in public as we see them to be in the home movies, the neighbours were able to persuade themselves that there was no compelling reason to act.

As is usual in this format, most shots were taken with nothing more than available light. Synch sound was recorded direct onto videotape, sometimes through a single microphone and on other occasions with a pair of clip-on mikes. The somewhat rough-and-ready quality of the pictures and the occasional imbalance in sound levels when Willa speaks to her family from behind the camera actually contribute to our sense of intimacy with these people. All in all the tape has something of the surface texture of a home movie, although from the plain evidence of its careful preplanning it is anything but that. The blend of the apparent casualness of the shooting style with the high professionalism of many of the tape's aspects (skilled technicians worked on its post-production) builds the viewer's confidence that Willa may not be an expert, but she is learning as she goes along and by the end knows full well what she is doing. And that applies not just to her skill as a filmmaker. One of the tape's strengths is the way that its aesthetics complement Willa's journey of self-discovery. To understand this, we need to describe briefly what happens. As she looks further into herself, and her family members reveal significant fragments of their history that she had not known, Willa becomes aware that the lives of each generation are connected by meaningful repeating patterns. First, she discovers that, although she broke the pattern inflicted by her stepmother and at no time inflicted physical injury upon her own children, they too had suffered grievously in their own childhood. As witnesses to her hysterical outbursts and drunken rages, they had felt responsible, as children often do, for the parent's suffering. Able now for the first time to share her remorse with them (and to make her discoveries stick by recording them on tape so that she can review and confirm them later), she eases some of the blocked channels for the love that they have found so difficult to share. Willa's initial reward is more horror when her daughter reveals that her father turned against her at the instance of his jealous second wife. He assaulted her over a three-year period before evicting her from the house at a time in her high-school career which wrecked her hopes of taking up the university place that was waiting for her.

Willa begins to see the mirror patterns that can run through damaged families and understands from what she has inadvertently done to her offspring that the abuser herself may be worthy of sympathy. This breakthrough is reinforced when she learns that Ferris, her stepmother, had herself been the victim of a horrible family life. She was the only daughter of a father who absented himself on the birth of the infant and a mother who drifted into alcoholism as a consequence of his desertion. Ferris seems to have ended up both parenting her mother and taking the blame for her condition onto herself – just as Willa's children did two generations later.

All this information gives Willa the courage to make contact with the old woman in the hope of understanding her better. Although she succeeds in working up the courage necessary to make the initial telephone contact, and then rings several times during the last weeks of her stay in Philadelphia, Ferris will not allow her to get any closer and declines a visit. But Willa discovers that even talking to her on the phone builds her comprehension as she listens to her stepmother's persistent lies and self-deceits. Her growing understanding eases the sting of the demonic image which has terrorised her all her life. She returns to London and moves out of her old flat. Her film closes with an image taken through doors opening out from the houseboat which she has made her home. As we look across the calm waters of the Thames, she tells us how her whole life has changed. For the first time in her adult life, she is able to sleep without nightmares and wake without dread. She feels in control as never before.

The style of this tape enriches its themes in addition to adding to our sense of its authenticity. There are amateurish aspects of the shoot such as the imperfect quality of the camera angles and sound recorded in the field. But these help convey in a deeply personal way the isolation of this brave woman as she maps and records what is to her (as to any individual who starts out alone on such a journey) the uncharted route to the terrified centre of what she must at first perceive as her unique, wounded self. However, the professional qualities the film exhibits in its editing and dubbing complement this with a feeling of knowing what needs to be done. This is justified when we find ourselves purposefully drawn into the realms of repressed memory complexes familiar in psychoanalysis. Willa combines knowledge of what she is doing (she has researched the subject and has launched a network for the care of former victims of child abuse) with a willingness to find her way intuitively. She is in effect practising auto-psychoanalysis with great success.

The family history that Willa Woolston and her sisters recover resembles the darkest of fairy tales. From the sisters' perspective, Ferris has the characteristics of a witch, and in fairy tales witches are often connected with evil stepmothers (Jacoby 1992: 206–7). When the mother or stepmother figure is introjected as a devouring witch (as in the Grimms' 'Hansel and Gretel'), there a negative mother complex has been aroused. The Jungian analyst Marie-Louise von Franz cites the case of a woman patient who came to analysis with just such a negative complex. It derived from her mother's animus problem which had driven the parent to complain endlessly to her family how much she regretted having married and had children. Like Willa (and presumably Ferris before her), this patient grew up perpetually reminded that it was wrong for her to be alive (1993: 51–2). Willa's opening words in her diary are, 'All my life, the first sensation as I wake has been fear. For no reason, no cause, I just felt apprehension, dread.' This duplicates the feelings of von Franz's patient who was frightened of everyone. Von Franz identifies existential fear as one of the basic enduring problems in adults who have not received enough maternal love when children (1993: 205–6). As intensely destructive as a witch, the mother figure in both instances has inflicted a form of living death on her daughter. In both cases the mother suffered a severe animus problem and this had transferred to the daughter. The animus often embodies in a woman the concealed masculine aspects of her personality. A girl typically projects her animus onto the father in childhood and in due time transfers it to other men such as a lover. No surprise, then, that Willa's own animus has been injured as has her daughter's. Willa's adult life prior to making the programme had been marked by a series of turbulent relationships with men and the consequent emotional turmoil and drunken rages caused her own children great distress.

Like all archetypal figures, however, the negative mother can sometimes reverse its terrible powers. Jacoby and von Franz both cite the Russian fairy tale 'Vasilisa the Beautiful' in which the Baba Yaga, an awesomely grisly witch, unexpectedly helps the hero, showing him the way forward like a magician endowed with profound knowledge (Jacoby 1992: 207; von Franz 1993: 172–3). By the end of *My Demons: The Legacy*, although the impetus comes from Willa and her sisters, the other side of Ferris's face has been revealed. Knowledge of the older woman's suffering helps Willa to integrate her own negative mother complex emotionally rather than merely intellectually, and endows her with a new authority (see von Franz 1993: 207).

Willa Woolston put herself through an invaluable therapeutic experience. But was her programme likely to have offered anything of the sort to the audience? Two features acknowledge its impact. Firstly, the editorial controllers of *Video Diaries* anticipated that *My Demons: The Legacy* (like some other programmes in their slot) would touch a need in certain viewers and ought to be accompanied by back-up. Indeed they had provided such back-up after Willa's first diary, *My Demons*, and it had been much in demand. A closing announcement drew attention to an address for correspondence and telephone helplines already open for callers who might feel in need of support. After *Video Diaries* this became standard practice in British terrestrial broadcasting where programmes might stir anguish in people who had been through similar experiences to the subjects.

Secondly, *My Demons: The Legacy* is a gruelling experience for the viewer. Its direct address to the viewer and the terrible history it recovers trigger overwhelming emotional responses in those who see it in its entirety, the majority of whom will have had no personal experience of a tormenting mother. The grief that the programme arouses can then in part be attributed to the empathy with which Willa expresses the rediscovered agony of those defenceless children – children who include her own former self. But in large part the programme works at depth because it activates two archetypal figures and situations. The first is indeed the child. An archetypal image encountered by many individuals as a key symbol in therapy, it can reveal to the patient his or her earlier self. Its recovery into memory can present analysands with the opportunity to understand, by seeing themselves as they once were, the roots of what may have been continuing trauma. In Willa's case, the readily understandable repression of the emotional pain that invested the appalling memories of her childhood stood in the way of her recovering from that trauma. By reconnecting Willa with her roots, her rediscovered child self assists her recovery. It is possible that in witnessing her rediscovery of forgotten memories, viewers may, as it were in parallel with her emotions, intuit that they themselves have forfeited much in the transition to adult consciousness.

Metaphorically the Terrible Mother, the second archetypal image in play here, represents nothing less than the devourer of her own offspring – the power an overpowering parent can exert to suck dry her children's psychological individuality.[4] Hence she is the obverse of the fertile, nurturing Earth Mother. For Jung the collective *imago* of the mother had exactly this profound ambivalence (felt throughout Willa Woolston's diary). The mother is a figure known in one manifestation or another to all, whatever their individual experience of being parented. As an archetypal *imago*, she signals the need for the young to break away from the mother's psychologically stultifying embrace in order to enter adulthood. Willa Woolston progresses, therefore, in a way which many of her viewers will intuitively recognise. She not only makes the break from the old woman devouring her life but also seems finally to have let go of her much-loved and long-mourned birth mother.

The direct address of naked psychological autobiography is one mode of contemporary documentary which unquestionably has the power to stir the viewer's emotions at a deep level and allow issues that time has obscured to spill unbidden into the conscious mind. It exposes anybody who engages with the deeply felt products of another person's imagination to the risk of emotional tumult. Some viewers will indeed (as Woolston's producers anticipated) be shocked by the reawakening of unwelcome trauma. Others may be tempted to emulate Willa Woolston and start out on their own journeys of self-discovery. Yet others again, the present writer included, will experience the need to reassess with their adult offspring their own past family histories as parents.

4 Comparable damage can be done by an overmastering father.

Chapter 8

Westerns, local and global imperialism

Introduction

I want to commence my observations on this enduring genre from the thought that the Western on screen constitutes a primary locus in which through much of the last century battle was joined for what was taken to be the collective soul of the United States of America. To me this seems the key to the genre's formidable strengths and also to its weaknesses.

The focus on the idea of the North American national identity encapsulated in the Western is clarified in the comparison with Brazilians' experience of collective identity. Roberto Gambini has argued that his nation suffers from a serious problem in lacking a myth of origin. As a consequence its people are ashamed of their remote past, which they regard as a black hole. They have instead built an identity dating from 1500 with what they call 'The Discovery' – an event which would more accurately be referred to as the invasion. The nation's history is based on the false premise that it began with the Portuguese Conquest. This has serious consequences for the structuring of the collective consciousness and, as a knock-on effect, for the way Brazilians relate to the deep layers of the collective unconscious. Gambini argues, 'Since we deny our ancestral origin, we distort it . . .' (1998: 150). Had this not occurred, Brazilians could have developed a vibrant synthesis, both practical and spiritual, between European and Amerindian ways of being; but no such synthesis was ever achieved.

Gambini's rueful account of Brazilian cultural history resonates edgily with the North American experience because significant features of their histories run parallel. Until the late twentieth century the Western furnished a myth of origin that was profoundly Euro-centred. It was a rewriting of history into legend that suited the white male perspective but had little to say to those women who were not willing to find their consciousness through the psyche of men. It did not address the experiences of Asian migrants; and (with rare, honourable exceptions) it had nothing whatsoever to say to the dispossessed original inhabitants of the continent. These omissions were catastrophic in their long-term consequences because, as Gambini says, 'All of mankind's great questions were worked on and solved by the indigenous peoples inhabiting the New World since pristine times' (1998: 150). Issues such as survival, conquering hunger, human relations, material culture, moral concerns and the nature of the universe – all these observations, and many others made over endless repetitions, added up to a wisdom very distinct from that of the European incomers. It was the stuff from which soul was made only to be destroyed by the invasion (Gambini 1998: 150–1). This was a consequence too of the near eradication of Native American culture in the USA.

Cultural provenance

If Western movies do indeed constitute a primary locus in which the struggle for the collective soul of the USA has been fought out and that struggle implicates its characters, how does it involve the deep psychology of the audience? Does the Western of the early twenty-first century differ from its predecessors in ways which reflect changes in the audience's circumstances and reveal psychological shifts associated with those societal changes?

After the genre had (once again) been declared dead at the start of the twenty-first century, the release of some fine movies in 2003 indicated that it had not lost its box-office capacity to engage substantial audiences – a reminder how deep its roots run into collective emotions. Those roots sustain boldly-drawn archetypal images that energise the Western's highly charged myths. Since we are discussing a genre that has grown a strong timber of resilient iconography, the archetypal images it deploys are both its established boughs and the nodal points from which new growth buds. Archetypes themselves do not change (or if they do, then at an evolutionary pace, far too slow to be detected in the human life span). Archetypal images, however, are more exposed to the erosions of time and culture than the forms that they can only fill out provisionally: images (archetypal or not) are of necessity woven from the symbolic strands which societies develop in order to communicate. Although archetypal images feel sovereign to people experiencing their power, they are not immutable and do alter under sustained social, cultural or ideological pressure (Wehr 1987: 93–4). As in any long-established generic form, therefore, both continuity of meaning and its evolution can be seen in the Western by examining the provenance of its imagery.

By 2004, the Western had occupied the screen (albeit with several gaps) for 100 years; but some of its sources were much older. The first Western novel, James Fenimore Cooper's *The Pioneers*, an immediate success, was published in 1823 but the literary heritage of two of the genre's significant thematic strands can be traced back to a seventeenth- and eighteenth-century British vogue. The upper classes of that era enjoyed odes that celebrated the rural idyll of the self-sufficient gentleman-farmer who had withdrawn from the stews of city life. In leading this vogue, Ben Jonson and Andrew Marvell revived delightfully the odes of Horace (*ca.* 13 BC), and countless clumsy poetasters thereafter copied their luminous example. Parallel to this sub-genre runs the pastoral tradition contemplating the shepherd's existence in the meadows. Here is an imagined life for a man (or occasionally a woman) which would be perfect were it not spoiled by human frailty and vice. Alexander Pope worked in this mode in 1704, tracing its usage back through Edmund Spenser and Sir Philip Sidney to the *Eclogues* of Horace's contemporary Virgil and thence to the third century BC *Idylls* of Theocritus.

Spiritual provenance

The pastoral idyll and the celebration of the self-sufficient farmer lie close to the themes of many great Western movies – none more so than *Shane* (1953). Why should this seemingly bizarre connection have such potency? Because, of course, in its English language reworkings, the rural ideal took its original energy less from secular literary sources than the Bible. Therefore the commanding image underlying the idyll was a highly charged symbol, vividly present in the minds of immigrants from Europe even before their arrival. It carried the sacred energy of an ancient, religiously and mythically charged image cluster which had crystallised in its Christian form in the idea of Paradise. This vision of the promised land resonated with meaning for those who moved to take up new land in the West. And it gave a particular spiritual credence to that historic migration (see Smith 1970: 123–32).

Gambini notes that Portuguese men had also landed in Brazil with a Paradise fantasy in their heads – an enormous and very dangerous fantasy, which certainly included a vision of naked and willing women in a place where everything was permitted. There (as in North America) this dream-land was for the exclusive enjoyment of white men, never for the Indians. Indeed, the Conquest was an absolutely masculine and phallic endeavour, its twin symbols the cross and the sword. Coupled with this, the refined feelings expressed by the great Portuguese love poets of the time were absent in the new territory. Instead of the positive anima whom the poets described, the invaders brought a fantasy which reflected unbridled greed and lust. The anima figure they had in mind was the whore, and Indian women have had to carry this projection to this day (Gambini 1998: 156–8).

The dominant ideology of the North American immigrants of the sixteenth and seventeenth centuries was Protestantism rather than the Catholic faith that dominated immigrant communities in Latin America. In the North, many of the newcomers came in family and community groups to settle and find new lives rather than return to the motherland. Gambini indicates in contrast that Portuguese men went to Brazil unaccompanied by family. There they bred with Indian women who thereby lost their place in their own community. As hybrids, the offspring were not accepted in their mothers' community and were treated as pariahs in Portugal should their fathers be repatriated and take them there (Gambini 1998: 156–7). The Church actually became so concerned about miscegenation and its consequences that it imported white prostitutes from Portugal from 1533 (and with them syphilis) (1998: 158). These factors make the parallel between the North American and Brazilian experiences less pronounced. Nevertheless, sexual relations between peoples usually follow the mass migration of unaccompanied men. And as we shall see, the dark whore is a recurring archetypal figure in the Western, juxtaposed to the pure, fair-haired woman. The genre's robber barons in the USA may not send gold to Europe, but they surely do steal the land.

Libido and the land

In the North American states, the Paradise image cluster metamorphosed into a seductive notion that the new territories were the garden of the world and that they could be made into the new Eden by the labour of an honest people. In its metamorphosis, that idea's potency extended the biblical symbolism of the garden as the blessed place, a Paradise on earth, to include in the cluster the farm, the smallholding, the wilderness, nature and even the desert. Looking at the image cluster from the perspective of analytical psychology, we can read it as an emerging symbol of an idealised, collective self. It was a sacred icon which took on its own distinctive warp from the political and cultural exigencies of the white North American experience.

There can be no question that influential American writers of the late eighteenth century such as J. Hector St John Crèvecoeur and Thomas Jefferson were steeped not only in the Bible, but also in the English literary tradition. But there was a formative difference in their New World circumstances. By this time, England was crowded by comparison with America and much of the arable land had been brought into private ownership. Where the owners were not themselves farmers, they acted as landlords renting to tenants. So the idea that the good life might be enjoyed by a farmer in retreat from the urbanised world's corruption was never practicable for more than a handful of rich gentry owning large estates. Rather, it was fashionable among an educated English elite as a nostalgic remembrance of the countryside which many had left when migrating into the towns. In contrast, eighteenth- and nineteenth-century American writers could contemplate a vast continent believed to be replete with untouched and wonderfully fertile land, there for the taking. For a time it seemed possible to a man such as Jefferson that the ideal could be made actual in Virginia – or nearly so.

If it is correct to assert that Western movies constitute a primary locus in which the struggle for the collective soul of *white* North America has been fought out, the question arises why the entry to Eden should be represented as a matter for struggle. The short answer is that the land has always been contested – both in historical actuality and the mythologised memories.

I have written elsewhere about the displacement of libidinous energy in the Western myth in the nineteenth and twentieth centuries. Eros, which would ordinarily attach man to woman, drew the Western male by main force to nature, such was the appeal of the pastoral ideal. The white hero (whether frontiersman, trapper or cowboy) dreads being trapped by marriage in the tedium of urban domesticity: he fears that the ambience of the dreary cow town will snuff out his masculine libido. Instead, his obsessive love of nature leads him to invest the wilderness with feminine qualities. Psychoanalytically interpreted, the resulting displacement makes for a dangerous, uroboric courtship of the Earth Mother. It inhibits the proper maturation of the Western hero's psyche and accounts for the often infantile nature of his relationships with white women. Furthermore, this quasi-incestuous love affair with nature was never untroubled because the new migrants could not ignore the awkward fact that there were other peoples already settled in the West. The latter had been there so long when the incomers reached their territories that they seemed to enjoy a bond with the land that Americans of European descent could not share. So the white man found a dark-skinned rival who had got there first and whose presence intruded on the newcomer's jealous love for the wilderness (Izod 2001: 40–1).

That rivalry troubled the psycho-sexuality of the whites themselves and their conception of Native Americans' nature. Since the new arrivals meant to possess the land by seizing it from its original inhabitants, they soon demonised the latter by intuitively making them the object of their collective shadow projection, as all peoples do with their enemies when they prepare to go to war. These racist shadow projections endured long after the end of the Indian wars and tainted the Western genre, where they remained a staple feature through much of the twentieth century. One consequence was experienced in North America no less than in the many other territories worldwide to which Europeans migrated in large numbers: the dark-skinned original inhabitants were laden with the burden of white sexual guilt and were thought of as licentious. The men were believed to be rapacious and to prefer white women to their own. For this reason, white women had to be defended against them. Meanwhile the dark woman was seen as sexually available (and therefore desirable) in ways that white women were not. This dichotomy lies at the root of the classical Western's somewhat coy characterisation of the good woman as blonde, chaste and fair, and the bad woman as dark, brunette, over-sexed and at risk of being killed in recompense for her libidinous temerity (Izod 2001: 41).

Marginalising the carriers of the unconscious

Either way, the impact of woman as anima is almost always severely slighted. Although she should function as an archetypal image whose power can lead a man's ego-consciousness toward some insight into the contents of his unconscious (with a concomitant enrichment of his personality), in the Western her power was marginalised.

The splitting of the female image runs right through the genre until well into the third quarter of the twentieth century. The male hero cultivates his strength (the power of his will) in order to defend from what are in fact his own split-off desires the chaste, civilised but rather bloodless woman who represents the only type he can accept as a marriage partner. In marrying her, he defends the urbanising culture that he despises but of which she is the steadfast representative. In short, we find that the white hero employs his highly-focused conscious will ultimately to resist the seductions (both benign and evil) of the unconscious (Izod 2001: 41–2).

The difficult endeavour to ensure that will should triumph had affected the representation of Native American peoples. Yet Luigi Zoja observes that, paradoxically, white Americans hunger for indigenous culture. He notes that this culture is at odds with the dominant form of narrative invented by Hollywood. The latter relies upon purposeful action and anchors the personality type of the modern hero: 'We are presented with men and women who choose, who align themselves with the powers of goodness, who entrust its redemption to wilful action, and who never doubt its final triumph' (1998: 41). The white Western hero is the criterion of this type. But the problem with which in the long term this narrative form confronts audiences is that it lacks ambivalence. Like Christianity itself, it 'shows no toleration for opposites that forever intertwine, the one around the other' (Zoja 1998: 36). Hollywood's dominant form gives the audience no help in facing 'everything within us that is paralysed by ambivalence, hypnotised by mystery, and fearfully immersed in eternal contemplation of the uselessness of all the greatest efforts of the will' (1998: 37–8). Applied to Hollywood's output in its entirety, Zoja's argument is rather too sweeping; but it does marry with my own observation of the cultural values typically represented by Western heroes. Through much of the twentieth century they bring about the triumph of Logos and power over Eros; of the conscious mind over the unconscious; and of the focused will to *become* over the diffuse, emotionally free experiencing of *being*.

According to Zoja, redress for this one-sided view of things is readily found in Native American culture and the discourse of Indian chiefs such as Joseph and Crazy Horse (Zoja 1998: 41–2; and see Rayner 1979: 14–15):

> The Hollywood hero strives for justice when his rights have been offended; the Indian Chief knows that life is the seat of drama, not of justice, and prepares himself in all tranquillity for the next blow of

> destiny . . . The Hollywood hero believes in the supreme power of will; the Indian Chief, like the tragic hero, believes that will counts for nothing . . . The Hollywood hero is ingenuous; the Indian Chief is wise.
> (Zoja 1998: 42)

Thus, Zoja argues, America's need to listen to the voices of its native peoples is not only a historical necessity – it reflects a need of modern collective consciousness. Gambini's (1998: 153) evaluation of Brazilian experience supports this position: 'Consciousness looks for its eternal other, the unconscious. Our ego searches for its other, an ego no longer identified with shadow and persona, but one striving to express the self. The quest for the other is always archetypal, and for [Brazilians] *this other is the Indian*'. Brazilian access to the Indian as other is, as we have seen, almost lost because of the degree of destruction of native culture. The other is not integrated and has become a renegade in the psyche and in its own land (Gambini 1998: 153–4). Once again, the resemblance to the North American experience is marked, and Gambini's words anticipate much that is found in Ron Howard's *The Missing* (2003).

The need for a nation to listen to the voices of its native peoples is also a moral obligation. Issues of morality have usually numbered among the main ostensible concerns of the Western but until the last quarter of the century such concerns seldom focused on interracial morality. Classical Westerns made prior to the 1950s focused on the stark contrast between good and evil to such a degree that they left a mark on the collective memory. A sign of this appears in the essays of those undergraduates in film studies who to this day refer to characters as 'black hat' and 'white hat'. Students can be taught how both moral issues and iconography in countless Westerns made since 1950 became more subtle than in earlier films, but some of them find it impossible to hold onto those nuances, such is the pull of black versus white archetypal conflict.

How can this occur (particularly given that in the genre the bad was often personified by Indians), if Zoja is right in identifying an appetite for Native American culture? One explanation lies in the long reach of Christian ideology. The moral absolutes read into even those Westerns which should properly be interpreted altogether more sensitively are sustained by an inflexible epistemology that sets black against white. Terms that originate in morality overlap onto race and, from a white perspective, were long mapped back onto 'whites', allegedly that colour in skin and morality, and 'black' people ditto. Historically the Western has overwhelmingly been racist. The notable exceptions to the general rule struggle against the tide so that examples of Westerns reflecting American Indian culture are to this day few and far between. Are the latter definitive of modern American culture as Zoja would anticipate? Or rather, is the Western still for many in the audience, as it predominantly was through the past century, a site of resistance to Native American culture – a site of resistance, perhaps to the needs of the white unconscious?

Allegory

Westerns are often interpreted by those who want to look beyond their surface as licensing allegorical readings. A similar mode of interpreting texts flourished in the Renaissance when readers of allegories moved skilfully through such texts as if they were switching between thematic strands. The nature of those strands was predetermined to the extent that readers would have expected to discover behind the entry level of narrative, character, imagery and action firstly, moral readings; secondly, Old Testament readings; and thirdly, New Testament counterparts to those older stories. Thus allegory in this period depended on pre-existing texts. These might draw from Greek or Roman myths and tales, but it was the Bible that shaped the other readings, both authorising and constraining the reader's interpretations. The writer would proceed from the assumption that the fiction should disguise but remain faithful to the source stories – biblical or classical – upon which it overlaid the fantasy world of the allegorical narrative. All the strands would be in play, though with continuously shifting intensity.

Biblical exegesis no longer has its former force for audiences. Today, archetypal images and the emotional charge they carry function in the Western as a potent attraction, drawing spectators' attention to what may reward their investigation. It fits with the shift away from the Bible's overmastering authority that the morality of Westerns does not in the first instance derive from antiquity nor even the historical period in which they are set, but from needs generated for both filmmakers and their audiences by present-day circumstances. Such needs and appetites are heavily influenced both by culture and by psychological projections. That helps explain why, in the Western, characters, story and imagery are so structured as to accommodate, often actively to invite, readings that engage simultaneously on more than one 'level'. It also helps explain why the allegorical mode is effective. It can weave into Western mythology strands drawn from a number of interconnected thematic areas or *topoi*. Hollywood productions usually do this tactfully so that the spectator can find gratification in the story (including the action, the nature of the characters and the fate that befalls them) without being obliged to explore the deeper levels. However, those deeper levels frequently supply the storyline with its resonance. Thus this genre provides a semi-constant but evolving armature around which may be wound readings bearing on moral questions, politics (both societal and familial), economics, psychology and spirituality.

At the surface is found the entry level of action and character development. Whether or not a given film claims to be a re-enactment of history, the entry level will have mythologised events of the past to meet (or occasionally to revitalise or even challenge) the cultural expectations of the present. This notwithstanding that many Westerns claim a measure of realism. However, they usually justify that claim by revising the accepted conventions of the genre rather than by any detailed representation of, say, a cowhand's working skills. In practice, fantasy (whether concealed or not) usually dominates the genre, its effect being to shape allegorical and symbolic readings of the myth. Those readings are given structure by the surface elements – narrative, character development, iconography and style.

Kung Fu, moral and political allegory

An example which makes this process obvious is found in 'The Ancient Warrior' (dir. Robert Butler, 1973), an episode from the series *Kung Fu* (Warner Bros Television). The fact that the Western was rendered deliberately strange by this series – which sought to capture a particular market segment at that historical moment – makes its constituent elements peculiarly visible. Its strangeness arises from a Hollywood conjunction truly weird seen from 30 years' distance. Bowderlerised Chinese traditional teachings blend with the more familiar trappings of the Western. The obviously Caucasian David Carradine plays an itinerant Buddhist monk, Kwai Chang Caine – the hero. To mention only the most dominant built-in contradiction, whereas the Western is inherently violent, Caine supposedly observes pacifist principles. The producers deal with this discrepancy by having the baddies resort to the usual Western mayhem with fists, boots and guns; meanwhile Caine abjures force until pushed beyond a man's (i.e. a westerner's) limits of endurance. The series manages to elide demonstrations of Caine's finely honed skills as a martial arts expert with notions of pacifism because a hero who never carries a gun is so rare in this genre as to seem pacifist.

In 'The Ancient Warrior', Carradine's monk rescues an ageing tribal leader (Chief Dan George) from some local rednecks who are tormenting him. The old man, last of his people, is looking for his sacred burial ground so that he can die in peace. Caine agrees to accompany him on his search. However, the chief discovers his chosen place in the main street of Purgatory, a town populated by bigots. The dying man possesses deeds that prove his claim to the entire territory and stands on his rights. So Caine's skills as peaceable representative and martial arts defender are soon drawn on. Because the town had eight years earlier been the site of warfare between Native Americans and the ultimately victorious white residents, many of the latter hate the people who fought against them and inflicted a number of fatalities before their own bloody defeat. It falls to Caine and the older and less paranoid residents of the town, led by the judge, to negotiate for the rights of the chief.

The elements of fantasy (a white fantasy at that) are all too plain here but, despite its superficial strangeness, the narrative does preserve the underlying structure of the good going up against the bad – albeit with *dramatis personae* (the chieftain and the Buddhist monk) from whose perspective the point of view is focused – characters who would have been inconceivable in the Western a decade earlier. Three factors licensed this extraordinary development. First was the respect won in 1967 by Chief Dan George himself as representative of the wronged dignity of his people in Arthur Penn's film *Little Big Man*. Second, that film's release and the transmission of *Kung Fu* coincided with an era of growing consciousness of white American racism against Native American peoples, as burgeoning support for the Civil Rights Movement indicated. The third factor was the disruption of conservative American morality caused by the Peace Movement's resistance to the never-ending Vietnam War. The disaffected would indeed have comprised the principal target audience for the series.

These factors lead us toward two *topoi* that in one form or another recur in many Westerns. Firstly, the stoic suffering of the main character invites a reading bound in with the genre's concern for moral issues – unmistakable in 'The Ancient Warrior'. Secondly, that reading takes energy from, and feeds it back into current political matters of high significance to the domestic audience at the date of release. By 1973, the Vietnam conflict had for some years bred conflict in the USA, manifesting in mass demonstrations in Washington, disruption of the Democrats' 1968 Chicago Convention, student sit-ins on a number of campuses and the shootings at Kent State University. The wider background to 'The Ancient Warrior' was plainly enough the belief which had gathered considerable popular support by the early 1970s that there must be a better way of negotiating differences that did not depend on the futile deployment of maximum force – whether at home (*cf.* the rednecks' hatred of the Native American chief) or abroad (*cf.* the facile contempt on the part of Purgatory's law officers for the peaceable Oriental monk).

Political correspondences were registered in 'The Ancient Warrior' with telling specificity. The people of Purgatory are policed by a certain Sheriff Pool, a bigot and a tyrant who ensures no one forgets the massacre. Although formally answerable to the mayor and a citizens' committee, this sheriff rides roughshod over the law's niceties, backed by his strong-arm deputies. Caine witnesses one of these deputies obeying orders and shooting in the back a man who has challenged the sheriff. When Caine confronts Pool with the evidence, the latter baldly asserts, 'A man does what it takes. The knack for survival is what makes for a good sheriff.' Given the political epoch, this is a significant rupture from the supposed readiness of sheriffs to die in the pursuit of their duty as custodians of the law.

In 1973, the 'Pool' on most Americans' minds was Watergate, the political scandal in which Richard Nixon was floundering. Attempting to rescue his presidency from allegations that he had authorised dirty tricks against his Democrat opponents in the 1972 presidential election campaign, he was sinking ever deeper into the political and moral mire by obstructing justice in the interests of self-preservation. The sheriff, whose first name is Aldon ('all done'), satirises Nixon. He has all the President's skill in fostering collective paranoia against Reds (Indians = Communists) and all his talent for whingeing self-justification. Resigning after the citizens' committee votes for the Ancient Warrior, Pool utters his own political epitaph, the Nixonian echoes of which ring plainly: 'These are violent times. Being a sheriff isn't easy. I think you'll find that out when you try to replace me.' Meanwhile the political associations of the episode are made the more persuasive by the elderly figure of Judge Marcus, a fictional ghost of ex-President Lyndon B. Johnson (who had died in January 1973). Playing to Johnson's record as a president who had worked for the advancement of civil rights (while glossing over his responsibility for escalating the Vietnam war), the judge advocates forgiveness of past military slayings and recognition of the Ancient Warrior's rights.

Although political allegory does not often take the form of so precise a microcosm as in 'The Ancient Warrior', the impact of distinctive policies and national moral values that certain American leaders stood for can be traced in some Westerns made during and after their administrations. Those films may offer a framework for their audiences to get behind current dominant ideologies, as in Wayne's endorsement of defiant anti-Communism in *The Alamo* (1960), or may provide (albeit generally semi-concealed in allegorical terms) an oppositional or satirical stance, as with *King Fu*. Philip French, who first advanced this thesis, discerned qualities of style and content which he argued characterised a liberal Kennedy Western, observing that it might have a slightly diffident hero capable of change and development. *Butch Cassidy and the Sundance Kid* (1969) can be placed in such a frame, in its case as a post-Kennedy Western. And it seems reasonable to to add *Kung Fu* to that cycle. French juxtaposed this type to the conservative and aggressive traits typical of films like *The Alamo* made in emulation of Senator Barry Goldwater's hard right-wing values (1977: 28–31). French wanted to suggest 'a link between contemporary pressures of various kinds and an existing body of material which is constantly subjected to them' (1977: 41). My own objectives are firstly to discover whether a comparable link can be demonstrated between the early twenty-first century Western and political values currently dominant in the USA and secondly to consider whether such links run deep enough to link the psychology of fictional characters to collective apprehensions of the audience.

Landscape and economic power

Westerns frequently centre on the ownership and use of land. I have referred to the genre's allegorical representation of territory in so far as it evokes readings that attend to sacred, psychological and political issues. However, as a recurrent and obsessional *topos*, the land also incorporates economic issues. The Western seldom allows respect for characters who do not own property – one of the factors that denies heroic stature to townspeople (excepting only sheriffs and marshals). It is also the usual subtext to the driving out of Native Americans from their homelands: notwithstanding their symbiotic relation with nature and their prior claim to dwelling there, they don't *own* the land in any form recognised by capital. Indeed, the loose derivation of many Western plots from the historical battles for land makes them fitting vehicles for allegorical reflections on the functioning of capital. So it seems likely that property will continue to be fought over on screen unless either the dominant capitalist ideology of the USA or the demography of its peoples should change out of all recognition.

Just as literary pastoral was once written for the educated, few of whom would actually have been working the land, so commercial factors always ensured that Western movies found the bulk of their audience not with cowboys but among town dwellers. While few of the latter would ever have been involved in battles over the ownership of large areas of land, in 1953 (the year George Stevens's film was released) *Shane*'s smallholders had their urban equivalent in the young families who were using their postwar affluence to become home owners, many of them in the suburbs that were springing up around major cities across the USA. *Shane* associated love of family and the cherished garden smallholding with redemption, while linking greed with damnation – an allegorical frame which readily mapped onto the new suburban values of the time. Although *Shane*'s newly-settled small farmers have legal rights to their property, they are threatened by the rancher who tries to drive them off the land in order to secure ownership of the entire territory. Ryker (Emile Meyer) reckons that they are stealing his land. His monstrous greed has the characteristic of irresponsible corporate capital – seizing property and taking profit without regard for the small man. Such action would have been strong in folk memory for many in the USA 20 years after the great depression of the 1930s. In addition, projected fear of the bankers who held liens on so many recently purchased suburban homes may also have vested in Ryker's demonic figure.

The film encapsulates Ryker's mania in day-for-night shots which also capture a kind of nobility. His white-maned head stands out against a cerulean moonlit sky whose vast acres he means to possess. His avarice cannot hide his hubristic passion – his sense that the land is *owed* him. So his greed is offset by the tragic qualities of a Lear who simultaneously knows but cannot allow himself to know what the future is bringing. His mania adds a not insignificant colouration to the film's optimism. Whatever the ruthlessness of Ryker, the audience is clearly positioned to see that the sane management of capital must be altered to accommodate the interests of 'smallholders'.

The same thematic territory was revisited in Anthony Mann's *The Man from Laramie* (1955). In this film relentless corporate greed must marry the restraint of the small enterprise to be humanised. Ranch owner Alec Waggoman (Donald Crisp) is another incipiently blind Lear figure who learns only when his sight is gone to see the true futility of all that he has amassed. By then both his spoilt son and the foreman he almost adopted are dead, indirect victims of his tyrannical need to control everything. Only when his life's ambitions have been destroyed through relentless acquisitiveness does he find the prospect of ease in the arms of the forgiving woman whose small neighbouring ranch he has coveted for years.

In 1985, Warner Bros released Clint Eastwood's *Pale Rider*. The film was modelled on *Shane* and Coy LaHood (Richard Dysart), the owner of a mining outfit, is Ryker's equivalent. However, the slack-jowelled LaHood's rapacious avarice is wholly self-absorbed. Since he runs a company, he too represents corporate greed as well as personal vice; but he lacks Ryker's tragic qualities and there is no hint of past glory about him. His operation uses hydraulic mining techniques which not only threaten the living of small-claim miners in the valley below, but rape the environment. Although the state legislature is discussing moves to outlaw this invasive technique, the only effect on LaHood is to make him drive his men harder to extract every ounce of gold the land holds before the law stops him. Thus Eastwood's take on corporate culture in the mid-1980s is gloomy in the extreme. His young hero Megan describes LaHood's site as Hell. When the mystical Preacher (Eastwood) wreaks apocalyptic revenge on the enterprise, the film plainly indicates that ecological irresponsibility is sacrilege. But it goes further by suggesting that human agency alone is not strong enough to curb the appetites of corporate capital.

In this, *Pale Rider* resembles the pessimism of *Comes a Horseman* (1978) which is set in the mid-1940s. Alan J. Pakula's small-scale ranchers Ella Connors and Buck Athearn (Jane Fonda and James Caan) manage to fend off the tyrannical cattle baron J. W. Ewing (Jason Robards), the latter having tried for years to bully or seduce Ella into surrendering her land to him. Thus far the familiar pattern is unchanged, but an oil corporation takes possession of Ewing's ranch in payment of his debts to them. The film ends with J. W. dead and Ella and Buck building a new life on her place. But the happy ending is literally undermined by the oil company which is drilling from Ewing's place beneath her land. Although the company's managing director has been murdered by J. W., corporate enterprise is not arrested by human calamity.

Not all Westerns have featured heroes opposed to corporate capitalism, but the exceptions tend to prove the rule. Ralph and Donna Brauer show that the TV series *Bonanza* based its storylines squarely around the protection of massive property rights – less than surprising when one knows that the sponsor of this most successful show was one of the world's largest corporations of that era, General Motors. The Brauers remark that the Ponderosa, the Cartwrights' ranch, is the size of a state. Far from allowing free access, the family police it, and in episode after episode drive off anyone who crosses its perimeters. The Cartwrights represent corporate power; and the law, in the shape of the local sheriff, answers to them. An arrangement which would foretell disaster in almost any other Western film or television series is here accommodated into the societal order because it suited corporate enterprise (Brauer and Brauer 1975: 121–6, 132–7).

Open Range

Open Range (Kevin Costner, USA, 2003), a slow-moving film that rewards the audience with its restraint, dignity and grace, returns to the more familiar mode in excoriating corporate greed. Here an Irish immigrant, Denton Baxter (Michael Gambon), is the ranch owner. He has purchased the town of Harmonville and the land for miles around. Along with property he has bought the Law too. His massive wealth has corrupted him, like Ryker and LaHood. Also like them, he rides roughshod over laws that give rights to the less powerful. Despite the fact that free grazing was still lawful in 1882, Baxter has his men kill drovers should his threats not deter them from grazing cattle on his land. He represents capital running riot with addictive greed. Nothing about his pustulous soul attains to tragic dignity.

In order to drive another group of cattlemen from his territory, Baxter deliberately starts a conflict with them when Boss Spearman (Robert Duvall) and Charley Waite (Kevin Costner) send their dependable hand to town for supplies. Baxter orders his hands to pick a fight with Mose (Abraham Benrubi) and the thugs injure the big man badly, albeit at painful cost to themselves. Outraged, Boss and Charley repay Baxter's hirelings with like treatment. But Baxter escalates the hostilities with relish and has his hired gun kill Mose and beat the apprentice Button (Diego Luna) near to death. For Boss and Charley, the ensuing showdown – as Baxter masses his forces against the two of them – is motivated less by the need to protect their livelihood (though that is one of their purposes) than by fierce moral anger.

The crisis that slowly engulfs the two men as the conflict with Baxter further intensifies tests their ten-year friendship. Pressure causes them to talk with unaccustomed openness to the doctor's assistant, the kindhearted Sue Barlow (Annette Bening). Only now, after ten years riding together, does Charley discover that Boss Spearman was once married and took to cow punching after losing his wife and child to typhus. For his part, Charley has kept secret the dreadful past that haunts him. As he now tells Sue, his soul is a battle ground. He fought during the Civil War in a unit which operated behind Confederate lines, killing both civilians and soldiers and doing whatever it took to shake the enemy. In the present crisis, the trauma of those murders resurfaces and swamps him (as William Munny's memories unsettle him in *Unforgiven*). He loses control of his killer instincts so that Boss, to save opponents who do not deserve to die, must twice step in front of Charley's gun. The older man's selfless courage forces Charley to discover again the difference between morally justified killing and murder.

The conflict with Baxter and his men (like most of the conflicts with rancher barons mentioned above) helps trigger in Boss and Charley an individuation process resembling that which many screen cowboys have undergone since the psychological Western evolved in the mid-1950s. Fostered by interaction with other characters and plot events, it brings about in the heroes a maturation or individuation with two related aspects. Firstly, it opens the individual to a deeper (often astonished) understanding of himself. And secondly, it reveals to him that he is 'individual' in the antique sense of 'indivisible' – that he is more alike to than different from his fellows. Indeed, the tension between the claims of the individual and those of the collective can often vividly be seen in the Western. Hence the genre screens with particular resonance in times of nationally felt disturbance, as when mass paranoia is aroused (formerly directed at Communists, lately against terrorists) or war is waged (whether armed or psychological). The tension between the claims of the individual and those of the collective underscores the genre. How a Western resolves those tensions often reflects the ethos of its era.

The Western (and, more broadly, mainstream Hollywood cinema in general) is good at limning spiky ego-centred differences between characters that at first make the members of a team hostile to each other. As the action proceeds, various exigencies (usually the overwhelming opposition of an enemy) reveal to them that they have much in common at the level of emotions and the potential hitherto latent in their semi-conscious desires, fears, loves and loathings. Their underlying moral traits may also harmonise. Of course, such bonding linked only the male victors in twentieth-century Westerns, a narrative outcome that legitimised a psychologically imbalanced generic regime lacking full-blooded integration of the feminine. It produced a dynamic prepared to counterbalance either war or paranoia only by force and will – the psychological fortes of the genre through the last century.

Open Range refreshes this familiar pattern. Contrary to the established norm, Boss and Charley seem at first to be closely attuned in temperament. But as the crisis develops, crucial underlying differences in their psychological orientation emerge, rooted in their dissimilar experiences of life. These differences are eventually subsumed into profound harmony when they share a readiness to die, and later (after they survive Baxter's villainous posse) when Charley learns, like the older man, how to live. It is notable in this connection that some of the townspeople eventually overcome their fears and also go against Baxter and Pool. These are presumably people, as

Jim Kitses suggests (2004: 26), who have recognised the force of Charley's line, 'You may not know this, but there's things gnaw on a man worse than dying.' The reawakened courage of these citizens underlines the healing processes of the final conflict.

The characters are sharing a process of individuation which both deepens their consciousness of self and connects them to their fellow beings. That process accords with Jung's thoughts about the opening out to scrutiny of complexes that had previously been unconscious. Nor is it out of kilter with the American Dream, founded as it was on strong family and religious values. There is, nonetheless, an apparent paradox in the Western's condemnation of large corporations and preference for the small-to-medium-sized enterprise. This shows itself in the demographics of the audience, many of whom will be connected with large organisations in both the capital market and the publicly-funded sector. Such organisations have size and influence which would make it easy to stereotype them as impersonal exploiters of wage earners on one side of the sales counter, and of consumers on the other. It is therefore necessary to ask whether the Western, no less than its literary predecessors, is in this additional sense a form of pastoral because it is also founded on an escapist nostalgia.

Open Range is a revealing case in point. Boss and Charley win their war, but decide to leave the range and return to Harmonville once their herd has been driven to market. Boss will adopt Button as his son and take over the town bar (whose proprietor, one of Baxter's henchmen, was killed in the final gunfight). Both the family and the bar are enterprises on a small, human scale which the audience can easily identify as plausible containers for psychological investment and development. Significantly, the film does not specify what will happen to Baxter's vast acres. In this it is typical of Westerns that end in defeat for the baron of capital but gloss over the economic consequences, focusing instead on the victory of 'small' people like the Starretts. Even *Comes a Horseman* does not explicitly show what will happen to Ella's property, but leaves audiences to work it out, provided they can be bothered to follow through a logic which will undercut the apparently happy ending. It is not hard to see why a utopian solution appropriate to the thrust of the genre (namely that a vast landholding should be broken up and sold off in small parcels) would be implausible. If the outcome of the fictional events were to accord with America's economic history, it would require that great ranches be bought up by even larger corporations. But such a resolution would fatally damage the economic individualism to which the Western myth is tied. Therefore, when the genre invokes economic issues, it remains pastoral.

In other aspects, however, the Western does connect purposefully with societal reality. Political allegory operates in both *Open Range* and another 2003 release, *The Missing*. The lawman who obeys Baxter's orders in organising men to go against the free grazers is Sheriff Poole (James

Russo). His name and self-justifying language echo the Sheriff Pool of 30 years earlier in 'The Ancient Warrior'.[1] At first a puffed up, menacing figure, this Poole collapses under pressure to reveal himself as an absurd, vacuous personality. Where the earlier character invited comparison with Richard M. Nixon, the vicious lackey in *Open Range* can be seen as a hit at George W. Bush, a president lampooned by his opponents as both empty-headed and the servant of big business.

Westerns reflect current perceptions of the family, alterations in which change the genre. Every drover in *Open Range* has lost his family; they now comprise an all-male unit with Charley playing 'son' to Boss and 'uncle' to Mose and Button. The all-male family is not unusual in the Western: examples include the Earps in Ford's *My Darling Clementine* (1946) and the motley bunch led by Sheriff Chance (John Wayne) in Hawks's *Rio Bravo* (1959) which numbers among its members Walter Brennan playing Stumpy as a nagging 'wife'. Such families are, of course, out of kilter (as Leigh Brackett plainly knew when satirising the male characters she created for Hawks's film); but there is no guarantee that they will be put to rights when the action is over. Henry Fonda's Wyatt Earp leaves town to cleanse himself of his crimes before he can think of seeing Clementine again. And although the delicious Feathers (Angie Dickinson) does finally corral Chance in *Rio Bravo*, she must trick him to do so; meanwhile the rump of the male family remains intact based around 'mother' Stumpy.

Open Range and *The Missing* are early twenty-first century Westerns that discarded none of the genre's traditional concern with power, but changed their female characters' access to it. They thereby not only reflected shifts in American society but also moved toward establishing a better balance for the genre as between anima and animus images. Sue Barlow in *Open Range* and Maggie Gilkeson (Cate Blanchett) in *The Missing* have substantial roles as lead women which require them neither to be self-effacing nor adept at trickery. Instead both of them have full and active lives. They address men as their rightful equals.

In addition to running her brother's household, Sue practises as a nurse and treats the drovers' casualties. In her intelligent kindness she cares for mind as well as body, encouraging the men to talk about themselves. Boss reveals his marriage, and this rare moment enjoying a woman's empathy touches him. With his memory of past happiness revived, he urges Charley to take a chance and tell Sue he loves her rather than walk away shamed by his past.

Sue's inner strength is formidable. A typical Western heroine would urge her man to avoid killing, and might back away from him if he used his gun. Sue, although the compassionate voice of reason, knows that a time comes

1 The shared name may be an in-joke for cognoscenti of the genre.

when compromise is impossible and fighting is justified (French 2004b). She eases the torments of Charley's soul by showing him that he is a good man at heart and that what he has done as a killer does not bar him from her love (see Kitses 2004: 27).

Sue Barlow's incorporation in the new order of family life synchronises with a series of animus displacements. Baxter is gunned down in the final confrontation. Boss, Baxter's benign opposite, his nurturing impulses restored, will father young Button. In his role as bartender, Boss will become the town's new moral and civic patriarch, annulling the late landowner's mad greed. Meanwhile Sue's gentle brother, Dr Walter Barlow (Dean McDermott), though one of the town's good citizens, is substituted in her life by Charley. By the time the action concludes, both men limp, a plain hint at Oedipal imbalance needing correction. Charley's previous renunciation of family was explicit; while Walter and Sue, both in their forties and living relics of their parents' family, should have found life partners long ago. When Charley finally realises that he is not unfit to marry Sue, we can see that each is completed by the other. He recovers his feminine side, softens and opens out.[2] She finds a man to contain her animus, as befits her erotic needs. No less significant in terms of the earlier discussion, establishment of the family unit implies shared individuation such that in *Open Range* the victors' bonding does not exclude women. In developing the genre's timeworn pattern, the film concludes by legitimising a psychologically balanced group that flourishes only because the feminine has been fully integrated.

Emancipation in the Western?

Two factors make *The Missing*'s Maggie Gilkeson significant in the genre's development. Firstly, she presents a further extension of the role of women in the Western. Secondly, the way that she and the Native American characters are presented invites the question whether in psychoanalytical terms women are taking on some of the healing roles which in the history of the Western it has been so difficult for American Indian characters to fulfil. Are women protagonists such as Maggie and Sue (Native Americans having for the most part been refused this role by filmmakers and audiences alike) now acting as psychopompi for white male heroes and putting them in touch with the unconscious – a connection resisted by screen cowboys for a century? Are Western women healing the split in the Western hero's psyche?

Maggie cooks and cares for her daughters and her lover, runs a farm and heals the sick. She is another formidable woman with a strong sense of

2 The middle name to which Charley only admits when preparing to die is Travis. With its source in 'traverse', it complements the idea of his being at a crossroads.

purpose who also, since her father walked out and her mother died, carries the unconscious for her family. The consequences of abandonment hurt so deeply that she has to keep rage on a tight leash. Nevertheless she has the courage to make her father feel the heavy burden he unthinkingly dumped on her. She confronts him so forcefully as to make him taste the complexes that govern her personality. So doing, she provides him, no less than the Western genre itself, with rare insight into a woman's psyche.

Comparison of Maggie Gilkeson with some of her recent screen ancestors sketches the evolution of women's roles. In 1988 David Jacobs and Robert Porter created a television series *Paradise* (Lorimar Television). It featured several significant role changes that reflected progressive American society of the 1980s rather than the 1880s. These included the Chinese American family whose members play an active part in community life and Ethan Cord (Lee Horsley), the gunfighter protagonist, who has single parenting thrust on him by the death of his sister. A young widow, Amelia Lawson (Sigrid Thornton), manages the bank. Her sardonic tongue militates against any sexual attraction which her good looks might otherwise have encouraged in Ethan. She abhors Ethan's profession, but helps him out of compassion for the four children who have been bequeathed by his dying sister to an inadequate father. An influential figure in the community, Mrs Lawson represents a clean break from patriarchal domination. Having said that, the adventures of Ethan as gunfighter and reluctant parent remain the focus, and to this extent, *Paradise* does not depart from the Western's traditional centring on the male hero as fulcrum.

We have already seen that *Shane* and *Pale Rider* share several thematic foci; but their inflections differ, with consequences for the women's roles. The earlier film adopted the point of view of Joey Starrett (Brandon de Wilde), the 8-year-old son of the smallholders threatened by the rancher. When Shane (Alan Ladd) fights Ryker and his men, Joey, like other Western lads in the 1950s, learns the moral lesson that killing an opponent marks one with the stain of murder. By contrast, in *Pale Rider* the wholesale slaughter of the villains is an apocalyptic cleansing by an avenging angel. Eastwood substitutes a pubescent girl, Megan Wheeler (Sydney Penny) for Joey. Her moral education concerns not killing (still men's work) but the nature of love. Megan and her mother will be the carriers of an insight into the ways that the secular and the sacred are linked through the forms of love.

In *Shane* as in *Pale Rider* and many other Westerns, mystical questions lie behind moral issues. Both films link the ethics of the community's conduct to questions of domestic morality. The domestic moral crux centres on a spiritual crisis for the women, who become confused by unexpected passion. Marion Starrett (Jean Arthur) has an honest, loyal affection – a domesticated love – for Joe (Van Heflin), her decent but unexciting husband. Theirs has been an untroubled patriarchal marriage mirroring the mid-twentieth-century American ideal. When powerful feelings for the gunman stir in her heart, they bewilder her. By degrees, she grasps that Shane has a mystical nature; and eventually she realises that her love for him is different from that in her marriage. Through him she intuits a sense of the sacred and eventually realises that the love in her marriage, although experienced with a lesser intensity and not glowing with numinous presence, does not lack sanctified qualities.

At the story level, Shane is a gunfighter first and foremost, and only through the interpretation of discreet symbolism can be read as having the qualities of a white knight embodying some, but only some, of the attributes of a Christ. It happens differently in *Pale Rider*. Megan, having had her dog killed in a raid by LaHood's men, prays for a miracle. The Preacher rides out from the icy mountains, reaching the miners' settlement in response to her summons just as Megan reads Revelations 6, 8. He is one of the four horsemen of the Apocalypse. To dispel any doubt that he must be a spirit, we are shown that he long ago took several bullets through the heart.

Like Marion Starrett, Megan's mother Sarah Wheeler (Carrie Snodgrass) has domesticated feelings for Hull Barret (Michael Moriarty), another decent and mundane man with whom she lives. Also like Marion, and in common with Megan, she feels an attraction of a different order to the Preacher.[3] For Sarah the issue is not how to differentiate two kinds of love but whether she should marry Hull and forego the religious intensity of passion she would experience with the Preacher. The night before he rides out to save the mining community, the Preacher does take Sarah as his lover.

Spirit touches body and momentarily animus and anima connect. Then, setting aside his dog collar and transformed as the gunfighter into the Angel of Death, the Preacher destroys LaHood along with his hoodlums and hired killers before returning to the mountains' ice and snow. Eastwood's character intensifies the paradox that previously ensnared gunfighters such as Shane who kill to save a community. However, he takes this paradox to a wholly different conclusion. Instead of leaving his hero crippled by guilt as required by a god who is exclusively good, Eastwood vests him with numinous duality: he is a figure with divine power who encompasses the opposites in one, being both good and evil.

Meanwhile Sarah's encounter with the sacred power he embodies has settled her yearning heart. Speaking of herself as having been confused, she now recognises that her passion for a numinous figure who encompasses the twin extremes of love and vengeance must be of a different order than that which makes for a devoted bond between ordinary people. The knowledge frees her to accept Hull's proposal.

3 Megan, lacking the older woman's circumspection, approaches the Preacher directly; but he tells her that 14 is too young for sexual experience (a teaching which angers the girl).

While the women learn the danger of trying to draw the Absolute into their daily lives, the decent men with whom they are partnered are completely unaware of the painful conundrum facing their dear ones. Intriguingly, however, the barons of capital are enslaved by the same impossible passion to grasp the Absolute – but in their case it battens malignantly on total possession of the land rather than love. Ryker may have been touched by awe at the power of Nature that he wishes to grasp in his fever to own all his eyes fall on; but LaHood has no sense of awe at all – his is a joyless hubris.

Thus through a question that starts with morality – whether Marion and Sarah should remain loyal to their partners or give way to temptation – both films access a deeper sphere of allegory, the spiritual. Nonetheless in each case it is still a male figure, albeit a spirit, who instructs the women. All the same, in attaining a degree of insight which their menfolk do not, Marion, Sarah and Amelia Lawson reveal the stirring of animus in the genre with an energy that could not indefinitely leave its male protagonists untouched.

Eastwood's next Western, *Unforgiven* (1992) provides an indication of the kind of change that endowing female characters with greater power can induce in the male hero. The wife of Will Munny (Eastwood) has died before the story begins, leaving him to scrabble a living as a pig farmer and bring up their two children. Her legacy to him has been the moral code with which she rescued him from the drunken abandonment of a professional killer's existence and by which he now tries to live. Although the thought of murder now revolts Munny, the reputation gained in his former life attracts a would-be gunslinger with a proposition. The persuasions to vanity which the young man proffers do not of themselves touch Munny, but his grinding poverty eventually does tempt him to go after the bounty payable for one last killing.

Throughout what proves to be a grim venture taking vengeance on cowboys for the knifing of a whore, his divergence from the path approved by his wife triggers hellish visions of those he has killed, traumatising him. Complications in the mission convert what he had imagined as a simple shooting into a hideous bloodbath. A posse capture, torture and slay the friend who has ridden with him, after which Munny in cold revenge massacres those tormentors. When the whole gruesome business is done, he returns to his children. The end title reports rumours that he later moved to San Francisco and made his living as a storekeeper. It seems safe to assume that the force of his wife's teachings has endured and her authority over his moral and spiritual life, though tested to the ultimate degree, is firmly restored at the end.

The anima-animus balance in the genre was thus being recast. Alterations in the roles of women as distinctive as in *Unforgiven* not only affected their screen relationships with men but also had consequences for the roles that male protagonists played and the nature of the Western male psyche. Although Will Munny could not sustain his new personality without first undergoing an anti-heroic journey into Hell, throughout his killing mission he was aware that his wife had guided him toward a personal rebirth. Having put his new life in peril, he seems, in recoiling from his crimes, to have recovered her gift on his return to the family.

The Missing: complex allegory for a new era

The plot of Ron Howard's 2003 film recalls John Ford's celebrated *The Searchers* (1956) in which the racially bigoted loner Ethan Edwards (John Wayne) obsessively hunts the Comanche who slaughtered his family and stole his niece. But as Michael Wilmington says, despite some direct references, *The Missing* is no slavish homage but 'a picture that often seems to be a critical, modernist response to *The Searchers*: a feminist, pro-Native American variation on the theme' (2003).

As mentioned, Native Americans in Westerns bore the projection of White America's fear and hatred of its enemies through most of the twentieth century. As a once visibly distinct people, they were made the all-too-convenient displaced focus of collective political paranoia. That theme is re-examined for the twenty-first century in *The Missing* when Lieutenant Ducharme (Val Kilmer), a white Southerner who commands a company of soldiers, laments that whites are consorting with Indians and there is no longer any telling who is who. It is true that the various communities in the film have lost their old, hard-edged borderlines and a few individuals are at ease with interracial contact. But while Ducharme has observed the fact, like all bigots he has no understanding of what racial mixing means for society as a whole, let alone for his own conduct. He utters his complaint only moments after summarily ordering his troopers to execute a man without trial. Because 'Indian' and 'guilty' are conjoined terms in Ducharme's dictionary, he has taken it as proven by circumstance that the long haired man found in the house of a murdered white family is the Indian who has killed them. But Ducharme's deductions about Samuel Jones (Tommy Lee Jones) are wrong on both counts. Here is one of many reflections in *The Missing* of the politically complex American society watching the movie. The New Mexico on screen comprises a mix of bigots in the old mould (belonging to every community) intermingled with people who have learned to live in harmony with other races.

Samuel Jones is Maggie's father, a psychologically complex figure, no less edgy than his conflicted daughter. This 'sorrowful mystic' has opted to live with the Navajo and Apache, adopting their culture and costume (Burr 2003). He left his family 20 years earlier, accounting for his disappearance with the story of a man who followed a hawk away from his home and never returned because the bird did not turn back. His Apache friend Kayitah (Jay

Tavare) puts it another way, describing him as an unquiet spirit. Either way, Samuel is some kind of visionary, but he suffers the contempt of both whites and Indians for embracing a mixed culture and denying the boundaries that bigots like Ducharme believe should separate the races.

Samuel has come back to Maggie ostensibly for treatment of a torn ligament. He does not admit until much later that he is required to be kind to his family as part of a tribal cure for snake bite. So he has brought money to help the grandchildren he has never known. But Maggie cannot forgive the years of loss and angrily insists he move on as soon as she has treated him. He rides into town to dull with whisky the pain that this unanticipated rejection causes him, and is thrown into jail as a drunk Indian. Not for the last time in this film, buried emotions burst to the surface. They link to an unexpected plot twist, and calamity will soon oblige the reluctant Maggie to ride with her father.

As Sandford says, Samuel knows how to walk the line between the two worlds (2003); but his ability to open up to the collective unconscious keeps him restless. The poetic wisdom that comes from being drawn by the spirit world (its messenger the hawk) has endowed him with some shamanic powers but no domestic virtues: he has been the passing lover of several women, and a lousy father.

The disruption to family caused by Samuel's absconding has left deep traumas, particularly marked in Maggie who blames him for the death from exhaustion of her mother. The abandoned daughter heads a dysfunctional family in which the anima-animus relationship is radically altered from older Western norms. Although Maggie is physically strong, like her mother before her she is psychologically drained. She is also a wounded healer, simultaneously tough and vulnerable like Asklepios, the figure of Greek legend whom we encountered in Chapters 2 and 7. But whereas Asklepios could respond with empathy to the psychological needs of others because of his past suffering, Maggie's animus problems choke that ability in her. Samuel will attempt to cure the injured spirit, but Maggie is sceptical and deals only with physical ailments.

The generations in the family mirror each other in that the fathers of Maggie's two daughters are also absent – the first a forgotten lover, the other a husband who helped set up the ranch but then moved on. Lilly (Evan Rachel Wood) is an angry teenager desperate to escape her mother's hard-grafting life and racially contemptuous of her new grandfather. Young Dot (Jenna Boyd) has an equable temperament, suffers blows bravely when they fall, accepts her fate and gets on with life. Exhilarated by the fantasy that she might be Indian, she has inherited the best qualities of both Maggie and Samuel and, in her easy relations with her grandfather, helps repair the anima-animus relation.

The core drama of *The Missing* commences when Brake (Aaron Eckhart), Maggie's hired hand and lover, rides with the girls through snow fields to share a day's recreation in town. Maggie has no time for such fripperies and stays back to tend her cattle. But when her family fail to return before dark she watches through the night in deepening anxiety until one of the horses returns riderless just before dawn. She tracks them, and in the deadwood of the winter forest finds Brake's corpse suspended gruesomely from a branch, trussed in a cowhide bag. Lilly has been kidnapped and Dot left by the attackers as witness to the horror.

Maddened by grief, terror and loathing, Maggie gallops to town to get the sheriff's help. Projecting raging hatred onto her father, she believes he has ambushed her family in revenge for being driven from the ranch. But she soon discovers that the sheriff had already gaoled him for drunkenness before the killings occurred. The law officer, from within the usual pale of unquestioning white paranoia, assumes the attackers to be Apache who have jumped reservation. He complacently reports that the cavalry are in pursuit, although some days away. Meanwhile he insists his duties confine him and his men to town and refuses to pursue the killers despite being much closer to them than the military.

When Samuel is released, he rides back to the ranch, having read the raiders' tracks. They are travelling south to the Mexican border and not north, as the sheriff believes. Maggie accepts that he is the only person who can help her. With Dot refusing to be left with neighbours, intuiting that she needs her family more than safety at this time of crisis, the three of them start their search for Lilly. Their journey eventually takes them from the snowy landscape of New Mexico's north, with its heavy skies and black forests, to the equally harsh deserts and rocky canyons of the south. But where Ethan Edwards in *The Searchers* circled in a sea of unknowing for five years, Samuel leads his party rapidly in direct pursuit of the raiders: he knows from experience their *modus operandi* and purposes.

In fact, the raiding party differs from what Maggie (and the audience) expects. It comprises a mixed group of bandits, the greater number Apache but some whites. A few of the latter are captured civilians but most of the band are renegade soldiers still kitted out in their uniforms. Greed, not revenge, motivates these deserters. David Thomson is mistaken when he alleges that their leader, in every other way a vile character, must rape the teenage girls they capture (2004: 14). On the contrary, Chidin (Eric Schweig) forbids his men to touch the girls because they are to be sold into prostitution across the border and will bring a better price as virgins.

All this makes for a distinctive variant on the countless Westerns which allude to conflicts with Indians as though two forces, both homogeneous in make-up, were posed in simple opposition to each other. The rank and file soldiers resemble the raiding party in being thieving riffraff and no less motivated by greed. Instead of protecting property, they openly defy Ducharme's orders and loot the possessions of a murdered farming family. Ducharme himself resembles the sheriff in pomposity and incompetence.

Both men obey orders to the letter, even when doing so is fatuous. Ducharme's troop accidentally stumbles upon Maggie, Dot and Samuel when they are closing in on the kidnappers. However, they are on another mission and, although his men disobey him with impunity, Ducharme insists on following orders, refusing to detour and pursue the villains close by. Meanwhile the company actually ordered to track the raiders has been inaccurately briefed and is heading in the wrong direction. We witness an army focused on the wrong target, a society the several parts of which are in dispute with each other over what should be done, and self-interest governing almost everyone. It makes an interesting microcosm for the confused North American military and political strategies post September 11, 2001, Afghanistan, 2002 and the second Iraq War, 2003–4.

Let's follow the politico-military allegory further. Filmed by Salvatore Totino, the razor-sharp New Mexico landscape takes on a frightful edge during Maggie's dawn search for her family. As she forces her horse forward through creaking forests, the animal's terror is felt by Maggie and communicated to the audience. She finds a flayed cow, then the corpse of her Latino hired hand and, hanging from a tree, a heavy bag made from the beast's bloody hide. It turns to reveal her lover Brake's grotesquely trussed body. The raiders, deliberately striking starkest fear into their victims and gratuitously insulting them in death, are acting like terrorists. Unlike his men, their leader is motivated less by greed than by hatred. Chidin is a *brujo* or witch. He possesses supernatural powers and uses them to maim and kill, being able to do so even at a distance. He will later cast a spell of such virulence that it causes Maggie to sicken near to death. Steeped in evil, Chidin fits into the early twenty-first century American mould of the 'terrorist'. Our fictional villain can thus be read as an allegorical representation of white America's mental image of the guerrilla leader.

The Missing presents Chidin as commanding mystical power in the contest of evil against good. Like the avenging preacher in *Pale Rider*, he is a mana personality:

> Mana . . . pertains to the extraordinary and compelling supernatural power which emanates from certain individuals, objects, actions and events as well as from inhabitants of the spirit world . . . [It] can attract or repel, wreak destruction or heal, confronting the ego with a supra-ordinate force . . . This is the quasi-divine power which adheres to the magician, mediator, priest, doctor, trickster, saint or holy fool – to anyone who partakes of the spirit world sufficiently to conduct or radiate its energy.
>
> (Samuels *et al.* 1986: 89)

Mana figures are important because they enable a person to project power at a time when that is a necessary step in confronting the ego with the nature of the inner self (Samuels *et al.* 1986: 89–90). In *Pale Rider*, Sarah's encounter with the Preacher does indeed empower her to realise her true nature. And Maggie's fight for life against Chidin, although it threatens her with obliteration, has similar psychologically fortifying consequences when she survives.

This struggle is not a face-to-face encounter but comes after the rescuers close on the raiders and are preparing an ambush. Dot accidentally gives their presence away. In the scramble to escape as Chidin's men come after them, Samuel warns against leaving anything behind, but Maggie's hairbrush falls from her bag. The family get away, but the witch uses hair from the brush to make a fetish, exerting malign power through it to destroy Maggie. In the contest which ensues for Maggie's life and soul, Samuel uses his shamanic powers. But he cannot match his opponent's strength and needs help, getting it from three sources. The family has in the interim fallen in with Chiricahua friends of Samuel. Kayitah and his son Honesco (Simon Baker) were attempting to free the young man's bride from Chidin when the raiders shot Honesco. Maggie attends to the wound, but begins to sicken herself. Samuel recognises that she has fallen under the *brujo's* influence and insists that (despite her resistance) she don an Apache necklace.[4] Kayitah assists by gathering healing herbs and performing rituals to counter the fetish while Dot reads out passages from the Scriptures. Far from this signifying a clash of cultures – of Christianity and Indian beliefs, of European medicine and tribal healing – cooperation between the two traditions is essential to their hard-won victory over Chidin's evil.

Maggie's cure is effected when Honesco places a hand on her brow. He too is a healer, now wounded, a young man of sweet and courageous disposition. Maggie recognises his purity, a poignant revelation for her. Earlier she had warned Dot not to sit near the injured youth for fear of the diseases that Indians carry. Now Honesco's healing gesture helps break through her racial prejudices. The playing out of the contest for her soul enriches her psyche in another way, though she is not fully aware of what has happened. Scarred by negative mana, she can now distinguish her father's weaknesses from the pure evil by which she has been attacked. Her relationship to her animus begins to ease.

Religious resonances in the scenario accentuate the sense that the characters' fates are shaped by myths deriving from diverse sources. Samuel bears the name of a constant warrior against evil, the devout prophet called by God to his service. Maggie's given name is Magdalena, recalling the first person to whom Jesus spoke after his resurrection. Her father's use of her full name has a prophetic quality since he himself is to die twice. His first

4 It contrasts with Chidin's necklace: tintype photographs of his captives, icons of his power over them.

death occurs when, facing overwhelming odds, he and Kayitah try another sortie against the *brujo*. Samuel is captured and Chidin mockingly offers to make him an Indian in death, promptly hurling him into a pit. The sardonic promise comes true in the sense that while Samuel lies injured and dying, his old psychopomp the hawk (which for Native Americans is the carrier of divine energy) swoops down and catches his attention.[5] Samuel focuses all his energies and asks it to lead him out of the valley of death back to his family. This is his rebirth, the new life granted to some heroes, the reward for having sacrificed everything for love.

With Maggie refusing to leave Lilly even though it may cost both Dot's and her own life, Samuel next prepares for one last assault against the enemy camp. Kayitah having been killed in the earlier raid, his corpse had been left lying on a boulder like a sacrifice on an altar. Now he too is 'reborn' with the dead man circling the camp on horseback. However, this return to life is no supernatural intervention (Dot is hidden under the warrior's blanket) but Samuel using a trickster's 'magic' on Chidin's people to gain time so that Maggie, Honesco and he can take up attacking positions. The trick works, they kill many of the raiders, free the captives and make their escape. However, Chidin and his remaining men pursue them relentlessly. With night coming on, Samuel leads the party to a promontory where the exhausted girls can rest while the adults keep the menacing kidnappers below their guns.

Before the final battle, father and daughter reconcile, Maggie recognising that she would have had no chance of recovering Lilly had it not been for her father. The battle itself takes place by night above a rocky canyon worthy of an Anthony Mann Western such as *Winchester 73*; but in a reversal of the device that Mann applied to several James Stewart roles, here the good hold the high ground. Just as hellish shadows in dreams and myths often force their way up from below and out of the unconscious into consciousness, so Chidin, most evil of bandits, worms his way irresistibly upwards under fire from Samuel and Maggie. The vile figure's relentless labour recalls the foray of John Milton's Satan toward the newly created world:

> So eagerly the Fiend
> Ore bog or steep, through strait, rough, dense, or rare,
> With head, hands, wings, or feet persues his way,
> And swims or sinks, or wades, or creeps, or flyes . . .
>
> (*Paradise Lost* II, 947–50)

The outcome of Chidin's fight would not, however, have been countenanced by Milton. *Paradise Lost* extolled the power of the Father 'to

5 The bird's magical powers are implicit in its colour-reversed image.

dissolve/ Satan with his perverted world' (XII, 546–7) so that good shall triumph over evil. But when the *brujo* attacks Maggie (the shadow animus making a murderous foray under cover of the dark), Samuel (in his role as redeemed, positive animus) comes to her aid and wrestles with the witch at the cliff edge. The ferocity of the battle banishes the men's sense of place, time and circumstance and they fall locked together to their deaths. Thus in *The Missing* (as opposed to *Paradise Lost*) we find a variant of the idea of dualism that we met earlier. Here good and evil, despite the occasional dominance of one or the other in their endless strife are, in the long perspective, in balance. Such a reading is supported by the fact that two of Chidin's men escape the final slaughter as does fine young Honesco. Forces from either side survive to fight another war.

The present war frees Maggie to return home leading a train of teenage girls and resume life with her daughters. In the personal domain of the hero, the psychological map of what has occurred is extraordinary for the Western genre. We first met Maggie when her animus was uncertainly projected onto her lover Brake; but the deeply repressed image of her father indicated an unresolved animus problem (confirmed by hints that she had taken a number of lovers). When the father surfaced, intense tribulation immediately overwhelmed her. A truly evil male shadow was unlocked in Chidin, not only an anti-father but also a racially nightmarish figure who destroyed her chosen animus by killing Brake. This activation of her archetypal shadow and the conflict that followed allow Maggie eventually to discharge the negative energies that had vivified her repressed parental and racist animus. With all these men dead, her animus has been internalised and at least partly integrated, an indication reinforced by the sweet presence of Honesco in the otherwise all-female group of survivors.

Maggie will head her own family, perhaps enlarging it by taking under her wing some of the teenagers whose families have been slaughtered by Chidin's men. Heading the family: that of itself is rare for a woman in a Western, yet another indication how the new assertiveness of women in western society has altered their psychological typing and therefore their functions in this genre. Once again we see how the rebalancing of gender roles in the Western (and behind them, of anima and animus) connects with the displacement of evil. The vitality of Chidin as a mana personality is significant in this respect since, according to Samuels *et al.*, 'as an ideal and incorruptible image [it] is essential to the process of initiation after which one has a renewed sense of individuality' (1986: 90).

A demon stalks the global ranch

Since film is a public medium it is appropriate to look beyond the domain of the personal to interpret the myth-charged imagery which the mana personality generates for the collective sphere. As an 'ideal and incorruptible image', Chidin has the purity of undiluted evil. This is where the allegorical equivalence resonates with Osama bin Laden's image in the USA. After September 11, 2001, the latter was not generally perceived as a cold-blooded, quasi-military strategist with political goals – an idea which might plausibly have been generated by reflection on the objectives behind the massacres he allegedly masterminded. Rather, the Bush administration fostered an image of a man demonically driven by insane hatred of all things American and good.

In the UK the idea was much discussed after the events of that terrible day that it was a wake-up call dragging the USA into a world (a sphere both of politics and the imagination) from which it had successfully isolated itself. That insulation from the grim horrors of organised guerrilla conflict had since the late 1960s been all too apparent from the other side of the Atlantic. The resuscitation then of IRA activity and the surfacing of various other groups deploying terror (such as the Red Army Faction in West Germany and ETA in Spain) familiarised Europeans with this dire, extra-democratic side of politics; but most North Americans were impossibly innocent of these horrors, as 9/11 finally taught. Now in the wake of those fearful events and the national trauma they delivered, it seemed sensible to ask whether there was something anguishingly painful happening in the collective American psyche for which Osama bin Laden and (in the allegorical world within *The Missing*) Chidin were dark and powerful agents.

The abhorrent nature of the murderous events of 9/11 cannot be mistaken; but it was not a necessary consequence of those horrors that Evil incarnate must be perceived as lying behind them. No such personified demon animated collective responses in Britain to atrocities carried out by either the IRA or its Protestant counterparts despite the rage, despair and grief that those attacks caused. The issue is particularly relevant to the Western because the genre habitually addresses America's leadership culture. As the world's dominant empire, the USA was through most of the twentieth century controlled by a profoundly masculine culture of Logos-centred power. In the movie genre, the endless contests for the land (Indian wars, the Civil War, range wars, even occasionally the War for Independence) are not sufficiently explained by the much mythologised history of the West. For the conflicts continued to rage on screen more than a hundred years after the frontier closed. As we have seen, read in terms of the expansion and consolidation of capital, these conflicts revealed a split between ranchers and smallholders. On the surface, the latter win, but the cattle barons, whatever their personal fates, never suffer the breakup of their vast properties. Change the focal plane, and it is possible to read these fictional contests over land as allegories for the massive expansion of American political influence. The small guys – American domestic concerns – seem to win; but, interpreted in this register, the monstrous, greedy figure who buys up and oppresses the West stands for global imperialist expansion, never completely exterminated. Now the genre has called up a demon in the menacing presence of Chidin, an archetypal figure which offers itself as the monster's shadow.

It is a principle of Jung's thinking about collective archetypal images that they enter the public domain when needed in order to correct an imbalance in the psychological disposition of large numbers of people. He observed that when archetypal images were given undue supremacy and reified they invariably converted to their contrary in order to balance the psyche. Thus, psychologically speaking, an absolute 'Father in Heaven' must call forth the devil (1935: 235–6). Conservative America of this era has its 'Father in Heaven' (George W. Bush) assuring it that America is always right, is the greatest nation on earth and has God on its side. There is little room for doubt that bin Laden's image is the devil; but the question that cannot yet be answered is whether it (or its future displaced substitutes) will have the potential to act as a corrective to a long-standing imbalance in dominant ideology.

The political and psychological climate in which *The Missing* was released makes the conjunction between the emergence of Chidin (the potent negative mana personality) and empowerment of Maggie (acceptance of feminist values in the Western) particularly interesting. This is the more significant in that Samuel is unable to defeat Chidin without the help of Maggie, Kayitah and Honesco. The film's Chiricahua are fine warriors but also gentle and sensitive friends. In short, this contest with evil calls for the deployment of both 'male' and 'female' values, linking Logos power to Eros kindness and cherishing. Kayitah and Honesco represent an ideal since the personality of each blends the characteristics of both Logos and Eros – a balance which Maggie has learnt from them by the end. That their hard-won mutual respect underlines the anti-racist thematic strand of the film hardly needs further emphasis. This allegorical reading of *The Missing* as referencing the collective psychological consequences of American involvement in the Middle East, implies that the deployment of Logos alone (imperialist policies backed by overwhelming but badly targeted military force), far from suppressing or obliterating the demon, has indeed summoned him.

This reading of the film can be projected forward as implying that a combination of Logos authority with active Eros (which at the very least entails an effort at understanding and appreciating others' values) might have a better chance of deflating the demon's rage.

Conclusion

Taking *The Missing* as a test case, then, if the interpretation offered in the previous chapter is persuasive, it is appropriate to recognise that Jungian theory contributed to our understanding of the way the film is framed and informed by a particular conjunction of history and psychology. *The Missing* offers insights, through a structure that licenses allegorical readings, not only into pre-existing North American social and political tensions continuing into the twenty-first century's early years but also the traumatising effect on the national psyche of September 11, 2001. However, recognising that much still leaves unanswered the central question with which we started out. To reduce it for the moment to the circumference of this one film, it is still necessary to account for the interesting fact that hardly anyone – American or not – has read Chidin as an allegorised stand-in for bin Laden.

A partial explanation might lie in recognition that film reviewers, as opposed to academic scholars, have to work fast and to tight word limits. They may cover six or seven films each week. Under those circumstances it is not surprising that, with the exception of a small and honourable cadre, most hack through the work and take their cues and much of their information from studio publicity. Nor do studios make a practice of drawing attention to the possible allegorical significance of their movies lest the product appear too intellectually challenging to be good entertainment. Their diffidence likewise inhibits from independent thinking the many reviewers who merely relay entertainment industry messages: they offer little more than a plot summary, an assessment of the actors' performances and (to demonstrate that they really do possess freedom of judgement) a valedictory cheer or boo.

Needless to say, there are factors of greater significance in play here. A further partial explanation for what is 'missing' might be attributed to the sensibilities of distributors (long ago reified as policy). Studios tend to relish controversy only when it centres on personal relations. The suggestion that an affair has started or ended between stars on a movie set; rumours of animosity between the director and leading players; the tantrums of writers bewailing that their original story has been ruined in translation to the screen – all such important issues nicely ferment the oxygen of publicity. Such off-screen dramas complement the preferred focus for mainstream movies on the pains and joys of the individual. These same studios, however, are notoriously reluctant to provide a platform for political controversy of the kind that might have been generated by making explicit any connection between Chidin and Osama bin Laden. They seldom reverse this position unless confident that controversy will enhance a movie's profitability. The difficulties Michael Moore encountered in 2004 when negotiating release for *Fahrenheit 9/11* make the point; and *The Missing* was not treated as one of the exceptions.

With the exception of *Barry Lyndon*, readings of all the films analysed in the foregoing chapters have been illuminated by Jungian methodology. They have been shown to resonate with archetypal figures or mythical stories. In most cases, the films offered spectators the *opportunity* to feel emotions deep enough to reach beyond the wholly conscious sphere of the mind. Yet, although individuals in the audience may have been affected deeply, in most cases few signs appeared that sufficient numbers of people were so engaged as to to make their emotional or intuitive responses felt in the public sphere. On the basis of the preceding analyses, I can only safely claim that two types of film have the ability to stir deep emotions and make a lasting psychological impact on large sectors of the audience. It seems necessary that the audience be overwhelmed by affect if the psychological impact is to be felt by large groups rather than individuals. However, that alone is not a sufficient precondition for such an effect.

Luke Hockley (2004) has used a Jungian perspective productively to explore how feeling and emotion have equally important roles to play in the experience that audience members take from their cinema-going. He reminds his readers that Jung distinguished between emotion (or affect) and feeling. Affect refers to an involuntary inner perturbation or nervous agitation (whether painful or pleasing, whether overwhelming or confined to bringing about a subtle shift in mood) that may be caused by immediate experience. Feeling, on the other hand, is voluntary in being a function that is under the individual's control. Its role is discriminatory in that it evaluates what the subject has experienced (Hockley 2004: 73–4, 77). Hockley cites Samuels *et al.* (1986: 11): 'One has command over feeling, whereas affect intrudes against one's will and can only be repressed with difficulty. An explosion of affect is an invasion of the individual and a temporary takeover of the ego'. Hockley affirms that the act of viewing films involves an emotional response – as the preceding chapters have confirmed. However, he goes further and argues that the experience of cinema will also eventually involve discrimination because by definition that has to be exercised when the evaluative feeling process kicks in (2004: 84–5). In support of his case, he cites Jung debating whether an individual's 'real' personality is found either in its emotionally excited or its normal state. Jung made the point that the ego is still the same ego no matter which of these states it may be in, 'even though it displays a differential attitude to these psychological happenings' (1923: 514):

> In the affective state [ego] is unfree, driven, coerced. By contrast, the normal state is a state of free will, with all one's powers at one's disposal . . . In this latter state an understanding becomes possible, because in it alone can one discern one's motives and gain self-knowledge. Discrimination is the *sine qua non* of cognition.

Hockley argues that before cinema-goers take the full experience of a film, their egos alternate from the affective to the normal state. Although in front of the screen they may be driven by emotions that are not necessarily comfortable, they are usually kept in their seats by the combination of two factors. These are, firstly, the collective nature of the experience and, secondly, the knowledge that affect in the cinema endures for a much shorter time than in daily life. Only after the screening is over can the ego, released from the affective state into which the film shifted it, return to the normal state and begin to discriminate. But that return to a state in which the ego exercises its judgement freely is, Hockley concludes, inevitable. One psychological function of experiencing cinema is to offer us the potential 'to understand why certain films move us, overtake us, and overwhelm us [so that] the psyche becomes increasingly differentiated – the films have the capacity to help us understand more fully who we are' (Hockley 2004: 85).

It seems to me a wonderful advantage for cinema-goers that they may relish movies for their entertainment (which is undoubtedly integral to the films' deeper functions) and also advance through them the differentiation of their psyche the better to understand themselves. However, although desirable, I think this outcome by no means an inevitable consequence of movie-going. David Hewison has made the point that mastering symbols powerfully presented on the big screen is not always possible for patients whose ego is splintered or only partially developed. They may find that such symbols are playing with them rather than the other way round (2000: 291–3).

I now want to revise my earlier position and suggest that between these two opposing positions there is an intermediate area of collective experience in which some cinema-goers neither master for personal differentiation the material that has moved them nor suffer a pathological response that threatens the ego. I have in mind what happens when individuals evaluate a film they have seen while sharing a powerful on-screen experience. Cinema draws much of its power from collective experience: screen genres depend for their existence on this phenomenon. The sense of participation with others in the auditorium will be vivid for many people even before they discuss a film with others who have seen it. That sense of enjoyment shared is also of great significance in the evaluation of a movie – witness the importance we place on learning the opinions of others, be it by word of mouth or review. When a person's ego returns to its normal state from the affect-driven excitation it experienced in the cinema, it is difficult to conceive that it could do so without the individual recalling the shared emotions that the film created. The recollection of affect (which may well revive those emotions) surely must flow over into and profoundly colour the process of evaluation. Jung remarked that as between affect and feeling 'the dividing line is fluid, since every feeling, after attaining a certain strength, releases physical innervations, thus becoming an affect' (1921: 411). Indeed it is worth remembering that we are discussing the *feeling* rather than *thinking* function of spectators. At its most basic, people's evaluation of a film may amount to no more than an attempt to register whether they liked or disliked it, with perhaps a half-formed notion as to why.

It follows that the individual's evaluative process is not *necessarily* one in which discrimination takes on the positively charged characteristics implied in the quote from Jung cited above and picked up by Hockley. Certainly it may foster individuation, as with the emotions aroused by Kubrick's *2001: A Space Odyssey*. When they evaluated that film through the feeling process, many viewers found themselves drawn to a deeper appreciation of the heroic journey of sacred discovery indicated in the film's title – a form pre-existing in epics, myths and stories of humans become gods. However, feeling can just as readily link an emotionally charged experience into pre-existing matrices of bigotry or hatred as into the *temenos* (or sacred precinct) where wisdom is enhanced. I referred in Chapter 8 to the racism historically endemic in the Western. The collective psychological energy imbuing that ideological matrix prepared the way for feeling evaluations which in turn were developed into what I regard as the misreading of *Open Range* as a celebration of neo-conservative values.

These examples make it clear that an individual's evaluation of a movie cannot be divorced from that of his or her collective. This is not to say that the individual has to feel or evaluate according to the dominant values of the day. But where a film (as with some potent genre productions) arouses strong shared emotions, those emotions may contribute to the forming of a dominant feeling. Where such culturally embedded values are highly charged, however, there collective evaluation may first feed off and then reinforce inflated states of collective consciousness – whether positive or negative, progressive or conservative, paranoid or liberated. In short, it may reinforce collective, unseeing, shadow projections – for example upon people of other genders, races, nations and religious beliefs. The process of evaluation cannot be innocent of societal influences any more than any other aspect of human culture. Having said this, collective evaluation can in some cases contribute to collective differentiation. It may also be strong enough to challenge received ideas and conventions. As was suggested in the Introduction, it is necessary to speak not only of the positive potential of what might be described as auto-therapeutic work but also of the risk of inflation in the reading of the film. This as true for the collective as for the individual. Where quasi-religious themes are in play, there exists a real danger that enthusiasm fired by emotion may overwhelm the conscious discriminatory processes of not only the individual but also the collective – and may do so for good or for evil. *The Missing*, however, illustrates yet another way in which individual spectators and collectives can respond to psychological overload.

Art house movies and authored films can arouse strong empathetic responses in individual viewers, but their appeal seldom extends so widely as to justify describing their audiences as manifesting group psychological affect arising from the cultural unconscious. To some degree this may be simply because audiences for such films are much smaller than for blockbusters. The largest part of the cinema-going population in the United Kingdom and North America excludes itself when press previews marry with marketing material, talent interviews and word of mouth reports to the effect that enjoyment of a film depends on the spectator bringing to bear a measure of cultural experience. Hints that a film is in this way 'difficult' in its subject matter or mode of address are enough to restrict the English-language audience to those who consciously enjoy puzzling over signs and meaning in the cinema. In general, authored and art films play to minority audiences and do not generate the collective cultural buzz of genre movies (partly propagated by marketing, but also a product of audience response) because they lack the genre film's thoroughly familiar cultural template which makes the basis for an uncomplicated evaluation by audiences. On the other hand, spectators' evaluations of such films can often be formed somewhat more freely because their feelings are subject to a lesser collective pressure than that exerted by blockbuster audiences.

Two types of film discussed in the preceding chapters have the potential to affect spectators in large enough numbers and with sufficient power to make it possible to see audiences as having enjoyed an experience that touched both the collective conscious and the cultural unconscious. These are first-person documentaries and genre movies. The former address viewers directly and can convey to the spectator personal, lived emotions that are embedded in the life histories of the subjects, themselves, of course, the directors. On the surface this small sub-genre could hardly be more different from the great genres of mainstream screen fiction; but both offer spectators the pleasures of ritual repetition. This thought is commonplace in respect of genre since the constituent films that make up any one kind must by definition reveal recognisable similarities to some elements of their antecedents. However, the concept of ritualised repetition is an innovation in relation to first-person documentary. Willa Woolston's *My Demons* could not have presented viewers with the opportunity for repetition in the same way as a generic production because no such film had ever previously been made. Her programme nevertheless draws spectators into making a guided, ritualised return to open up their own repressed secret dreads. Those terrors will obviously not connect with spectators' actual life experiences unless like Woolston herself they suffered childhood abuse. Instead, just as Freud recognised that patients' reports of sexual relations between themselves as children and their parents were not invariably historically accurate but could be the product of imagining, so some spectators find that this film summons nightmares which terrorise them in their fantasy life. The confluence of the film with viewers' fantasies has the power to tug the latter toward empathic relation with Woolston and stir painful emotions.

The confluence of film and fantasies is thankfully not confined to instances in which viewers' fears are aroused. It may also occasion the resuscitation of desires – for example, the yearning for personal growth or achievement, often dreamed but never realised. This seems to be the factor which endowed Steve Feltham's year-long watch by the shores of Loch Ness with some of the qualities of a sacred vigil and made his video diary so attractive. In both instances spectators' evaluative feelings are likely to be drawn empathically toward productive differentiation of formerly unconscious contents; but it has to be allowed that *My Demons* might trigger nightmare recollections or fantasies of gross parental abuse which could overwhelm feelings.

The second type of film which we encountered that can powerfully affect large audiences comprises generic productions with compellingly emotive storylines. Because the broad parameters of genre movies can in part be anticipated, experiencing them has some of the qualities of ritual. The makers of every genre film acquire with the form a heritage that gives them the opportunity to rework long-established archetypal narratives, characters and images in ways that will tap deep currents of meaning for their audiences. That occurs because those devices (with all the greater strength the more visionary the work) arise from and in return engage with impulses emerging from the unconscious of not only the film's makers but also its spectators. It follows that genre films also deal in fantasy. It is a main factor in their sometimes being experienced as having the sacramental characteristics described earlier.

The link between first-person documentary and genre feature film lies therefore in the confluence of film and *autochthonous* fantasy. In *autochthonous* fantasy the originating energy stems from below in the unconscious and forces upward into consciousness where, as we have seen, it makes itself known through symbolic material. The arousal of such fantasy-based material, if it is to be triggered by a genre production, must hook the attention of a substantial fan base. Once again, then, the concept of the cultural unconscious comes into play. By focusing and amplifying shared fantasies, a thriving genre provides a continuity of myth that goes some way to compensate for the ephemeral nature of screened images. Continuity is tied to change so that cultural, social and political shifts in the audience's lives are reflected in each particular film but the genre as a whole continues to articulate with underlying archetypal energies that change their colouration more slowly than the plots alter.

It seems to be possible for images, characters and story events charged with affect to be pulled in contrary directions during evaluation even though they are found in a single text. This phenomenon appears to be a function of the kind of culture-driven feeling process I have described. Some spectators looking only for entertainment and reinforcement of culturally and politically conservative values from *Open Range* did not feel its subtler nuances. They arrived at a simplified understanding of the film by surrendering to the pull on the imagination of old generic stereotypes, reducing its themes to black versus white, good versus evil – in this case nothing more than a traditional conflict of the drovers' party against the cattle baron and his hirelings. Conceding that *Open Range* was read by some in rough and ready a manner as a pro-Bush Western, we have to recognise that many others read the film's underlying themes as renouncing those same values.

The fact that such a casual, reductive reading of *Open Range* is possible might help account for its popularity compared with *The Missing*.[1] No such simplified reading of *The Missing* can be made; at every point it would frustrate neo-conservative desires for a simple story clearly articulated with the genre's old racist values. The most persuasive explanation of the popular failure to identify the allegorised absent terrorist in this film presents us with yet another way spectators may respond to psychological overload. It further justifies focus on the cultural unconscious rather than collective consciousness.

Something more than intense political controversy alone must have been the cause of Chidin's Other passing without comment. When, not without a battle, Michael Moore managed to secure distribution for *Fahrenheit 9/11*, the film augmented an angry political row between those who found execrable any pre-second-term election slur on George W. Bush and those of contrary disposition who were enthusiastic about this uninhibited lampoon. However, Moore's film analysed policies of the Administration that had been a focus of sharply divided political debate for three years. Those policies were exceptionally contentious and firmly lodged in the public domain (that is, in collective consciousness). The case of *The Missing* was

1 By way of comparison, in theatrical release *Open Range* took $58m at the North American box office and *The Missing* $27m (Internet Movie Database 2003a, b) – the former a respectable return, the latter figuring it as a small, independent film.

different because it threatened to raise a demon. Just as individuals blank out and repress a fearful memory or a painful complex, so too impressions collectively held can be wiped out when a devastating social trauma has been suffered. The fearsome collective trauma of 9/11 cordoned off Osama bin Laden in the popular psyche as a repressed image of execrable terror. The trauma isolated his image in the deepest shadow and blocked collective conscious recognition. In the wake of the horror, most American movie-goers could not allow themselves to see that Chidin confronted them with a thinly disguised representation of their demon. Repression arrested what might otherwise have been a productive differentiation of the film's melodramatic fantasy villain. That in turn might have enabled audiences of *The Missing* better to understand dominant currents in the conservative American psyche.

It is worth reminding ourselves that the phenomenon of cultural repression is not new in movie culture. In the 1950s North American paranoia over the threat of Communism had something of the quality of today's fear of terrorism. Films like John Ford's *The Searchers* or Don Siegel's *Invasion of the Body Snatchers* (neither very popular on first release) were not at the time widely recognised as invoking the menace of Communism. Although the attribution of political allegory to them and some other genre movies of that epoch is now commonplace, it seems probable that they were the objects of a cultural repression comparable to that which slighted *The Missing*'s impact.

Tentative conclusions can be drawn from the Jungian analyses of the foregoing selection of films. Most of them revealed an archetypal symbolism capable of being activated to touch the individual's unconscious. The archetypal qualities of these films did indeed engage my own emotions – something that must occur if a Jungian reading is to have any merit beyond that of a mechanical amplification of signs. Much Jungian work on films (including my own) has been devoted to amplifying symbols, to reading them within the framework of Jungian theories of archetypes and human psychology, and to authenticating the reading in the emotion-charged imaginative experience of the writer. At its best, such a programme of study brings into the light treasures gathered, not without difficulty, during an intense personal journey.

The authored films investigated in this book tended to encourage this kind of reading. And, it should be added, nothing innate to the first-person documentary or the genre film inhibits personal readings of this kind. Work in the Jungian tradition, however, always keeps an awareness of the collective in focus. When we turn to consider the public response to the two kinds of film which seem to engage a wider audience at a deep level, we see that the first-person documentary also works in the private sphere, not least because it is televised. It can affect viewers with overwhelming emotional force but, when it uses direct address to the viewer, probably leaves fewer openings for creative misreading than genre films. Woolston's film, though it reached viewers privately, touched both collective consciousness and the cultural unconscious. It did so riding a wave of concern that arose over child abuse in the 1990s which was no less psychologically rooted in western culture of the time than based on case history.

A more ambivalent picture emerges in the case of genre films. Such films, because of their ritual quality, are more likely than any others to engage energies active not too far beneath consciousness in the cultural unconscious. Where the cultural unconscious is stirred, a film may arouse strong emotions in large numbers of the audience or touch on a collective repression. The force of emotional arousal or repression may then be such that it does not wholly lie within the power of filmmakers to control or even direct it. It should be no great surprise, when we recall Jung's observations on the power of emotions, that their widespread excitation in audiences can lead to mixed responses. Some spectators will take the force of archetypal and symbolic representations more or less as the filmmakers intended; others will appropriate a film to their own world view. Although this occurs rather dramatically (the darkened movie theatre as panic room) where moral hysteria is exploited by the tabloids, it is not solely dependent on cynical orchestration designed to escalate the moment. As we saw in connection with the Western, spectators, both singly and in groups as fans, are capable of reading archetypal images not as actually presented in their on-screen textual setting but so that they fit unquestioned stereotypes with which those spectators enter the cinema. Conversely, repression, as in the case of *The Missing*, can blank evidence from collective recognition.

Filmography

THE ANCIENT WARRIOR
(Robert Butler, USA, 1973)
Episode 15 from the television series KUNG FU

Production company: Warner Bros Television
Series created by: Ed Spielman; *developed by:* Herman Miller
Producer: Jerry Thorpe
Screenplay: A. Martin Zweiback
Director of photography: Richard L. Rawlings
Editor: Gary Griffen
Art director: Gene Lourie
Sound: William Randall
Music: Jim Helms
Leading players: David Carradine (Kwai Chang Caine), Chief Dan George (The Ancient Warrior), Victor French, Denver Pyle, G. D. Spradlin, Will Geer
Running time: 49 minutes

BARRY LYNDON
(Stanley Kubrick, UK, 1975)

Production company: Hawk Films, Peregrine
Distributor: Warner Bros
Executive producer: Jan Harlan
Producer: Stanley Kubrick
Screenplay: Stanley Kubrick. Based on the novel by William Makepeace Thackeray
Director of photography: John Alcott
Production designer: Ken Adam
Editor: Tony Lawson
Art director: Roy Walker
Set designer: Vernon Dixon
Costume: Ulla Britt Søderlund, Milena Canonero

Sound recordist: Robin Gregory
Sound editor: Rodney Holland
Music: Irish traditional music: The Chieftains; excerpts from work by Johann Sebastian Bach, Frederick the Great, Georg Friedrich Handel, Wolfgang Amadeus Mozart, Giovanni Paisello, Franz Schubert and Antonio Vivaldi – adapted by Leonard Rosenman
Narrator: Michael Hordern
Leading players: Ryan O'Neal (Barry Lyndon/Redmond Barry), Marisa Berenson (Lady Lyndon), Patrick Magee (Chevalier de Balibari), Hardy Kruger (Captain Potzdorf), Gay Hamilton (Nora Brady), Marie Kean (Mrs Barry), Diana Koerner (Lischen), Murray Melvin (Reverend Samuel Runt), Frank Middlemass (Sir Charles Lyndon), Godfrey Quigley (Captain Grogan), Leonard Rossiter (Captain Quin), Leon Vitali (Lord Bullingdon), Dominic Savage (Young Bullingdon)
Running time: 187 minutes

BESIEGED/L'ASSEDIO
(Bernardo Bertolucci, Italy, 1998)

Production companies: A Fiction and Navert Film in co-production with Mediaset
Distributor (film): Alliance Releasing (UK)
Producer: Massimo Cortesi
Screenplay: Clare Peploe, Bernardo Bertolucci. Based on a story by James Lasdun
Director of photography: Fabio Cianchetti
Editor: Jacopo Quadri
Production designer: Gianni Silvestri
Pianist for David Thewlis and music arranger: Stefano Arnaldi
Sound: Maurizio Argentieri
Sound editor: Sandro Peticca
Music: Alessio Vlad, excerpts from work by Wolfgang Amadeus Mozart, Edvard Grieg, Johann Sebastian Bach, Alexander Scriabin, Ludwig van Beethoven, Fréderic Chopin, John C. Ojwang, Papa Wemba, Salif Keita, Coro Bondeko, John Coltrane, Ry Cooder, Ali Farka Toure, Empire Bakuba, A. Ambrosino, G. Savino
Leading players: Thandie Newton (Shandurai), David Thewlis (Jason Kinsky), Paul Osul (Winston), John C. Ojwang (peripatetic musician), Cyril Nri (priest)
Running time: 93 minutes

THE CRUISE: Le Grand Buffet
(Christopher Terrill, BBC1, 1998)

Executive producer: Olivia Lichtenstein
Camera: Christopher Terrill

Film editor: Julie Buckland
Sound: Jonathan Mitchell, George Foulgham
Music: John Harle
With: Jane McDonald
Running time: 29 minutes

THE DREAMERS
(Bernardo Bertolucci, UK/France/Italy/USA, 2003)

Distributor (film): Fox Searchlight Pictures
Production companies: Recorded Picture Company, Peninsula Fiction
Producer: Jeremy Thomas
Screenplay: Gilbert Adair based on his novel *The Holy Innocents*
Director of photography: Fabio Cianchetti
Costume designer: Louise Stjernsward
Production designer: Jean Rabasse
Editor: Jacopo Quadri
Supervising sound editor: Mark Auguste
Music supervisor: Janice Ginsberg
Leading players: Michael Pitt (Matthew), Eva Green (Isabelle), Louis Garrel (Théo), Robin Renucci (Father), Anna Chancellor (Mother), Jean-Pierre Léaud and Jean-Pierre Kalfon (themselves)
Running Time: 116 minutes

EYES WIDE SHUT
(Stanley Kubrick, UK, 1999)

Production companies: Warner Bros, Hobby Films, Pole Star
Distributor: Warner Bros
Executive producer: Jan Harlan
Producer: Stanley Kubrick
Co-producer: Brian W. Cook
Screenplay: Stanley Kubrick, Frederic Raphael inspired by Arthur Schnitzler's 'Traumnovelle'
Director of photography: Larry Smith
Editor: Nigel Galt
Production designers: Les Tomkins, Roy Walker
Art directors: Kevin Phipps, John Fenner
Sound recordist: Edward Tise
Supervising sound editor: Paul Conway
Music: Jocelyn Pook; Dmitri Shostakovitch, 'Jazz Suite, Waltz 2'; Georgy Ligeti, 'Musica Ricercata II; Wolfgang Amadeus Mozart, 'Requiem, KV 626'
Leading players: Tom Cruise (Dr Bill Harford), Nicole Kidman (Alice Harford), Sydney Pollack (Victor Ziegler), Julienne Davis (Mandy), Marie

Richardson (Marion Nathanson), Vinessa Shaw (Domino), Todd Field (Nick Nightingale), Rade Sherbedgia (Milich), LeeLee Sobieski (Milich's daughter), Leon Vitali (mock cardinal), Alan Cumming (desk clerk)
Running time: 153 minutes

LIDO
(Lucy Blakstad, BBC2 1996)

Producer: Lucy Blakstad
Director of Photography: Michael Eley
Underwater photography: Mike Valentine
Film editor: John Dimwoodie
Sound recordists: David Welch, Tim Watts
Dubbing mixer: Michael Narduzzo
Post production: Marc Eskenazi, Vincent Narduzzo
Music: Andy Cowton
Modern Times *series editor:* Stephen Lambert
Running time: 49 minutes

THE MISSING
(Ron Howard, USA, 2003)

Production companies: Revolution Studios/Imagine Entertainment
Distributors: Columbia Pictures (USA)
Columbia TriStar Films (UK)
Executive producers: Todd Hallowell, Steve Crystal
Producers: Brian Grazer, Daniel Ostroff, Ron Howard
Screenplay: Ken Kaufman, based on the novel *The Last Ride* by Thomas Eidson
Director of photography: Salvatore Totino
Art director: Guy Barnes
Editors: Dan Hanley, Mike Hill
Costume designer: Julie Weiss
Sound recordists: Travis Call, Frank Fleming
Supervising sound editor: Anthony J. Ciccolini III
Music: James Horner
Leading players: Cate Blanchett (Magdalena 'Maggie' Gilkeson), Tommy Lee Jones (Samuel Jones), Eric Schweig (Pesh-Chidin), Evan Rachel Wood (Lilly Gilkeson), Jenna Boyd (Dot Gilkeson), Val Kilmer (Lt. Jim Ducharme), Aaron Eckhart (Brake Baldwin), Simon Baker (Honesco), Jay Tavare (Kayitah)
Running Time: 136 minutes

MY DEMONS: THE LEGACY – A Video Diary
(BBC2, Willa Woolston, 1992)

Camera, sound recording and editorial control: Willa Woolston
Technical training: Bob Tolputt
Series editor: Jeremy Gibson
Series producer: Bob Long
Producer: Emma Read
Film editor: Alice Forward
Dubbing mixer: Peter Brown
With: Willa Woolston, her sisters and children
Running time: 76 minutes

OPEN RANGE
(Kevin Costner, USA, 2003)

Production companies: Touchstone Pictures, Cobalt Media Group, Beacon Pictures, Tig Productions
Distributors: Buena Vista Pictures, Touchstone Pictures, Winchester Film Distribution
Screenplay: Craig Storper based on the novel by Lauran Paine
Executive producers: Armyan Bernstein, Craig Storper
Producers: Kevin Costner, Jake Eberts, David Valdes
Director of photography: James Muro
Editors: Michael J. Duthie, Miklos Wright
Production design: Gae S. Buckley
Art direction: Gary Myers
Sound editor: Richard Dwan Jr, Frederick H. Staly
Sound designer: Scott Sanders
Music: Michael Kamen, Julianna Raye
Leading players: Robert Duvall (Boss Spearman), Kevin Costner (Charley Waite), Annette Bening (Sue Barlow), Michael Gambon (Denton Baxter), James Russo (Sheriff Poole), Diego Luna (Button), Abraham Benrubi (Mose Harrison), Dean McDermott (Dr Walter Barlow)
Running time: 138 minutes

S1MØNE
(Andrew Niccol, USA, 2002)

Production companies: New Line Cinema, Niccol Films
Distributors: Cinergia Ltd., Entertainment Film Distributors, New Line Cinema
Executive producers: Bradley Cramp, Michael De Luca, Lynn Harris
Producer: Andrew Niccol

Co-producer: Daniel Lupi
Screenplay: Andrew Niccol
Director of photography: Edward Lachman
Editor: Paul Rubell
Production design: Jan Roelfs
Art direction: Sarah Knowles
Sound recordist: Jeremy Peirson
Sound design and supervising sound editor: Richard King
Music: Samuel Barber, Carter Burwell, Gary Schreiner, Curt Sobel
Leading players: Al Pacino (Viktor Taransky), Winona Ryder (Nicola Anders), Elias Koteas (Hank Aleno), Jay Mohr (Hal Sinclair), Catherine Keener (Elaine Christian), Evan Rachel Wood (Lainey Christian), Pruitt Taylor Vince (Max Sayer), Rachel Roberts (Simone)
Running time: 117 minutes

STEALING BEAUTY/IO BALLO DA SOLA
(Bernardo Bertolucci, Italy/UK/France, 1995)

Production companies: Fiction Cinematografica, Recorded Picture Company, UGC Images
Distributor (film and video): Twentieth Century Fox
Producer: Jeremy Thomas
Story: Bernardo Bertolucci
Screenplay: Susan Minot
Director of photography: Darius Khondji
Editor: Pietro Scalia
Production design: Gianni Silvestri
Art direction: Domenica Sica
Sculptures: Matthew Spender
Music composer/conductor: Richard Hartley
Leading players: Liv Tyler (Lucy Harmon), Sinead Cusack (Diana Grayson), Donal McCann (Ian Grayson), Jeremy Irons (Alex Parrish), Jean Marais (M. Guillaume), Carlo Cecchi (Carlo Lisca), Stefania Sandrelli (Noemi), Francesco Siciliano (Michele Lisca), Rachel Weisz (Miranda Fox), Joseph Fiennes (Christopher Fox), Roberto Zibetti (Niccolò Donati), Ignazio Oliva (Osvaldo Donati), Jason Flemyng (Gregory), Leonardo Treviglio (Lieutenant), Rebecca Valpy (Daisy Grayson)
Running time: 113 minutes

Guide to further reading

On Jung

Jung, C. G. (ed.) (1964) *Man and His Symbols*. London: Arkana Paperback (1990).
Samuels, Andrew (1985) *Jung and the Post-Jungians*. London: Routledge.
Samuels, Andrew, Bani Shorter and Fred Plaut (1986) *A Critical Dictionary of Jungian Analysis*. London: Routledge & Kegan Paul.
Young-Eisendrath, Polly and Terence Dawson (eds) (1997) *The Cambridge Companion to Jung*. Cambridge: Cambridge University Press.

On post-Jungian analyses of film and television

Hauke, Christopher and Ian Alister (eds) (2001) *Jung and Film: Post-Jungian Takes on the Moving Image*. Hove: Brunner-Routledge.
Hockley, Luke (2001) *Cinematic Projections: The Analytical Psychology of C G Jung and Film Theory*. Luton: University of Luton Press.
Izod, John (2001) *Myth, Mind and the Screen: Understanding the Heroes of our Time*. Cambridge: Cambridge University Press.

Bibliography

Adams, Michael Vannoy (1997) 'The archetypal school', in Young-Eisendrath, 101–18.

Barthes, Roland (1973) 'Myth Today', in *Mythologies*. St Albans: Paladin.

Baum, Kathleen E. (2001) 'The Ghost of Christmas Past in *Eyes Wide Shut*'. Paper delivered at the American Comparative Literature Association Conference 'Topos/Chronos: Aesthetics for a New Millennium', University of Colorado at Boulder.

Beebe, John (1990) 'The Notorious Postwar Psyche', *Journal of Popular Film and Television*, 18(1) (spring): 28–35.

—— (1996) 'Jungian Illumination of Film', *Psychoanalytic Review*, 83(4) (August): 579–87.

—— (2001) 'The Anima in Film', in Hauke and Alister, 208–25. Revised 1992 essay.

Bennett, Catherine (1999) 'Women Behaving Not Very Badly', *The Guardian*, 18 March.

Bertolucci, Bernardo (1996) 'Conversation avec Anne Wiazemsky', *Nouvelle Revue Francaise*, 520: 20–39.

Billen, Andrew (1997) 'Sun, Sea and Shandy', *New Statesman*, 29 August. www.findarticles.com/cf_0/m0FQP/n4349_v126/20141352/print.jhtml, downloaded 18 January 2001.

Bolen, Jean Shinoda (1985) *Goddesses in Everywoman: A New Psychology of Women*. San Francisco: Harper & Row.

—— (1990) *Gods in Everyman: A New Psychology of Men's Lives and Loves*. New York: Harper Perennial.

Bradshaw, Peter (2004) '*The Dreamers*', *The Guardian*, 6 February. http://film.guardian.co.uk/Reviews/, downloaded 12 February 2004.

Brauer, Ralph with Donna Brauer (1975) *The Horse, the Gun, and the Piece of Property: Changing Images of the TV Western*. Bowling Green, OH: Bowling Green University Popular Press.

Brooks, Xan (2004) '*Stealing Beauty*', *The Guardian*, 5 February. http://film.guardian.co.uk/Reviews/Front/, downloaded 12 February 2004.

Burr, Ty (2003) 'Howard's Western is "Missing" something', *Boston Globe*, 26 November. http://www.rottentomatoes.com, downloaded 26 March 2004.

Carotenuto, Aldo (1989) *Eros and Pathos: Shades of Love and Suffering*. Toronto: Inner City Books.

Casement, Ann (ed.) (1998) *Post-Jungians Today: Key Papers in Contemporary Analytical Psychology*. London: Routledge.
Chatsworth, Sally (1999) '*Besieged/L'Assedio*', *Sight and Sound*, 9(5) (May): 40.
Chetwynd, Tom (1993) *Dictionary of Symbols*. London: Aquarian Press.
Ciment, Michel (1983) *Kubrick*, tr. Gilbert Adair. London: Collins.
Clarke, Arthur C. (1968) *The Promise of Space*. Harmondsworth: Penguin (1970).
Cluny, Claude Michel (1976) 'Le film du mois: Le temps retrouvé: notes sur *Barry Lindon* de Stanley Kubrick', *Cinéma* (Paris) 214, (October): 92–101.
Combs, Richard (1976) '*Barry Lyndon*', *Monthly Film Bulletin*, 43(504) (January): 3–4.
Cook, Nicholas (2000) *Analysing Musical Multimedia*. Oxford: Oxford University Press.
Dempsey, Michael (1976) '*Barry Lyndon*', *Film Quarterly*, 30(1) (fall): 49–54.
Ebert, Roger (2004) '*The Dreamers*', *Chicago Sun-Times*, 13 February. http://rogerebert.suntimes.com/apps/pbes.d11/section?category=REVIEWS, downloaded 13 February 2004.
Feeney, F.X. (2004) 'Le Temps Retrouvé: Bernardo Bertolucci's beautiful dreamers', *L.A. Weekly*, 6–12 February. http://www.laweekly.com/ink/04/11/film-feeney.php, downloaded 12 February 2004.
Finkelstein, Joanne (1991) *The Fashioned Self*. Cambridge: Polity Press.
Forbes, Jill (1992) *The Cinema in France after the New Wave*. London: bfi and Macmillan.
Fredericksen, Don (1979) 'Jung/Sign/Symbol/Film', Part 1, *Quarterly Review of Film Studies*, 4(2) (spring): 167–92.
—— (1980) 'Jung/Sign/Symbol/Film', Part 2, *Quarterly Review of Film Studies*, 5(4) (fall): 460–79.
—— (2001) 'Jung/Sign/Symbol/Film', in Hauke and Alister, 17–55. Revised version of the two earlier essays.
French, Philip (1977) *Westerns: Aspects of a Movie Genre*, revised edn. London: Secker & Warburg/British Film Institute.
—— (1999) 'Keep your shirt on . . .', *The Observer Review*, 12 September: 7.
—— (2004a) 'We just can't ménage without you', *The Observer*, 8 February. http://film.guardian.co.uk/Reviews/, downloaded 12 February 2004.
—— (2004b) '*Open Range*', *The Observer*, 21 March. http://film.guardian.co.uk/Reviews/, downloaded 30 March 2004.
Frith, Simon (1999) 'Politics and the Experience of Music', *Sosiologisk årbok*, 2: 217–31.
Gambini, Roberto (1998) 'The Challenge of Backwardness', in Casement, 149–62.
Grimal, Pierre (1991) *Dictionary of Classical Mythology*. London: Penguin.
Grady, Pam (2002) Review of *S1møne*, in *Reel.com* cited at www.rottentomatoes.com, downloaded May 2003.
Gray, Richard M. (1996) *Archetypal Explorations: An Integrative Approach to Human Behavior*. London: Routledge.
Gross, Larry (1999) 'Too Late the Hero', *Sight and Sound*, 9(6) (September): 20–3.
Harlan, Jan (dir.) (2001) *Stanley Kubrick: A Life in Pictures* (three-part documentary).
Haro (2002) Review of *S1møne*, in Haro Reviews the Movies, www.haro-online.com/movies/simone.html, downloaded May 2003.

Hart, David L. (1997) 'The Classical Jungian school', in Young-Eisendrath, 89–100.

Hauke, Christopher and Ian Alister (eds) (2001) *Jung and Film: Post-Jungian Takes on the Moving Image*. Hove: Brunner-Routledge.

Hayward, Susan (1993) *French National Cinema*. London: Routledge.

Henderson, Joseph L. (1984) *Cultural Attitudes in Psychological Perspective*. Toronto: Inner City.

Hewison, David (2000) '"Loving the Alien?" A response to John Izod's "Active imagination and the analysis of film"', *Journal of Analytical Psychology*, 45(2) (April): 287–93.

Hillman, James (1988) *Suicide and the Soul*. Dallas, TX: Spring Publications.

Hockley, Luke (2001) *Cinematic Projections: The Analytical Psychology of C G Jung and Film Theory*. Luton: University of Luton Press.

—— (2004) 'Watching Films: The Affective Power of Cinema', *Harvest*, 50(2): 72–86.

Hopcke, Robert H. (1995) *Persona: Where Sacred Meets Profane*. London: Shambhala.

Houston, Penelope (1976) *'Barry Lyndon', Sight and Sound*, 45(2): 77–80.

Insdorf, Annette (1978) *François Truffaut*. Boston, MA: Twayne Publishers.

Internet Movie Database, The (1999) *Eyes Wide Shut*, www.imdb.com/title/tt0120663, downloaded May 2003.

—— (2003a) *Open Range*, www.imdb.com/title/tt0338188, downloaded March 2004.

—— (2003b) *The Missing*, www.imdb.com/title/tt0316356, downloaded March 2004.

Izod, John (1992) *The Films of Nicolas Roeg: Myth and Mind*. London: Macmillan.

—— (2001) *Myth, Mind and the Screen: Understanding the Heroes of our Time*. Cambridge: Cambridge University Press.

Jacoby, Mario (1992) 'The Witch in Dreams, Complexes and Fairy Tales: The Dark Feminine in Psychotherapy', in Mario Jacoby, Verena Kast and Ingrid Riedel, *Witches, Ogres, and the Devil's Daughter: Encounters with Evil in Fairy Tales*. London: Shambhala.

Jordan, Marion (1983) 'Carry On . . . Follow that Stereotype', in James Curran and Vincent Porter (eds) *British Cinema History*. London: Weidenfeld & Nicolson.

Jung, Carl Gustav (1907) 'The Psychology of Dementia Praecox', in *The Psychogenesis of Mental Disease, The Collected Works*, Vol. 3, 2nd edn. London: Routledge (1991).

—— (1921) *Psychological Types, The Collected Works*, Vol. 6, rev. edn. Princeton, NJ: Princeton University Press (1976).

—— (1923) 'Psychological Types', in *Psychological Types, The Collected Works*, Vol. 6, rev. edn. Princeton, NJ: Princeton University Press (1976).

—— (1931a) 'On the Relation of Analytical Psychology to Poetry', in *The Spirit in Man, Art and Literature, The Collected Works*, Vol. 15. London: Routledge & Kegan Paul (1966).

—— (1931b) 'Marriage as a Psychological Relationship', in *The Development of Personality, The Collected Works*, Vol. 17. London: Routledge (1991).

—— (1935) 'The Relations Between the Ego and the Unconscious', in *Two Essays on Analytical Psychology, The Collected Works*, Vol. 7, 2nd edn. London: Routledge & Kegan Paul (1966).

—— (1939) 'Conscious, Unconscious, and Individuation', in *The Archetypes and the*

Collective Unconscious, The Collected Works, Vol. 9, 1, 2nd edn. London: Routledge & Kegan Paul (1968).
—— (1942) 'On the Psychology of the Unconscious', in *Two Essays on Analytical Psychology, The Collected Works*, Vol. 7, 2nd edn. London: Routledge & Kegan Paul (1966).
—— (1946a) 'The Psychology of the Transference', in *The Practice of Psychotherapy, The Collected Works*, Vol. 16. London: Routledge (1985).
—— (1946b) 'Analytical Psychology and Education', in *The Development of Personality, The Collected Works*, Vol 17. London: Routledge (1991).
—— (1948) 'The Phenomenology of the Spirit in Fairytales', in *The Archetypes and the Collective Unconscious, The Collected Works*, Vol. 9, 1, 2nd edn. London: Routledge (1968).
—— (1949) 'Foreword to Neumann: "Depth Psychology and a New Ethic"', in *The Symbolic Life, The Collected Works*, Vol. 18. London: Routledge & Kegan Paul (1977).
—— (1950a) 'Psychology and Literature', in *The Spirit in Man, Art and Literature, The Collected Works*, Vol. 15. London: Routledge & Kegan Paul (1966).
—— (1950b) *Aion, The Collected Works*, Vol. 9, 2, 2nd edn. London: Routledge & Kegan Paul (1968).
—— (1951) 'The Psychology of the Child Archetype', in *The Archetypes and the Collective Unconscious, The Collected Works*, Vol. 9, 1, 2nd edn. London: Routledge & Kegan Paul (1968).
—— (1952a) *Psychology and Alchemy, The Collected Works*, Vol. 12, 2nd edn. London: Routledge & Kegan Paul (1968).
—— (1952b) *Symbols of Transformation, The Collected Works*, Vol. 5, 2nd edn. London: Routledge & Kegan Paul (1981).
—— (1954a) 'The Archetypes of the Collective Unconscious', in *The Archetypes and the Collective Unconscious, The Collected Works*, Vol. 9, 1, 2nd edn. London: Routledge & Kegan Paul (1968).
—— (1954b) 'On the Psychology of the Trickster-Figure', in *The Archetypes and the Collective Unconscious, The Collected Works*, Vol. 9, 1, 2nd edn. London: Routledge & Kegan Paul (1968).
—— (1954c) 'Psychological Aspects of the Mother Archetype', in *The Archetypes and the Collective Unconscious, The Collected Works*, Vol. 9, 1, 2nd edn. London: Routledge & Kegan Paul (1968).
—— (1954d) 'On the Nature of the Psyche', in *The Structure and Dynamics of the Psyche, The Collected Works*, Vol. 8, 2nd edn. London: Routledge & Kegan Paul (1969).
—— (1956a) *Symbols of Transformation, The Collected Works*, Vol. 5, 2nd edn. London: Routledge & Kegan Paul.
—— (1956b) *Mysterium Coniunctionis, The Collected Works*, Vol. 14, 2nd edn. Princeton, NJ: Princeton University Press (1977).
—— (1957) 'Commentary on "The Secret of the Golden Flower"', in *Alchemical Studies, The Collected Works*, Vol. 13. London: Routledge & Kegan Paul (1967).
—— (ed.) (1964) *Man and His Symbols*. London: Arkana Paperback (1990).
Karten, Harvey (2002) Review of *S1møne*, www.all-reviews.com/videos-4/simone-2.htm, downloaded May 2003.

Kavaler-Adler, Susan (1996) *The Creative Mystique: From Red Shoes Frenzy to Love and Creativity*. London: Routledge.

Kehr, Dave (1999) '*Besieged:* A triumphant homecoming, and certainly Bertolucci's most personal film in a decade', *Film Comment*, 35(2) (Mar–Apr): 6–8.

Kilborn, Richard (2000) 'The docu-soap: a critical assessment', in John Izod, Richard Kilborn and Matthew Hibberd (eds) *From Grierson to the Docu-Soap: Breaking the Boundaries*. Luton: University of Luton Press.

Kilborn, Richard and John Izod (1997) *An Introduction to Television Documentary: Confronting Reality*. Manchester: Manchester University Press.

Kitses, Jim (2004) 'Forgiven', *Sight and Sound*, 14(4) (April): 24–7.

Konigsberg, Ira (1996) 'Transitional Phenomena, Transitional Space: Creativity and Spectatorship in Film', *Psychoanalytic Review*, 83(6) (December): 865–89.

Mailer, Norman (1968) *The Armies of the Night*. Harmondsworth: Penguin.

Maslin, Janet (1999) 'Bedroom Odyssey', *The New York Times*, 16 July. http://query.nytimes.com/search/, downloaded 20 July 2005.

McAuliffe, Jackie (2001) www.jackiemcauliffe.net/interviews.html, downloaded 17 January 2001.

McDougal, Stuart Y. (2001) 'Password "Fidelio."' Paper delivered at the American Comparative Literature Association Conference 'Topos/Chronos: Aesthetics for a New Millennium', University of Colorado at Boulder.

Miller, Mark Crispin (1976) '*Barry Lyndon* Reconsidered', *The Georgia Review*, 30(4). www.visual-memory.co.uk/amk/doc/0086.html, downloaded 30 November 2001.

Morgan, Margery (1980) *Bernard Shaw, Pygmalion*. London: Longman.

Moss, Stephen (1998) 'Movie Shots', *The Guardian*, 7 October, G2: 4.

Neumann, Erich (1954) *The Origins and History of Consciousness*. Princeton, NJ: Princeton University Press (1973).

Nichols, Bill (1971) '*Il Conformista*', *Cineaste*, 4(4) (spring): 19–23.

—— (1994) *Blurred Boundaries: Questions of Meaning in Contemporary Culture*. Bloomington, IN: Indiana University Press.

Ogle, Tina (1998) 'Oh, what a perfect day', *Radio Times*, 4–10 July: 25–7.

Orwell, George (1941) 'The Art of Donald McGill', in *Critical Essays*. London: Secker & Warburg (1960).

Ovid (1955) *The Metamorphoses*, tr. Mary M. Innes. Harmondsworth: Penguin.

'Photographing Stanley Kubrick's *Barry Lyndon*' (1976) *American Cinematographer*, 57(3) (March): 268–75, 320–1, 338–40.

Purdon, Noel (1971) 'Bernardo Bertolucci: two or three things I know about him', *Cinema* (London), 8: 6–15.

Rayner, William (1979) *Chief Joseph and his People*. London: Collins.

Rhodes, Steve (2002) Review of *S1møne*, www.all-reviews.com/videos-4/simone-2.htm, downloaded May 2003.

Ross, Benjamin (1995) 'Eternal yearning', *Sight and Sound*, 5(10) (October): 42.

Rourke, Brian (2001) 'Visualizing the Enlightenment: Film Narrative and Social Space in Stanley Kubrick's *Barry Lyndon* and Jacques Rivette's *The Nun*.' Paper delivered at the American Comparative Literature Association Conference, University of Colorado at Boulder.

Rushing, Janice Hocker and Thomas S. Frentz (1991) 'Integrating Ideology and

Archetype in Rhetorical Criticism', *Quarterly Journal of Speech*, 77(3) (November): 385–406.
—— (1993) 'Integrating Ideology and Archetype in Rhetorical Criticism, Part II: A Case Study of *Jaws*', *Quarterly Journal of Speech*, 79 (February): 61–81.
Sachleben, Mark and Kevan M. Yenerall (2004) *Seeing the Bigger Picture: Understanding Politics Through Film and Television*. New York: Peter Lang.
Samuels, Andrew (1985) *Jung and the Post-Jungians*. London: Routledge.
—— (1993) *The Political Psyche*. London: Routledge.
—— (2001) *Politics on the Couch: Citizenship and the Internal Life*. London: Profile Books.
Samuels, Andrew, Bani Shorter and Fred Plaut (1986) *A Critical Dictionary of Jungian Analysis*. London: Routledge & Kegan Paul.
Sandford, James (2003) 'The Missing', *Kalamazoo Gazette*, www.rottentomatoes.com, downloaded 30 March 2004.
Scott, A. O. (2004) 'When To Be Young Was Very Sexy', *New York Times*, 6 February. http://query.nytimes.com/search/, downloaded 12 February 2004.
Screen International (2002a) 'Box Office: North America', 1370 (30 August): 33.
—— (2002b) 'Box Office: North America', 1371 (6 September): 37.
—— (2002c) 'Box Office: North America', 1372 (13 September): 29.
Shaw, George Bernard (1916) *Androcles and the Lion, Overruled and Pygmalion*. London: Constable.
Sineux, Michel (1976) 'Maestro, musique!' *Positif*, 186 (October): 36–41.
Sklarew, Bruce (1999) 'Returning to my low-budget roots: an interview with Bernardo Bertolucci', *Cineaste*, 24(4) (Sept): 16–19.
Sklarew, Bruce, Bonnie S. Kaufman, Ellen Handler Spitz and Diane Borden (eds) (1998) *Bertolucci's* The Last Emperor: *Multiple Takes*. Detroit, MI: Wayne State University Press.
Smith, Henry Nash (1970) *Virgin Land: The American West as Symbol and Myth*. London: Harvard University Press.
Smith, Murray (1995) *Engaging Characters: Fiction, Emotion and the Cinema*. Oxford: Oxford University Press.
Solomon, Hester McFarland (1997) 'The developmental school', in Young-Eisendrath, 119–40.
Sorell, Walter (1973) *The Other Face: the Mask in the Arts*. London: Thames & Hudson.
SpiceUpYourLife (2001) www.SpiceUpYourLife.org.uk, downloaded 17 January 2001.
Stables, Kate (2002) '*S1møne*', *Sight and Sound*, 12(11) (November): 55–6.
Stephenson, William (1981) 'The perception of "history" in Kubrick's *Barry Lyndon*', *Literature/Film Quarterly*, 9(4): 251–60.
Stevens, Anthony (1991) *On Jung*. London: Penguin.
Tacey, David J. (1997) *Remaking Men: Jung, Spirituality and Social Change*. London: Routledge.
Tassi, Fabrizio (1999) 'Una storia d'amore, un inno al cinema: *L'Assedio* di Bernardo Bertolucci', *Cineforum*, 39(382) (March): 21–5.
Thompson, David (director/producer) (2003) 'Cinema, Sex, Politics: Bertolucci Makes *The Dreamers*', BBC4. tx. 8 February 2004.

Thomson, David (2004) 'The last frontier', *Sight and Sound*, 14(2) (February): 12–15.

Todorov, Tsvetan (1973) *The Fantastic: A Structural Approach to a Literary Genre*. Cleveland, OH: Case Western Reserve University Press.

Toulmin, Stephen (1990) *Cosmopolis: The Hidden Agenda of Modernity*. Chicago: University of Chicago Press.

TV Library (2000) www.tvlibrary.co.uk/pdb/p_16555.html, downloaded 19 January 2001.

Ulanov, Ann Belford (1971) *The Feminine in Jungian Psychology and in Christian Theology*. Evanston, IL: Northwestern University Press.

—— and Barry Ulanov (1994) *Transforming Sexuality: The Archetypal World of Anima and Animus*. London: Shambhala.

Vaughan, Dai (1983) *Portrait of an Invisible Man: The Working Life of Stewart McAllister, Film Editor*. London: British Film Institute.

Vincendeau, Ginette (2004) '*The Dreamers*', *Sight and Sound*, 42(2) (February): 41–2.

Vogel, Amos (1971) 'Bernardo Bertolucci: an interview', *Film Comment*, 7(3) (fall): 24–9.

Von Franz, Marie-Louise (1964) 'The Process of Individuation', in G. G. Jung, *Man and His Symbols*.

—— (1993) *The Feminine in Fairy Tales*, 2nd edn. London: Shambhala.

Wagstaff, Chris (1991) 'Theatre of Memory', *Sight and Sound*, 1(5) (September): 14–17.

—— (1994) 'Bernardo Bertolucci's Intravenous Cinema', *Sight and Sound*, 4(4) (April): 18–21.

—— (1996) '*Stealing Beauty*', *Sight and Sound*, 6(9) (September): 54–5.

Wehr, Demaris S. (1987) *Jung and Feminism: Liberating Archetypes*. Boston, MA: Beacon Press.

Whitehouse, Charles (1999) 'Eyes without a face', *Sight and Sound*, 9(6) (September): 38–9.

Wilmington, Michael (2003) '*The Missing*', *Chicago Tribune*, www.rottentomatoes.com, downloaded 30 March 2004.

Wollen, Peter (1992) 'Delirious Projections', *Sight and Sound*, 2(4) (August): 24–7.

Young-Eisendrath, Polly and Terence Dawson (eds) (1997) *The Cambridge Companion to Jung*. Cambridge: Cambridge University Press.

Zoja, Luigi (1998) 'Analysis and tragedy', in Casement, 33–49.

Index